Islamic Surveys

General Editor

C. HILLENBRAND

[redacted]

Islamic Names

Annemarie Schimmel

EDINBURGH UNIVERSITY PRESS

[redacted]

Edinburgh University Press
22 George Square, Edinburgh

Set in Linotron Trump Medieval
by Koinonia, Bury, and
printed in Great Britain by
Redwood Press Limited
Trowbridge, Wilts

British Library Cataloguing
in Publication Data
Schimmel, Annemarie, *1922–*
Islamic names. — (Islamic
surveys)
1. Islamic personal names
I. Title. II. Series
929.4'0917.'671

ISBN 0 85224 563 7
ISBN 0 85224 612 9 pbk

Contents

INTRODUCTION ix

I THE STRUCTURE OF A 'NAME' 1

ism or *ʿalam* - *kunya* - *nasab* - *nisba* - *laqab*

II 'BORN ON FRIDAY' 14

The naming of a child

III 'HELP FROM GOD' 25

Religious name-giving

IV 'MOTHERS OF THE FAITHFUL' 42

The naming of girls

V 'LIONS, MOONS AND ROSES' 50

The nickname or *laqab*

VI 'A NAME TOO HEAVY TO BEAR' 68

Changes and transformations of names

APPENDIX: Some notes on Turkish family names 80

NOTES 84

BIBLIOGRAPHY 94

INDEX OF PERSONAL NAMES 100

INDEX OF PLACES, ETHNIC GROUPS AND LANGUAGES 131

INDEX OF QUR'ĀNIC VERSES 134

GLOSSARY OF TECHNICAL TERMS 135

Editorial Note

In view of the wide range and complexity of the transliteration systems which exist for Arabic, Persian and Turkish, as well as for Urdu and other languages of the sub continent, it has been decided to maintain the author's original versions of Islamic names throughout. This policy also enables the reader to see a more accurate representation of the forms of the names as they have developed in the different areas of the Muslim world.

C.H.

Author's Note on the Transliteration

The orientalist will discover a discrepancy in the transliteration of compound names, and will find *Sharaf ad-dīn* and *'Abdul Latīf* instead of either *Sharaf ad-dīn* and *'Abd al-Laṭīf* or *Sharaf'ud dīn* and *'Abdul Latīf*. The reason for this inconsistency is that in common parlance names with *ad-dīn* are usually shortened to the first constituent element: *Shihāb*, or *Shihābi*, while the constructions with *'Abd* are very often split up into *'Abdul* and *Laṭīf*, which frequently appear as independent names. I therefore consider it more practical to use a 'mixed' transliteration than the 'correct' one.

As for Turkish names, they are usually given in the modern Turkish alphabet unless they are attested in classical sources. The main changes in the modern transcription are the following: *j* = *c; ch* = *ç; sh* = *ş; gh* = *ğ; q* = *k;* short *a* is frequently pronounced as a short *e*, the dipthong *au* rendered as *ev; d* at the end of the word or in reduplication becomes *t*. Thus, *Khālid* appears as *Halit, Jalāl ad-dīn* as *Celalettin, Taufīq* as *Tevfik, Aqqūsh* as *Akkuş*.

In the examples given in the text, A, P, T denote Arabic, Persian and Turkish respectively.

Introduction

One of the first Arabic stories I read as a teenager was this:

> Sharīk ibn al-Aʿwar entered Muʿāwiya's presence. He was ugly, so Muʿāwiya said to him: 'You are really ugly, but a beautiful person is better than an ugly one; you are *Sharīk*, 'companion', – but God has no companion; and your father is *al-aʿwar*, 'one-eyed', but a sound person is better than the one-eyed; how then did you come to rule your tribe?' He answered: 'You are *Muʿāwiya* – and what is *muʿāwiya* but a bitch that howls and make dogs howl? And you are the son of *Ṣakhr*, 'rock', but the plain is better than the rock; and you are the descendant of *Ḥarb*, 'war', but peace is better than war; and you are the descendant of *Umayya*, and what is *umayya* but 'a slave girl' in the diminutive? How did *you* become the Commander of the Faithful?'[1]

This story contains a number of important ingredients for the study of names and shows the importance people ascribed and continue to ascribe to proper names. The name is part of the person; rather, it is really the person; therefore, to know someone's name means to have power over that person. Did not God teach Adam the names of all things so that he might 'rule over them'? Names must not be mentioned in the case of great people and women; and Arabic, Persian and Turkish poets have never ceased singing of their beloved's beauty, but rarely without adding: 'I shall not tell her/his name!' Names are surrounded by a taboo; they carry *baraka*, blessing power, but can also be used for magic.[2] Everywhere one finds that by calling a child by the name of a saint or a hero (including film stars!) parents hope to transfer some of the noble qualities, the heroism or beauty of their patron to the child, and thus to make him participate in the patron's greatness. To change one's name means indeed to change one's identity: and hence the importance of a change of name in the case of conversion. Names can tell much about the likes and dislikes of people, about fashions and trends, about religious and political predilections, and thus a study of the nomenclature in any society is highly revealing.

It is, at the same time, a never-ending task. As Leone Caetani stated at the beginning of his *Onomasticon Arabicum*,[3] one could as well compose a complete dictionary of Arabic since almost every word has appeared, at some point in history, as a proper name. The same can be said for the Persian and Turkish areas, and for Muslim India. However, certain patterns can be discovered, and we shall try to give a modest survey of types of names as they occur in the world of Islam.

As early as 1854 the French scholar Garcin de Tassy remarked that one of the problems that embarrass those who want to occupy themselves with the history of the Muslim East, is the sheer quantity of names, surnames and honorific titles which one and the same person bears.[4] Indeed, at times one may become impatient when confronted with a full-fledged line of names – especially when they have to be catalogued: under which heading should one list *Najīb ad-dīn Abū Ḥafṣ ʿUmar ibn Muḥammad ibn al-Bayṭār ar-Rāzī*, to give a perfectly normal Arabic example? And where does one find *Khān Bahādur Nabībakhsh Aḥmad Khān Jamālī*?

Another problem which is especially likely to confuse the non-orientalist reader is the transcription of names, which is becoming more and more difficult with the growing number of Oriental scholars writing in European languages and adapting their names to English or French style. The large number of immigrants from the Muslim world – Turks, Arabs, Persians, Afghans, Pakistanis and so on – with their strange sounding names offer another challenge to Western people. The untutored reader of a newspaper or of a survey of Islamic history or literature would probably be quite surprised to learn that *Qāsim, Qassem, Gassem, Gacem, Kaçim, Casem, Kasim and Ghasim* are all in fact the same name, but transcribed differently, and how could he know, when opening a French or Turkish publication, or a German or English one, that the word *dawla* 'state', which forms the second part of so many titles, can also appear as *daula, dowle, dovleh, devlet* or *daulat*? Who understands why one *Ikrām ul-Ḥaqq* can delete the first part of his name and appear in the telephone directory as Mr *Huq, Haq, Haqq, Haque, Hak*? The Turkish way of transcribing Arabic and Persian words is particularly difficult for a foreigner to understand: *Taufīq* appears as *Tevfik, Khālid* as *Halit*, etc. A further problem arises as speakers of non-Arabic languages are often unable to pronounce correctly the Arabic letter *ḍ*, a deep *d*, and like to change it into *z*: thus *Ramaḍān* becomes *Ramażān* in the Persian-Turkish areas. Since many Indian languages exchange *j* and *z* as well as *s* and *sh*, we may encounter *Ramaḍān* in Bengal or Gujarat as *Ramjan, Murtaḍā* as *Murtażā* and *Murtajā*, and so on. The confusion between *s* and *sh* and the difficulty in pronouncing the hard Arabic *kh* correctly leads in India to transcriptions like *Ghousbux* for *Ghauth-bakhsh*. The sharp Arabic *ḥ* is sometimes lost, so that *Fatḥ ʿAlī* becomes *Fatali*, and some short vowels disappear altogether: *Sulaymān* can become *Sliman*, and *Abū Bakr* appears in North Africa in French transcription as *Boubker*. Even an Orientalist will probably take a deep breath before recognizing the great medieval saint *Abū Madyan* in the name *Boumédienne*.

The farther we are from the heartlands of Islam the more difficult is it to identify certain names. Among my Turkish friends there are some whose names are still an enigma to me, although I have learned that *Mügül* was nothing but an abbreviation of *Ümmü Gülsüm*, the Arabic *Umm Kulthūm*; and one wonders why a pretty girl is called *Samīna*, 'the fat one', until one realizes that only the transliteration of the Indian pronounciation of *thamīna* (the precious one) causes this mishap.

There is no dearth of books on Islamic names. In classical times numerous authors dealt with names, though mainly in connection with the correct pronounciation of transmitters of Prophetic traditions; and they compiled extensive works on *nisba*s and *kunya*s and other parts of an Arabic name. Every historical work offers an almost endless number of names and new combinations, in whatever Islamic language it may be written or with whichever period and country it may be dealing. Leone Caetani's monumental *Onomasticon* was never completed, but its first volume offers a most useful survey of types of names with numerous examples. The old articles by Garcin de Tassy and Barbier de Meynard in the *Journal Asiatique* are still worth reading and give an excellent survey of non-Arabic names as well. Studies by Arab scholars like H. al-Bāshā, with his extensive collection of names and titles, or I. Samarrā'ī's small but useful survey of Islamic names are good tools for the researcher; and studies in the nomenclature of a certain area, like P. Marty's rich article on Tunisian onomastics, are most welcome. Several papers about the development in modern Turkey exist, and a great number of special studies have been devoted to individual problems. Excellent guides are the articles on *ism, kunya,* and *laḳab* in the new edition of the *Encyclopedia of Islam*.

This book does not aim at an exhaustive treatment of names. We neither offer statistics, as A. K. Bihniyā has done in his survey of tens of thousands of modern Persian names, nor do we try to draw parallels with developments in other cultural areas, tempting as this might have been. Our aim is to offer some guidelines for the general reader, which may contain some interesting material for the orientalists as well. Much of the material is taken from modern sources such as newspapers, telephone directories (including that of North Yemen), and from discussions with numerous friends in Muslim countries. A wide collection of Turkish names, which I gathered in Ankara between 1954 and 1959, has been used; as has my unpublished study of Mamlūk names.

Many friends have answered my questions and contributed stories about names. Among them I must gratefully mention Dr Ziāuddīn A. Shakēb, of Hyderabad and London, who told me numerous stories and quoted a great number of examples from the Deccani Muslim tradition.

The late Sharīf ul-Ḥasan of Islamabad was another important source of information; he himself was keenly interested in names and family ties in the Indo-Pakistani subcontinent. Dr. Shams Anwarī Ḥusaynī of Cologne kindly informed me about some Persian traditions and guided me to important new Persian publications about Iranian nomenclature. Öner Önder of Bonn helped me with official lists of Turkish names from the Turkish consulate. Professor Ali S. Asani of Harvard contributed interesting remarks about Ismaʿili names in India and East Africa, and Professor Stefan Wild of Bonn answered some intricate questions about Arabic dialectical names. Professor Wolfhart Heinrichs and Dr Alma Giese, Harvard, were kind enough to read the whole manuscript and to offer valuable suggestions. My warm thanks are due to all these friends as well as to the many un-named people who, even by passing remarks, helped clarify one point or another.

I

The Structure of a 'Name'

Islamic names are formed according to a strict pattern, at least in the classical period of Arab civilization. The relevant articles in the *Encyclopedia of Islam* allow a comprehensive survey of the traditional forms and many remarks apply also to the customs of non-Arabs. Each name consists – in the sequence usually applied – of the *kunya*, that is the name *Abū x* (father of so-and-so), or *Umm x* (mother of so-and-so); the actual *ism*, that is the personal name (sometimes enlarged by a *laqab* with *ad-dīn*); then the *nasab*, one's relation to one's forefathers; then the *nisba*, pointing to one's native place, national or religious allegiance and the like, and finally the *laqab* (nickname), which later tended to develop into a proper name, or a family or clan name which could also be an honorific designation. Thus, a man might be called Abū'l-Maḥāsin (Jamāl ad-dīn) Yūsuf ibn Abī Yūsuf Ya'qūb al-Makkī al-Ḥanbalī az-Zayyāt. Often, the *laqab* with *ad-dīn* precedes all other names. We shall discuss these names briefly according to their forms, including Persian and Turkish usages, and then examine their peculiarities in more detail.

For the sake of convenience we begin not with the *kunya* but with the *ism*.

Ism or *'alam*.[1]

The proper name, *ism*, can consist of an adjective in any of its different forms, including participle or elative; of a noun (either concrete or abstract); or of a verb. Full sentences, as known in Hebrew names like Jonathan (Yahweh has given), do not occur in Arabic *ism*s. Verbs of incomplete action are used in Arabic; in other languages full verbal forms such as the imperative, or the past tense are also found.

Some Arabic *ism*s are fully declinable (having three grammatical cases), like *'Amrun*; others have only two case-endings such as *'Umaru* and those that are originally verbs of incomplete action, like *Yazīdu*. Some appear with the definite article: *al-Ḥasan*. In other cases the usage admits of both definite and indefinite forms, for example, one would address *al-Ḥasan* as *Yā Ḥasan*. A peculiarity of classical Arabic names is that a number of male names have a feminine form, such as *Mu'āwiya, al-Mughīra ibn Shu'ba, 'Urwa* and many more. In some cases, such as *al-Ḥārith* and *Ḥāritha*, masculine and feminine forms for males exist side by side.[2]

Qur'ānic and historical *ism*s are frequent and compounds abound, especially of *'abd* 'slave' with *Allāh* or one of the Divine names. Other combinations of nouns with *Allāh* (or a Divine name) like *'Aṭā Allāh*, 'God's gift', appear in great variety, particulary in the Muslim East. Many Persian and Turkish names were incorporated into Arabic nomenclature in the course of time; and Arabic, (especially Islamic) names found their way into all non-Arabic Muslim languages, especially in the upper classes.

Among the adjectives used in *isms* every conceivable form occurs. The active participle of the I verbal form, *fā'il*, such as *Khālid*, 'remaining', *Nāẓim*, 'arranging' occurs; further the form *fa'īl*, like *Sa'īd*, 'happy', *Zakiy*, 'pure', or, more emphatically, *Sa'ūd*, 'very happy'; further, the passive participle of form I, as in *Mas'ūd*, 'happy' or *Maḥfūẓ*, 'preserved', and of form II like *Muẓaffar*, 'victorious' or *Munawwar*, 'enlightened'. These latter forms are often used for both sexes. The active participle of form IV is also common, as in *Muḥsin*, 'beneficient' or *Mu'īn*, 'helping'.

Very widespread are adjectives of the form *af'al* which denote either the comparative/superlative as in *As'ad*, 'happier, most happy' or else signify colours and physical deficiencies, like *Asmar*, 'blackish brown', or *A'raj*, 'lame'. These have the feminine form *fa'lā: Samrā'*.

The use of adjectives for *isms* is common in Persian and Turkish as well: *Narmīn* 'soft', *Bihtar* 'better' (P), or *Şen* 'cheerful', *Kutlu* 'happy' (T).

Among the concrete nouns, animal *isms* abound, partly for the animal's characteristics or, in some cases, when the animal mentioned was the first thing seen after the baby's birth. To what extent old totemistic ideas survive, is an open question. Lions are especially frequent:[3] *Asad, Ghaḍanfar, Ḥaydar, Layth, Usāma, Ḍirghām, Shibl*; in Persian *Shīr, Shīrzād*, in Turkish *Arslān*. So too are *Fahd* (cheetah), *Namir, Nimr, Qablan* (T) 'leopard', *Bābur* (T) 'Tiger'. The bull, *thaur*, is also represented in Arabic names but occurs more frequently in Turkish as *bughā* with a great variety of compounds like *Altun-*, *Gümüş-*, *Kutlu-*, *Demir-bughā* (Gold, Silver, Lucky, Iron-Bull respectively). Foxes, *tha'lab* and wolves, *dhi'b, sirḥān* or *aus*, are again better represented in Turkish where *börü, kurt, bozkurt* (grey wolf) were often used. *Bseisa* (= *busaysa*) 'kitten' is found even among Bedouins, and one wonders why someone might have been connected with vermin such as *dharr* 'minute ant', *al-māzin* 'ant's egg', *al-furay'a* 'little louse' or *burghūth* 'flea)' Birds, especially predatory ones, are good omens for a brave boy, and the eagle, *'uqāb*, or its chick, *al-haytham*, and the falcon, *saqar, al-quṭāmiy*, appear in Arabic as does *'ikrima*, the dove. They are apparently an even more important part of Turkish names, where various types of hawks and falcons abound: *sunqur, balban*, *tughān, (dŏgan), tughril, tarlan, turgut* – often specified by *aq- (ak)* 'white' like *Aqdoghan*, or *qarā (kara)* 'black', *qarāsonqur*. The Persian *shāhīn, bāz*, and *shāhbāz* belong here too. All these names are known among Indian Muslims, but in the Subcontinent one finds also smaller indigenous birds like *tūta* (parrot) or *mīna*, the blackish meena bird.

Just as there seems to be no restriction in the use of animal names, plants too are used as *isms* both in classical and modern times,[4] be it the bitter colocinth, *ḥanzala* or *ʿalqama*; the watermelon, *biṭṭīkh*, or any kind of potherb like *basbes*, fennel, or *kumīn*, cuminseed (modern Tunisia). Names of flowers and tender plants are mainly given to women as we shall see in chapter IV.

All nature served the Muslims for names, beginning with the sun *(shams; Shemissa* is still in use in Tunis) and *āftāb, khurshīd* (P) or *Gün, güneş* (T) – to the moon (*badr* is the full moon; *māh* (P) and *ay* (T) occur often in combinations). Stars in general – *najm, akhtar* (P), *yĭldĭz* (T) – are used. So too are single stars and constellations, especially *Suhayl* (Canopus), or the Pleiades (*thurayyā*). The horizon (*ufuq*), the sky, (*āsumān* (P)), mountains (*jabal, dağ* (T)), the ocean (*baḥr, daryā* (P), *deniz, engin* (T)), rain (*yağmur* (T)), or lightning (*barq*) (A), *şimşek, yĭldĭrĭm* (T)) and many more are bestowed on children. In many cases, their original meaning is nowadays forgotten and they are used because of their connection with a famous hero, such as the name *Ḥamza* (the Prophet's uncle and hero of a widespread saga) whose original meaning, namely 'bean', nobody is likely to remember. Indeed, if one were to tell people the original meaning of many much-loved names they might well be rather shocked.[5]

Household goods are also used for *isms*. Ibn Qutayba, in the ninth century, mentions among others *salm* (a bucket with one handle), *ḥafṣ* (leather basket), *bakraj* (coffee-pot) and, more elevated, *an-naḍr* (Gold). Besides concrete names, abstract nouns are also often used for naming children.[6] They may point to virtues, like *Faḍl* 'Virtue', or to good wishes, like *Salāma* 'Wellbeing', *Naṣr* also with an article: 'Victory'. Almost every form of verbal noun could be used in this category, and some of them are commonly used for both men and women. We find forms such as in *Taufīq* 'success', *Iqbāl* 'good fortune', *Tawaddud* 'Love', *Irtiḍā* 'Contentment'. Other forms include *Rifʿat* 'Elevation' and *ʿIṣmat* 'Chastity, sinlessness', *Bahjat 'Splendour'*, *Nuṣrat* 'Victory', *Wadād* 'Love'. Again many of them are used for both sexes.

Abstract nouns are of course not lacking in non-Arabic languages, like *Umīd* (P) 'Hope' or *Armaghān* (P) 'Gift', *Uğur* 'Good luck' or *Ertēm* (T) 'Virtue'.

Present-tense verbs appear in Arabic as *isms*[7] like *Yazīd* 'he increases', *Yaʿīsh* 'he lives'. In Turkish, negatives occur like *qaymaz* 'he does not slide', which can also be interpreted as the participle 'not sliding'; and we find imperatives like *Güven* 'Trust!' or *Güngör* 'See the sun'. Positive forms are also common, like *Yener* 'he vanquishes, vanquishing', as well as optatives: *Dursun* 'May he stay'. Most tenses of the past are found in names like *Aydoğdu* or *Aydoğmuş* 'a moon was born', *Iltutmiş* 'he grasped the land', and many more.

Double names were formerly rare. Garcin de Tassy claims that in India only *sayyids* used them,[8] but it seems that they occur nowadays in all parts of the Islamic world, and among all strata of society. They sometimes lead to strange combinations such as *Bābak Ḥusayn* or *Yad Allāh Gayumarth* in Iran, where parents have tried to prove their allegiance to both the Islamic and the ancient Persian tradition; such mixed names occur also when the parents come from different religious backgrounds.[9]

Kunya or *agnomen*[10]

The *kunya, agnomen* is the designation of a person as father, *abū (abou, bū, abō,* genitive *abī,* accusative *abā*) or 'mother', *umm,* of so-and-so. Frähn in his study of the titles and cognomens of the Golden Horde (Kazan 1814) called it a hyionymicon, 'connected with a son's name'. On the other hand, as the *kunya* precedes the given name, Kosegarten called it *Vorname,* 'first name'. More studies have been devoted to the *kunya* in its different forms than to any other part of Muslim names. It is possible that originally the intention to honour someone by calling him or her after the firstborn son gave rise to the use of the *kunya* or, if the person was still young, the hope that they might be blessed with a child, especially a son. It may also be that the *kunya* was sometimes used to avoid pronouncing the given-name which is surrounded by a taboo: as a secondary name it was not considered to be a real part of the person, and hence to know it did not imply any danger for the bearer.[11] The fact that the term is derived from the same root as *kināya* (indirect expression), seems to point to the deeper meaning of the *kunya.* It may be that for this very reason many women are known only by their *kunya.* In some parts of the Islamic world, such as rural areas of Pakistan, husband and wife do not address each other by their proper names (*isms*) at all, but rather as Father of X or Mother of Z; or they prefer to avoid any name and use only a personal pronoun when speaking to each other (*tum, āp* 'you').

The use of the given-name was in any case considered improper, and thus the *kunya* was mentioned when one wished to honour someone (*at-takniya takrima*). It is therefore considered rather bad taste to use the *kunya* when speaking of oneself; and the refusal to be called by one's *kunya* is regarded as a sign of modesty.

Here a problem arose for the theologians: if the *kunya* was an honorific name, why then was the Prophet's worst enemy called (*Qur'ān*, Sūra 111) *Abū Lahab* 'Father of Flame', that is, with a *kunya*? (similar to *Abū Jahl*, Father of ignorance, the other outstanding enemy of the young Muslim community). The Quranic commentator, az-Zamakhsharī, explains the use of the *kunya* in this case by claiming that it is used as in names *Abū'l-khayr, Abū'sh-sharr* 'Father of good, or of evil' as implying that Abū Lahab was destined for hellfire. Another interpretation claims that God in the Qur'ān addressed His friends by their proper names, *ism*, like 'O Yaḥyā, O Dāūd!' while the *kunya* was reserved for His enemies.

As the *kunya* was meant as honour it was not customary in early Islam to give it to non-Arabs or to slaves. It was therefore a remarkable event when the Christian physician Jibrā'īl ibn Bukhtīshū' after successfully treating the ninth-century caliph al-Ma'mūn, was granted a *kunya* by the grateful patient; this *kunya* was *Abū 'Īsā*. This combination – *Abū 'Īsā Jibrā'īl* – sounds very odd, as if Gabriel were Jesus' father. Indeed, the very *kunya* Abū 'Īsā was disputed, as Jesus had no human father, and the caliph 'Umar had strongly disapproved of its usage; but even a leading traditionist (*muḥaddith*), at-Tirmidhī, did not object to being called by this *kunya*.[12]

The *kunya* was not to be used for socially inferior people, nor was it proper to address respected persons by their given name. This is reflected in an anecdote in the *Kitāb al-aghānī* of Abu'l Faraj al-Iṣfahānī, the famous tenth-century collection of stories and poems. The singer Ibrāhīm al-Mauṣilī was admired by crafty Iblīs (Satan) who exclaimed: '*Aḥsant yā Ibrāhīm!*' (Well done, Ibrahim!). Then, in the words of the incensed musician, 'my wrath increased and I said: First of all he entered my room without permission and wanted me to sing for him, and then he called me by my proper name (*ism*) and not by my *kunya* (as would have been correct)!' But such are the ways of the devil . . .

The *kunya* need not refer only to a son; many cases of *abū* with a feminine name are known from the first generations in Islam: *Abū Ruqayya Tamīm ad-Dārī, Abū Laylā, Abū Rīḥāna* and so on because 'one was proud to honour daughters and not, like the pre-Islamic Arabs, bury them alive.'[13] Names such as *Sulmā bint Abī Sulmā* show that the *kunya* indeed pointed to real daughters. Some *kunya*s were used so often that they turned into proper names: for example *Abū Bakr*, which figures in biographical dictionaries under *Abū*, not under another name to which it has been added as a *kunya*.

Some people had more than one *kunya*, 'one for war and one for peace', or *kunya*s that were used in different countries.[14] This was considered to be a mark of dignity, as in the case of the eighth-century

'Abbasid caliph Hārūn ar-Rashīd who was called *Abū Ja'far* and *Abū Muḥammad*.[15] Even people without children were often given a *kunya* although the caliph 'Umar (ruled 634-44), always very strict, disapproved of one Shu'ayb being called *Abū Yaḥyà* – 'and you have no son'.[16] Nawawī, however, devotes a whole chapter to the permissibility of inventing a *kunya* for a childless person: was not 'A'isha, the Prophet's young, childless wife called *Umm 'Abdallāh*?[17] That might refer to her relation with her nephew or, according to another version, to a miscarriage; for stillborn children were also given a name.

As slaves generally had no *kunya*, it was a sign of gratitude or respect for a faithful slave if his owner granted him one: when the caliph al-Mahdī (ruled 775-85) manumitted his slave, the poet Nuṣayb, he married him to a girl and called him *Abū'l-jafnā* (Father of the girl with curly hair).[18]

In the course of time certain *kunya*s were attached to certain proper names. A person called 'Alī would probably also be named *Abū'l-Ḥasan* or *Abū'l-Ḥusayn*; Abū 'Alī al-Ḥusayn also occurs. An Ibrāhīm was likely to be called *Abū Isḥāq* (Isaac) or *Abū Ismā'īl* (Ishmael) in consonance with the historical sons of Ibrahim (Abraham). 'Umar is often combined with *Abū Ḥafṣ*, as the caliph 'Umar's daughter Ḥafṣa was married to the Prophet (the caliph himself, however, had the *kunya*s *Abū 'Abdallāh* and *Abū Laylā*). A man called *Ayyūb* (Job) may receive the *kunya Abū'ṣ-ṣabr* 'Father of patience' in remembrance of Job's patient suffering. One can invent fitting combinations like *Abū'n-najm Badr* 'Father of the star, Full Moon', or *Abū'l-baqā Khālid* 'Father of eternity, eternal' where both parts of the name point to duration and eternity; or the *kunya* can be derived from the same root as the proper name (*ism*): *Abū'l-'izz 'Abdul 'Azīz*. These latter combinations, however, led to a different type of *kunya*, for the *kunya* was often used to express not only a reality – the existence of a child – but also wishes and blessings for the parents' happiness and the child's progress. The famous tenth-century litterateur as-Ṣāḥib Ibn 'Abbād sent a letter to an 'Alid to whom a son had been born: 'and his name, *ism*, be *'Alī* so that God may exalt, *yu'allī*, his memory, and his *kunya* should be *Abū'l-Ḥasan*, so that God may better, *yuḥsin*, his affairs!'[19] Although Abū'l-Ḥasan is a normal *kunya* for any 'Alī after the example of 'Alī ibn Abī Ṭālib, the Prophet's cousin and son-in-law, 'Alī's son al-Ḥasan, yet Ibn 'Abbād interpreted the name as an expression of hoped-for success.

Such metaphorical *kunya*s, to use Caetani's term, are frequent, and Kosegarten fittingly translates them with high-sounding Latin terms: *Abū'l-futūḥ* 'Pater victoriarium – father of victories', *Abū'l-Maḥāsin* 'Pater virtutes – father of virtues' etc. One often finds *Abū'l-barakāt* 'father of blessings', *Abū'l-faraj* '– of joy', *Abū'l-yumn* '– of happiness' etc. Such *kunya*s seems to be restricted to urban circles and are little known among Bedouins, as Caskel's studies prove.[20] In many cases the use of the definite article is fluctuating; the article being often connected with metaphorical *kunya*s: *Abū Naṣr* is 'father of Naṣr', while *Abū'n-naṣr* is 'father of victory'.

The *kunya* is sometimes shortened to *bū*: *Abū Isḥāq* (father of Isaac) becomes *Busḥāq*; or it appears in the accusative as *Abā*, *Bā*, thus in South Arabia and Iran *Abū Yazīd* becomes *Bāyazīd*, and *Abū Dharr* turns into *Bādharr*. In North Africa, *Abu'l* can be contracted to *Bel*: Abu'l-Ḥasan becomes *Bel Hasan*.[21] Some *kunya*s are disputed. We mentioned *Abū ʿĪsa* 'father of Jesus'; but the Prophet's *kunya*, *Abū'l-Qāsim*, also poses a problem; it should not be applied when the person is called Muḥammad. ʿAlī's *kunya*, *Abū Turāb* 'father of dust', has been interpreted differently by pious Shiites and the early adversaries of the fourth caliph.[22]

There is another aspect to the *kunya* as well. It 'reveals intellectual or moral qualities or defects, physical peculiarities, the custom of wearing specific garments or other objects, the habitual company of animals, or particular taste, or incidents in the person's life.'[23] The most famous representative of this type of *kunya* is *Abū Hurayra*, 'Father of a kitten', Muḥammad's companion around whose *kunya* numerous stories were woven; but one may also think of the Arab poet *Abū'l-ʿAtāhiya* (748-825/6), 'Father of craziness'. This type of *kunya* has often assumed all the characteristics of the *laqab* or nickname; in fact, the word *kunya* has lately come to designate family names, as in modern Damascus, or what formerly would have been called a *laqab* (as in the Maghrib).[24] If someone is called *Abū'd-dawāniq*, 'Father of farthings', as was an ʿAbbasid caliph, it points to his miserliness. *Abū ʿaṣīda (Bou asside)* can be someone who is fond of the sweet dish *ʿaṣīda* or at whose birth much *ʿaṣīda* was cooked and distributed to the poor.[25] A man in a Syrian village was called *Abū ʿiẓām*, 'Father of bones', because he regularly stole chickens to feed his children.[26] *Bou ras* (*Abūa's*) is someone with a large head; *Abū raqība* (*Bourghiba*) someone with an unusually long or short neck; *Borjel (Abū rijl)* a person with a deformed foot, *rijl*; while *Abū khashab* 'Father of wood' may be someone with a wooden leg.[27] One can call one's child *Bū Dīnār* for good fortune or because a piece of gold was found when he was born. Amazingly, the *kunya Abū Jahl* 'Father of ignorance', known from the Prophet's days, is today found in Yemen, as is *Abū ʿaṣr* 'Father of difficulty'. This kind of *kunya* is rarely applied to women, as their outstanding characteristics were not known outside their home; but they may have their own nicknames inside the women's quarters.

The *kunya* as a means of characterising persons and things is frequently used for animals, such as *Abū Ḥuṣayn* (father of the little fortress) for the fox, or *Umm arbaʿ wa arba ʿīn* (Mother of forty-four) for the centipede, but this usage need not concern us here.[28]

In recent times there has been an increasing tendency in Orientalist circles to designate as *kunya* not only the names formed with *Abū* and *Umm* but also those with *ibn* (son of). This use is found even in the great eighteenth-century dictionaries like the *Tāj al-ʿarūs*, but should be avoided.[29] Terms of relationship other than *abū* and *umm* belong to the category of *nasab* and form a special class of names, to which we now turn.

Nasab – 'lineage'.[30]

The *nasab* expresses the relation of a son or a daughter to his/her father or mother and is expressed in Arabic by *ibn, bin* for males, *ibnat, bint* for females, in the plural *banū* (genitive *banī*) and *banāt* respectively. Sibling relationships, brother, *akhū* (genitive *akhī*) and sister, *ukht*, also fall under this category. Someone may be called *akhū X* if his brother or sister is a well-known personality, as in the case of *ʿUmar akhū al-Juwayriyya umm al-mu'minīn*, the brother of Juwayriyya, one of the Prophet's wives, or *Ibn akhī ash-Shāfiʿī*, 'the son of [the famous jurist] ash-Shāfiʿīs brother', i.e., his nephew. Many persons in Islamic history are known by their *nasab: Ibn Sīnā* (980-1037) and *Ibn Rushd* (1126-98), to mention the most familiar ones. They appear in Western sources as *Avicenna* and *Averroes*. The twelfth-century physician *Avenzoar* of Seville is of the family of *Ibn Zuhr*; the *Avencerrage* family of Granada are the *Ibn as-Sarrāj*.

Sometimes the father's *kunya* is the point of reference: *Ibn Abī Laylā*, or *Umayya ibn Abī Umayya* for example. Often, the *nasab* refers not to the father or mother but to a more distant ancestor, especially when it expresses a profession like *Ibn as-Saʿātī* 'Son of the clockmaker', *Ibn az-Zayyāt* 'Son of the oil-man' or *Ibn al-Fāriḍ* 'Son of the notary'. It can also be formed with the father's or ancestor's nickname, *laqab*, as in *Ibn as-sikkīt* 'Son of the taciturn man' or *Ibn Dhī'l-liḥya* 'Son of the bearded man'. If a child is born of non-Muslim parents, one speaks of *Ibn* or *Bint ʿAbdallāh*. That is valid for most slaves too, including the military slaves (*Mamlūks*), in the Middle Ages. If the father was unknown a person could be called 'son of his father', like the famous governor *Ziyād ibn Abīhi* in early Umayyad history; or else he would be called after his mother.

This latter custom, however, is also found when the mother was noted for special traits, for instance when she was a foreigner. That is the case with ʿAlī ibn Abī Ṭālib's son from a slave girl, who became known as *Muḥammad ibn al-Ḥanafiyya*, the son of a woman belonging to the Ḥanīfa tribe. Similarly we find *Ibn al-Qūṭiyya* or *Ibn ar-Rūmiyya*, 'Son of the Visigothic, or, Byzantine woman'. In polygamous families, one of the wives might be remarkable in some way, so that her children would be named after her, as in the case of Marwān ibn al-Ḥakam known as *Ibn az-Zarqā'* 'Son of the blue-eyed woman'. Alternatively, the maternal family might be more important that the paternal line, as in the case of *Ibn Bint al-Aʿazz* whose maternal grandfather, *al-Aʿazz*, was a vizier, or *Ibn ukht Ghānim* 'son of Ghānim's sister'. The thirteenth-century Seljuq historian Ibn Bībī is called after his mother, *Bībī al-munajjima*, 'the lady astronomer'. Sometimes one finds simply *Ibn as-sitt* or *Ibn al-mar'a*, 'son of the lady', or, 'of the woman'; or full names, like *Ibn Maryam* 'Son of Mary' or professional names like *Ibn ad-dāyā* 'Son of the wetnurse'.[31]

For further extension of the *nasab* one may use the term *sibṭ*, 'grandson through the daughter' as in the historian *Sibṭ Ibn al-Jauzī*, whose mother was a daughter of the famous twelfth-century lawyer and theologian Ibn al-Jauzī and who was even called by the Turkish epithet *Qizoghlu*, 'the girl's son'. In *sayyid* families in non-Arabic areas we find *Sibṭ-i Ḥasan* (descendant of Ḥasan) or *Sibṭ-i rasūl* (descendant of the Prophet). Sometimes the word *al-ḥafīd* (the grandson) is used, especially when two scholars, or notables, bear the same name: *Ḥasan ibn ʿAlī ibn Ḥasan al-ḥafīd*.

The plural *banū*, often also in the genitive *Banī, Bnī*, is used for a family or a clan, as *Banū Isrā'īl*, 'the children of Israel' or *Banū Umayya*, 'the Umayyads'. The word survives also in Persian family names like *Banūʿazīzī* or *Banīfāṭima*. Among the Arabs, *āl* (family) is frequently found, like *Āl Hāshim, Āl Saʿūd* or *Āl Ṣabāḥ*. This *āl* can be shortened and then looks like the Arabic definite article as in *Alʿumar*. In Indo-Pakistani names one encounters *Āl-i Aḥmad*, 'Ahmad's family', to denote *sayyid*ship.

In North Africa the word *wuld*, (pl. *aulād, ūlād*) is used instead of *ibn*, like *Sī* (from *sayyidī*, 'my lord') *Ḥamza wuld Sī Aḥmad. Walad*, 'son', is also used in Iran, sometimes even as a proper name. Among the Berbers one finds *ait, at, eyt, īt* as in *Aït Aḥmad*, and the family of the *Ūlād Ṭāhir* may appear as *Iṭṭāhirān*. In modern Arabic the *ibn* is often left out, and Aḥmad ʿAlī is likely to be Aḥmad ibn ʿAlī, which can make a proper analysis of names difficult. As for Persian *nasab*, the most common way is to connect the son's name with that of the father by the *i* of the *iżāfet*; e.g. *Ḥusayn-i Manṣūr*. As this *i* is not written, forms like *Ḥusayn Manṣūr* emerge, and as in the Arabic Aḥmad ʿAlī the father's name is often understood to be part of the son's name – Ḥusayn ibn Manṣūr al-Ḥallāj is usually known as *Manṣūr* in non-Arabic areas. In India, one observes the tendency to drop the *i* of the *iżāfet* in most cases.

The Persian *pisar* (son) is rarely used in names, but the form *pūr* occurs, as in *Nādirpūr* or *Pūr-i Bahā*; the corresponding feminine is *dukht*, 'daughter', known to us from Turandot, that is, *Tūrāndukht*. In Persian families and countries under Persian influence the relationship is usually expressed by the suffix *-zāda*: e.g. *Muftīzāda* (Son of the Mufti), *Jamālzāda, Taqīzāda*. This is common among Indian Muslims, and is mostly found with titles, like *Nawwābzāda, Pīrzāda*. Women are then distinguished by the Hindi feminine ending -ī, and thus names like *Mubārakzādī* (daughter of Mubārak) appear.

In Turkey *zāde* is often used in leading families like the *Köprülüzade* or *'Āshiqpāshāzāde*, or with professions as in *Helvacīzade*, 'son of the sweetmeat confectioner'. It alternates however with the Turkish suffix *-oğlu*: and thus we have the famous folk hero *Köroğlu* 'Son of the blind one', the medieval ruling family of the *Ramazanoğlu*, or the *Yazīcīoğlu*, 'Son of the scribe'. For individuals, *oğlan* (son) was used in former times, as the names of folk poets like *Karacaŏglan* show. Families might also simply use the plural to express their common ancestry: *Ağzībüyükler* are those descended from someone with the nickname *ağzībüyük*, 'with a big mouth'. With the introduction of family-names in Turkey in 1934, many families dropped the traditional suffixes or changed the *-oğlu* into *-gil*: a *Necatizade* or *Necatioğlu* might become a *Necatigil*, a *Siyavuşoğlu, Siyavuşgil*. The suffix *-soy* (family), is likewise used in family names, as in *Cebesoy*, related to *cebe* (harness) and probably abbreviated from *cebeci*, harnessmaker.

In Pakistan, especially in Sind, the ending *-potrā, -pōtā* expresses the *nasab* in a family unit: the *Dāūdpōtās* are descendants of one Dā'ūd. Among the Pathans in Afghanistan and the North-West Frontier, the relevant suffixes for members of a clan derived from one ancestor are *-zay*, like *Yūsufzay, Saddōzay, Pōpalzay* (which suffix is dropped in modern times for practical reasons) or, in the case of larger clan units, the suffix is *-khēl*, like *'Īsākhēl, Miānkhēl* or *Kākākhel*.

Nisba or 'relation'

The *nisba* refers to the place of birth, residence or origin. It is formed in Arabic by adding *-iyyun* (*ī*), fem. *-iyyatun* (*iyya*) to the place-name or the tribal name: *Hāshim – al-Hāshimī; Baghdād – al-Baghdādiyya* (for a woman from that city). A person can have several *nisbas*: *Muḥammad ad-Dimishqī al-Kūfī* would be originally from Damascus but settled and became famous in Kufa.

Some names form irregular *nisbas*,[32] especially those with a long *ī* in the second syllable, which is replaced by a short *a*: a man from the tribe *Thaqīf* is *ath-Thaqafī*, a woman from the tribe *Ḥanīfa, al-Ḥanafiyya*. The *nisba* of the famous tribe *Quraysh* is *al-Qurashī*, which was later, especially in non-Arab countries, replaced by the 'regular' *Qurayshī*. Irregularities occur, especially in foreign names: the Persian cities *Rayy* and *Marw* form their *nisba*s as *Rāzī* and *Marwazī* respectively, *Yasi* in Turkistan gives *Yasawī*, *Herāt* not only *Herātī* but usually *Harawī*. The numerous *nisba*s which have been carefully collected by Muslim scholars in works like Samʿānī's *Kitāb al-ansāb*, reveal the extent of Islamic expansion at particular moments: scholars with the *nisba ash-Shāṭibī* (Xativa in Spain) and *al-Farghānī* (from the Farghana in Central Asia), *as-Sindhī* (from the lower Indus valley) and *at-Tartūshī* (from Tortosa), *al-Bukhārī* (from Bukhara) and *at-Tatwānī* (from Tetuan), *az-Zabīdī* (from Zabid in Yemen) and *ash-Shāhjahānābādī* (from Dehli) show the centers of Islamic culture – even though a *nisba* might be borne generations after the ancestor had left his original home. There are still *Landoulsi*, 'Andalusian' in Tunisia![33]

*Nisba*s can also denote someone's religious or legal persuasion: a follower of the school of Ibn Ḥanbal is a *Ḥanbalī*, an adherent of the doctrines of the Muʿtazila, a *Muʿtazilī*; a Shiite believing in the twelve Imāms is an *Ithnāʾʿasharī* (Twelver), and a mystic dealing with the philosophy of illumination, *ishrāq*, an *Ishrāqī*. The *nisba*s are often derived from professions in the plural: *qawārīrī* is someone who makes glass bottles, *kawākibī* someone who produces a special kind of nail. These names developed into real family names.[34]

The *nisba* can also refer to a proper name or parts of it, meaning 'belonging to so-and-so', like *Bakrī* from Abū Bakr, *Raḥīmī* from ʿAbdur Raḥīm, *Fakhrī* from Fakhraddīn, and one might adopt a *nisba* in order to show one's admiration for a certain hero, as the Indian scholar Shiblī (d. 1914) took the *nisba Nuʿmānī* out of respect for the great medieval jurist Abū Ḥanīfa *Nuʿmān*. The Sufis (the word itself is a *nisba* from *ṣūf*, 'wool') point to their spiritual allegiance by choosing the name of their fraternity like *al-Qādirī, ash-Shādhilī*, or the name of their master, *Reḥmānī* (from one ʿAbdur Raḥmān in modern India). No *nisba* was formed from the Prophet's name, and his descendants through Fāṭima and her husband ʿAlī are called *ʿAlawī*, i.e. Alids, or in special cases *Fāṭimī*; and they add *al-Ḥasanī* or *al-Ḥusaynī* to their proper names to show from which grandson of the Prophet they descend. Sometimes a *nisba* points to a custom of the bearer and is thus close to a nickname, as in the case of *Ibn al-Bismillī*, whose father, a sailor, would constantly say *Bismillāh*, 'In the name of God', and was therefore surnamed *al-Bismillī*.[35]

In compound names, *nisba*s are formed that take into consideration only certain letters of the original name: a person from Ḥiṣn Kayfā (in

Eastern Turkey) would be *al-Ḥaṣkafī*; one finds also *al-Bū'aqlī*, from Abū 'Aql, and in the Middle Ages forms like *al-'Abdurraḥmānī* were used because 'Abdur Raḥmān was no longer seen as a genitive construction. *Nisba*s from professions were equally ungrammatical – someone who was both a qāḍī and an amīr could be called *al-Qāḍamīrī*.

In modern times, when many *nisba*s have become real family names, women consequently use the masculine form and call themselves *Mūnā al-'Ajamī* or *Māgda Nuwayhī*, since the *nisba* is no longer alive. In Iran a long *ī* is used to form the *nisba*, like *Iṣfahānī, Tabrīzī*, so that the forms coincide with the Arabic *nisba*. In Turkey the *nisba* ending, mainly from place names, is *li*, which follows Turkish vowel harmony: *Ankaralĭ, Izmirli, Istanbullu*.

In Indo-Pakistan one will find the ending *-wālā*, (fem. *wālī*) to denote the same: *Poonawālā* is a man from Poona, *Dehliwālī*, a woman from Dehli, *Jāpānwālā* a merchant in Karachi who trades predominantly with Japan. The Sindhi equivalent is *-wāṛō, wāṛī*.

Laqab, nickname.[36]

The most colourful type of names are the nicknames, *laqab*, pl. *alqāb*. As a classical Arabic verse claims:

> Rarely do your eyes see a man
> whose inner meaning is not – if you only think!
> – in his *laqab*![37]

A *laqab* is given to a person to distinguish him from others who bear the same name, be it by age, status, or outward appearance. It can be honorific, (*tashrīfī*) or for purposes of identification, (*ta'rīf*), but also deprecating, for *taskhīf*; in this case it is usually called *nabaẓ*. The ancient Arabs apparently excelled in inventing nasty *alqāb* for their enemies, for even the Qur'ān warns them not to use pejorative soubriquets: *lā tanābaẓū bi'l-alqāb*! (Sura 49/11).

The custom of honouring someone by a specific name is traced back by Qalqashandī to the prophets, for Abraham was called *Khalīl Allāh*, 'God's friend', and Moses, *Kalīm Allāh*, 'the one addressed by God'. The Prophet Muhammad himself became known as *al-Amīn*, 'the trustworthy one', Abū Bakr as *aṣ-Ṣiddīq*, 'the most truthful one', and 'Umar as *al-Fārūq* 'the discerning one'.

Alqāb very often point to physical characteristics, such as *al-abraṣ*, 'the leper', or *al-Jāḥiẓ*, 'the goggle-eyed one', the *laqab* of the famous 'Abbāsid polymath. They can be derived from a profession, as *an-Najjār*, 'the mason'; from religious customs, as *az-Zāhid*, 'the ascetic'; or from an unusual expression of which the individual was fond. Incidents in one's life could also result in nicknames, as in the famous case of the pre-Islamic poet *Ta'abbaṭa Sharran*, 'he carried something evil under his arm' (which is interpreted as the demoness he carried off in the desert). As becomes evident from this example, *alqāb* can consist of a full sentence.

Some *alqāb* were given to attract good luck; thus a 'black malodorous slave' was called *Kāfūr*, 'camphor'. (Incidentally, the most famous Kāfūr in Arabic history had the *kunya Abū'l-misk*, 'father of musk'.) Other *alqāb* were opprobrious in order to avert the evil eye: the caliph al-Mutawakkil has an extremely beautiful slave girl whom he called *al-qabīḥa*, 'the ugly one'. It was possible to be called by different *alqāb* in different places, as in the case of the mystic al-Ḥallāj, a fact that was confusing for the Government of Baghdad.[37]

Many *alqāb* developed later into family names, like the Iraqi family *al-Malā'ika*, 'the angels', whose *laqab* was given to them because of their unity and kindness,[38] or the Turkish family *Peyniryemezgil*, 'clan of him "who does not eat cheese"'. Among those which developed into family names are the *alqāb* in non-Arab countries which define the bearer's clan or tribe, such as *Barlas* among the Turcomans, *Awān* in the Punjab, or *Afshār* among the Persians.

It was even possible to bestow a *laqab* posthumously: when Ḥanẓala was slain in the battle of Uḥud (625 A.D.) the Prophet called out '*ghasīl al-malā'ika*, washed by the angels', for the martyr does not require the normal ritual bath before burial.

The different kinds of *alqāb* will be analyzed in more detail in Chapter V.

II

'Born on Friday' – the Naming of a Child

'On Doomsday you will be called by your names and the names of your fathers – so chose beautiful (or, graceful) names!'[1] Thus said the Prophet, who also regarded messengers with a handsome face and a graceful name as a favourable auspice. It is therefore not surprising to find the word *Adīgüzel* (T) 'His name is beautiful' as a proper name in Malatya. According to another Prophetic tradition, the father has three obligations toward his son: to teach him to write, to select a good name for him, and to marry him off when he comes of age.[2]

The Prophet's pronouncement was directed against the ancient Arab custom of calling sons by frightening or harsh names like *Ḥarb* (War), *Ṣakhr* (Rock), *Murra* (Bitterness), or by names that were given to the child after the first object seen at the time of its birth. Who would like to be called *Qunfudh* (Hedgehog)[3]? Likewise, names given to children on account of their personal characteristics, as is particularly common among the Bedouins and in rural areas in general, were and often still are, appalling: *Suwayyid, Suwaydān* or *Asyūd* (from the root *aswad*, black) point to the infant's swarthy looks; *Gleimid* (= *julaymid*) compares the child to a small round pebble, *Gredhi* (= *juraydi*) to a 'young rat'. Such names would be used in an urban environment only as a descriptive *laqab*.

As outward signs are supposed to reflect the inner condition, children bearing such names were certainly unfortunate, for a beautiful name – so one thought – was also the expression of a beautiful character: *adĭ güzel tadĭ güzel,* 'Whose name is nice, his taste is also nice', as the Turkish proverb has it.

The name also has the important function of binding the child into the family unit.[5] And thus boys were in many cases called after a deceased grandfather, girls after a grandmother. If the grandmother was alive, she might select the granddaughter's name. Among the Arab tribes in early times the maternal grandfather's name was often given to a son. The classical reference for this custom is the statement of ʿAlī ibn Abī Ṭālib, whose maternal grandfather bore the name *Asad* 'lion'. In his father's absence his mother called the newborn child by a related name, as he himself stated: 'And I am the one whose mother called him *Ḥaydara* 'lion'.' After the father's return the name was then chaged to *ʿAlī*. According to Shia tradition, Abū Ṭālib had prayed near the mount Abū Qubays for a name for his son and was given a tablet with emerald script in which *ʿAlī*, 'who will become highest, *aʿlā*'' was written.[7] That the custom of naming a boy after his grandfather continued is evident from the entries in the biographical dictionaries where one may find numerous *Aḥmad ibn ʿUmar ibn Aḥmad* and similar genealogies. Often, a noun denoting 'successor' is given along with the father's or grandfather's name, such as *Khalaf, Makhlūf, Yakhlaf.* Nowadays, the grandfather's name has often become a family name: ʿUmar ibn ʿAlī ibn Muṣṭafā becomes *ʿU. Muṣṭafā.* In women's names one can also see this tendency to adopt the grandfather's name: *Umm Khālid bint Khālid* shows that a woman named her son after her father. Rarely, several children bear the same ancestor's name: Ḥusayn ibn ʿAlī ibn Abī Ṭālib called all his sons ʿAlī; the middle one, surnamed *Zayn al-ʿābidīn,* continued the line of the Shia imāms.

Sometimes a deceased uncle or aunt's name was given: the father's name appears only and not very often, when he died before the boy was born. The only exception is Muḥammad, a name which every male Muslim should bear; but one avoided naming too many individuals in a family by the same name, and even when a boy bore his grandfather's name he would often be called by a nickname, as was customary for example in Tashqurghan.[8]

In Turkey, and it is probably true for most other areas, the midwife gives the child a religious name, or *göbek adĭ* (umbilical name) while cutting the umbilical cord. Three days later the so-called *ezan adĭ* is given while reciting three times the *adhān*, the call to prayer, and whispering the name thrice into the child's right ear. Alternatively, the official name is given during the *ʿaqīqa* on the sixth day after birth: the *ḥadīth* collected by Nawawī recommend the seventh day.[9] People often seek the most blessed hour for performing this act, and the official name is usually chosen and given by a venerable personality such as an elderly member of the family. In Turkey the name-giving used to be the right only of the husband's family; in some Sindhi and Gujarati families the father's sister gives the name. A religious leader or, in rural areas, the landlord or owner of the village, was asked to name the child, or else an employee's patron. Badāūnī, the sixteenth-century Mughal historian, tells how he brought his newborn son to the Emperor Akbar, asking for a blessed name, and as the emperor was reciting during those days the invocation *Yā Hādī*, 'O Thou that Guidest Right!' he called the boy *ʿAbdul Hādī.* When Badāūnī returned home the imām urged him to have the whole Qur'ān recited to ensure a long life for the boy, but as he did not follow this advice the child died soon afterwards. Akbar also predicted the birth of the three sons of his commander-in-chief, the Khānkhānān ʿAbdur Raḥīm, and gave them Persian names even before they were born.[11] This, indeed, is not unusual especially in Shia circles, for it is said that the Prophet named Fāṭima's unborn child Muḥsin; but she had a miscarriage. However, according to popular opinion, the child at least had a name and could not accuse his parents at Doomsday of having left him without a proper name.[12] Among Ismailis the Aga Khan is often asked when visiting a place to select names for the children of pregnant women, and he gives them a male or female name for the future baby.

Although the father's actual name is generally not used for a son, he may be given a name that is somehow related to the paternal name. Thus when the father is *Ibrāhīm*, the son is likely to be called *Ismā'īl* or *Isḥāq*; a *Dā'ūd*'s son would probably be *Sulaymān* or vice versa, and similarly with *Ya'qūb* and *Yūsuf*, or *Yaḥyā* and *Zakariyā*. Often brothers are all called after the Qur'anic prophets if the father bears the name of a prophet. A similar harmony can be achieved with names consisting of *'abd* 'slave of' – and one of the Divine names: *'Abdul 'Aẓīm* 'slave of the Mighty' *son of 'Abdul Qawiy* 'slave of the Strong'. In non-Arabic countries this could lead to the invention of quite nonsensical names, provided they rhymed nicely: in Hyderabad/Deccan one *'Abdus Ṣamad* called his son *'Abdul Gunbad*, 'slave of the dome' (*gunbad* is a Persian word). Names with *ad-dīn* are used in the same way: *Ḥusām ad-dīn* (Sword of religion) *son of Sinān ad-dīn* (Spear of religion). *Ghulām Murtażā son of Ghulām Muṣṭafā* belongs to this category,and on a less lofty level the Mughal name *Qablān Beg ibn Shīr Beg*, 'Mr Leopard son of Mr Lion.' The record for this type of recurring pattern comes from the Deccan, where a gentleman by the name of *Abū'l-maḥākim Muḥammad Iḥsān Afżal ad-dīn Yūnus 'Abdul Muḥīṭ Shahīd Allāh Khān Bāsiṭ* had seven sons whose names were all constructed like his, so that one of them was *Abū'l-maḥāsin Muḥammad Muḥsin Rashīd ad-dīn Mūsā 'Abdul Muḥṣī 'Ubayd Allāh Khān Dhākir*.[13]

On the other hand the sons' names may follow the same grammatical pattern as that of the father: the sons of *'Ināyat Khān* appear as *Wilāyat, Hidāyat-, Shujā'at-, Karāmat-* and *Salāmat Khān!* Or else the names are formed from the same root letters: *Laṭā'if son of Laṭīf*. In some families the initial letter was used for generations, as in the royal Ghaznavid house with *Maudūd ibn Mas'ūd ibn Maḥmūd* (all passive participles).[14]

To call children by rhyming or related names is in any case quite common – whether it is the classical combination of *Ḥasan, Ḥusayn*, and *Muḥsin*, or *'Amr, 'Umayr*, and *'Āmir*. Thus, Amīr Pāyinda Khān of Kabul in the nineteenth century called all his sons from one wife by compounds of *dil*, 'heart': *Purdil, Sherdil, Kohandil, Mihrdil Khān*. In a pious Bengali family we find *Nūr al-hudā*, 'light of right guidance', *Shams aḍ- ḍuḥā*, 'Sun of the morning light', *Badr ad-dujā*, 'Full moon of the darkness', and *Khayr al-hudā*, 'Best guidance', with high-sounding expressions alluding to Qur'ānic verses. Two Pakistani musician brothers are called *Badr ad-dīn* and *Qamar ad-dīn*, 'full moon' and 'moon of religion' respectively. A recent book on child-rearing in Turkey even offers appropriate names for twins: two girls might be called *Serab (sarāb)* and *Mehtap (mahtāb)*, 'Mirage' and 'Moonlight', two boys, *Bülent* and *Levent*, 'High' and 'Young hero', or *Kutlu* and *Mutlu*, both meaning 'happy, fortunate'. In the case of boy and girl twins, their names can be taken from classical love-stories, like *Kerem* and *Aslĭ*, or consist of combinations like *Alev* and *Ateş*, 'Flame' and 'Fire'.[15]

As these names reflect the cultural interests of the parents they are likely to change from time to time. At different times different names are fashionable, partly because of popular figures of the time who have such names and partly for aesthetic reasons. As formerly the heroes of the faith or of early Islamic history were referred to in favourite names, it is now often political slogans and catchwords. A Turkish girl's name was *Anayasa* 'Constitution'; and *Nidāl* and *Kifāḥ*, meaning 'snatching away' and 'fight', appeared in Egypt during the Arab-Israeli war. Triplets born in Izmir, Turkey, were called *Hürriyet, Uhuvvet,*and *Musavat* (Arabic: *hurrīyat, ukhuwwat, musāwāt)*, 'Freedom, Fraternity, Equality'. Political figures lend their names to children; thus *Menderes* or his first name, *Adnan*, occurred frequently during the late 'fifties in Turkey where about the same time triplets in Egypt were named *Gamāl* (Gamāl ʿAbdun Nāṣir), *Nehru* and *Tito*.[16]

As in the West movie stars and singers – like Elvis – are commemorated in hundreds of names, so actresses and singers like *Umm Kulthūm* are now among the cultural heroes of young families, and in more than one family known to me a boy was called after a film star whom his mother admired while expecting him. Thus a westernized Ismaili family called their son *Omar* – a name otherwise avoided by Shiites – after the actor Omar Sharif, and among the Turkish workers in Germany famous football players are name-giving models. At present, there is on the one hand a growing tendency to invent new names for euphonic reasons (as in Egypt the girls' names *Hiyām* or *Sihām*, which actually means a camel's disease),[17] or to adopt Western names into the Islamic pattern and, with the mobility typical of our time, parents choose names which are easy to pronounce for foreigners and do not carry a negative or ugly meaning in English or German.[18] A Turkish boy with the beautiful name *Ufuk (ufuq* 'Horizon') would probably suffer terribly in an English-speaking country.

There are, however, still families in the Persianate world which aspire to a high style in names and call their children *Firdausī* or *Saʿdī* after the two great Persian poets; the number of *Iqbāl*s in Indo-Pakistan in homage to the great philosopher poet Iqbāl (1877-1938) is quite large, and recently, in the tendency to emphasize the Islamic heritage, classical Islamic names or high-sounding compounds are again becoming more popular.

The joy over the birth of a child, particularly a son, is expressed in all Islamic languages with names that correspond exactly to our Theodore, 'God-given'. In classical Arabic, *'Aṭā' Allāh, 'Aṭīyat Allāh* or *Hibat Allāh*, all meaning 'God's gift', are common; an Egyptian girl in our day is called *Minnat Allāh*, 'The gratitude owed to God'. This type of name seems even more widespread in the Persian and Turkish areas. Persians will use *-dād*, 'he gave', and call a boy *Allāh-dād, Ilāh-dād* or *Khudā-dād*, all meaning 'God gave'; it occurs also in combination with one of the Divine names: *Raḥmān-dād, Raḥīm-dād*, and even *Ṣabūr-dād*. One can also substitute *-bakhsh* 'gift' for *dād* (in Pakistan this is often spelled *bux*), and form names like *Allāh Bakhsh, Ilāhībakhsh* or even, with the old Persian word for God, *Yazdānbakhsh*.

In Turkish the idea of 'given' is expressed by the verbal form *virdī, birdī, berdī*, 'he gave', in regionally varying pronounciation: *Allāh berdī, Allāhvirdī* and often with one of the Divine names such as *Ḥaqqverdī, Khāliqbirdī, Jabbārbirdī, Subḥānverdī.* The combination with the Persian noun is also found: *Khudāberdī*, but predominant is the purely Turkish *Taghrībirdī* (*taghrī* being the Arabic transliteration of the Turkish *tangri, tengri*). Names like *Mengübirtī*, 'The Eternal has given' belong to this category. *Allāhberen*, 'God is giving', occurs in Iran in Turkish families.

In the Indian languages like Urdu, Sindhi and Panjabi the same principle is followed, with Indian verbs replacing the Persian or Turkish ones: *Allāh-diyā, Raḥīm-dinā, Dhāṇī-dinā, Allāh varāyō* '– has brought', *Allāh-rakhiyā*, '– has placed' or *Sa'in dinō* 'The Noble One has given' express the same feeling of gratitude as does the North African *Jābū Allāh* (= *jā'a bihi Allāh*), 'God has brought him.'[20] But what, one wonders, is the story of someone called *Dīw-dād*, 'given by a demon'? Is he a distant relative of *Ibn Jinnī*, 'Son of a jinn'?

The feeling of gratitude expressed in such names is not always directed toward the creator; it may be that the Prophet, a Shia imām or a saint is considered to have helped the parents who were waiting for a child.: *'Aṭā' Muḥammad* or *'Aṭā'Ḥusayn* are not rare in the Middle East; *Dād-'Alī, Ikrām 'Alī* 'Kindness of 'Alī' or *Haydarbakhsh* belong to the Shia nomenclature. *Nabībakhsh* 'Gift of the Prophet' is quite common in Pakistan, while *Ghauth-bakhsh*, 'Gift of The Help' (i.e., *'Abdul Qādir Gīlānī*), and *Qalandar-bakhsh (La'l Shahbāz Qalandar* of Sehwan) point to the saint whose intercession was requested to obtain a son. *Nūr-bakhsh* 'Gift of the Light' occurs in the Shia Persian Sufi tradition.

Another type of name expressing gratitude are compounds with words like *faḍl* (TP *fażl*) 'favor, grace' and the name of God, the Prophet, or an imām; they rank from *Faḍl Allāh, Faḍl al- Ghanī, -ar-Razzāq, -al-Mannān* and *Fażl Rabbī* (cf. Sura 27/40) to *Fażl Aḥmad* and *Fażl 'Alī* (sometimes abbreviated to *Fazlī*).

One may place here also names beginning with *iḥsān*, 'beneficence', like *Iḥsān rabbī* or *Iḥsān-i ḥaqq*, which are used, like those beginning with *'ināyat* 'providence' or *in'ām* 'kind gift', mainly in Indo-Pakistan. There, one encounters not only *'Ināyat ar-raḥmān or -ar-raḥīm* but even *'Ināyat-i Kibriyā*, 'Providence of the Divine Glory'. *In'ām ul-ḥaqq* and combinations with *luṭf* 'kindness' belong to the same category. Here too, the name Allāh can be replaced by one of the Most Beautiful Names: *Luṭf Allāh (Luṭfullāh), Luṭf al-Barī* etc. Even the word *fayḍ* (P *fayż)* 'emanation, overflowing grace' is used, as in *Fayż ar-raḥmān.*

Not only the parents' gratitude to God and the Prophet, or a saint, is expressed in names but also the hope for a long and happy life, for the Prophet urged his community to use names of good augury. *Barakāt* 'Blessings', *Sa'ādat* 'Felicity', *Ẓafar* 'Victory' may be chosen. In the Persianate world one will find – for both sexes – combinations with *khush*, 'nice', like *Khush-ḥāl* 'happy', *Khushdil* 'of happy heart' or else with *bih* 'good', like *Bihzād* 'Well born', *Bihrūz* or *Rūzbih* 'Good day', *Bihnām* 'Of good name', as well as *Nāmvar* 'famous', *Kāmrān* 'Successful' or *Farrukhzād* 'Of happy birth'.

In Turkish, combinations with *qūṭ*, 'happiness' are known from ancient times, like *quṭlugh* (modern *Kutlu*) 'happy', or *Uğur* (Good luck). *Aykut* and *Günkut*, (Happy moon and Happy Sun, or, Happy Day) are more recent variants. In former times, a Turkish boy might be greeted as *Aydoğmuş, Arslandoğmuş*, or *Gündoğmuş* – 'The moon –, a lion –, a sun is born' and wishes for his future life were expressed in heroic names like *Korkmas (qorqmaz)* 'Fearless', *Ürkmez* 'he does not shy away', *Yïlmaz* 'unyielding'. And when the founder of the Mughal Empire, Bābur, was preparing to conquer the north-west of India, he called his son *Hindāl*, 'Take India'. In this connection one may mention the custom of giving military names to boys: in Eastern Anatolia names like *Asker* 'soldier', *Binbashï* 'Major', *Alay* 'Regiment' can be found; and *Okumuş* 'Someone who can read,' certainly expresses a wish.[22] In Arabic, expecially in countries that formed part of the Ottoman Empire, Turkish titles like *Bāshā*, or *Shalabī* (= *çelebi*), 'Nobleman' can be found. They all are meant to ensure a glorious future for the child; and if after a long series of boys a long-awaited girl is born, she may be called *Masarrat*, 'Joy' or, in all languages, 'Wish' *Munyā* (A), *Ārzū* or *Armān* (P) or *Dilek* (T).

However, despite all these good wishes expressed in their names small children died all too frequently. As in the West 'earthy' names were sometimes used for a child born after many deaths. (cf as *Erdmuthe, Erdmann* in German) in order to bind the little soul to the earth before it can fly away, so the Muslims have a number of names which were originally meant to secure a child's life. There are also some customs to protect a child thus endangered. For example the child may be called by a name from roots meaning 'to live', such as *Yaḥyā* (from *ḥayya*, 'to live'), *Ya'mur* (from *'amara* 'to flourish') or *Ya'īsh* and the wellknown feminine *'Ā'isha* (from *'ysh* 'to live'). The combination *Abū'l-baqā Ya'īsh* is particularly strong, as *baqā* means 'remaining, duration'; *Yabqā*, 'he remains', from this same root also occurs. In the Persianate areas one finds *Jāvīd* 'eternal', or *Mānda* 'remained', while among the Turks *Yaşar (yāshār)* 'he lives' and even *Ölmez* (he does not die, immortal) occur; verbal forms from *durmak* 'to remain', are frequent, like *Duran* 'remaining', *Dursun* 'he/she may remain' or *Durmuş* 'has remained'. In the Indian environment, the root *jī*, 'to live', serves the same purpose – *Jiā, Jīnūn, Jīwa, Jūna* and their feminine counterparts *Jīan, Jīndo, Jīnī, Jīwī* are used in the Punjab.[23]

A good Muslim custom is to name the child *'abd*, 'servant of –' with one of those Divine names that point to eternity of life, like *'Abdul Ḥayy*, '– of the Living', *'Abdul Bāqī*, '– of the Everlasting' or *'Abdud Dā'im*, '– of the Ever-remaining', etc. One would also avoid giving the child the name of a family member or friend who has tragically died, and if someone in a group bears the name of an individual who has prematurely died one says in Konya: 'His name is the same, his age may not be the same'.[24]

Instead of giving a child, for whose survival one fears, a strong and positive name, one can also do the contrary, that is, call it by an opprobrious name to cheat the evil spirits that surround it and want to snatch it away. In Arabic one finds *Yamūt, Tamūt*, 'he/she dies', in the Punjab *Machhai*, 'Child of death'. In Tunis a name like *Chebinou* (= *shay' baynahu)* 'what is common between him (and a jinn)' is used[25] while among the Turks a child born after many children have died is often called *Adsïz*, 'without name', because as long as the child has no name, nobody can practice black magic against it.[26] (cf. *Balāsim* = *bilā ism*, 'without name' in Southern Iraq). In classical Arabic tradition names like *Murr*, 'bitter', *Kalb*, 'Dog' or *Ḥarb*, 'war' were supposed to frighten the jinn and are still used in Tunisia and elsewhere despite the Prophet's aversion to such names; likewise, names derived from the root *ghlb*, 'to be victorious', can be used to emphasize that the child will overcome the evil spirits.

As one often dresses up little boys in girls' clothes to distract the interest of the jinns, so one may also give them the ugliest possible names, for instance *Zibālah,* 'Garbage' (Egypt) or *Gonañra,* 'Dunghill' (Punjab). *Chilra,* 'Louse', occurs also in the Punjab.[27] *Kishile,* 'a piece of rough woollen cloth by which a pack animal's face is covered' (Khuzistan), belongs to this very widespread category.[28] And while *Bulāqī,* 'Nose-ring' (the sign of the married woman in northern India) is a perfectly honourable name for a woman it has a very negative connotation when given to a boy.[29]

Among the rites to ensure the life of an infant there is an interesting Tunisian custom which is also connected with names: a parent begs at the doors of forty men by the name of Muḥammad and buys a new dress from the money thus acquired, which supposedly protects the baby.[30] In the Punjab and elsewhere the infant is given to a *faqīr* and then begged back as a kind of alms. Children who have undergone such a ceremony can then be called *Ghulām Bhīk,* 'Servant of the beggar' or *Khayrātī* ('Alms'). The child can also be given away immediately after birth and bought back for a few cowries or coins, which is reflected in names like *Bechai* 'Sold' (Punjab) or *Satkandī* 'Seven cowries' (id.) In Turkey a woman was once called *Beşbine,* 'For five thousand'. Similar customs are known from Bengal and Afghanistan. In Tashqurgan in northern Afghanistan, a child that is considered to be in danger is passed between the jawbones of a wolf and then given the name 'Wolf', *gorg* (P) or *börü* (T).[31]

It is a moot question whether one should give a baby born next after a deceased child the name of the dead one, or avoid it; both customs are found – unless the new baby is simply called 'Substitute', *ʿiyāḍ* or *ʿauḍ.*[32] Should the family be afflicted by misfortune after a child's birth, one tends to change its name after consulting with religious specialists; the same is done in Turkish areas, especially Istanbul, when a child is nervous, naughty, or difficult to handle because (so one thinks) 'its name is too heavy for it'.[33]

An easy way to remember a child's birthday or at least the season during which it was born, is to give it a name that indicates the day or time of the year; just as we know people called Noël, Dominique, 'born on Sunday', or April. The names of the months serve the same purpose. *Ramaḍān* (Ramzān, Ramjān, diminutive Rumayḍān), the holy month of fasting, is particularly blessed and therefore often remembered in names. *Rajab, Shaʿbān* and *Muḥarram* occur likewise owing to their religious significance, while *Ṣafar* (as in *Ṣafar Khōja, Ṣafar Bey*) reminds the Shiites of the fortieth day after Imām Ḥusayn's martyrdom, and the Muslims in general of the beginning of the

Prophet's last illness. Children born in Ramaḍān may be called *Ṣā'im* (f. *Ṣā'ima*, 'fasting') or *Rūza* (P), *Oruç* (T), 'Fast'; and I remember a Turkish woman called *Sa'ime Oruç*. The name *Shahr Allāh*, 'God's month', can also be used for a child born in Ramaḍān. The name of the month can be combined with other names, like *Ramjān 'Alī* (Gujarat, Bengal); and the Persian, and even more Indo-Muslim, tendency to add *ad-dīn*, 'of the religion' to every conceivable noun leads to forms like *Rajab ad-dīn* or *Sha'bān al-milla* (*milla* = religious community).[34] In the Persianate areas *Mihrī* can be used for a woman born in the month of Mihr, September, and numerous are names for both sexes connected with *Ādhar*, March-April.

An Indian woman's name *Laylatulqadr*, shows clearly her birthday in the sacred night of Ramaḍān, and so does Mr *Ramzan Idi*'s name. It is a special joy when a child is born on one of the two feasts (*'īd*), especially on the *'īd ul-fiṭr* at the end of the fasting month. Thus names like *'Īdū, Īdō* (Panjabi), *Eid Muḥammad* (Baluchistan), *al-'Aïd, Bel-Ạïd, al-'Ayyād, 'Ayyādī*, or *'Ayyāda* (North Africa) occur frequently and so does the Turkish equivalent of *'Īd, Bayram*. If a boy is born on the *'īd al-aḍḥā*, 'the Feast of offering', during the pilgrimage season, he may be called *Baqr'īdī* (Punjab); and *Qurbānverdī* 'The Sacrifice has given' is found among Turks in Iran. A *Ḥājj* (Tunis), *Ḥājjī* (Iran) or *Ḥājjīgeldī*, 'The pilgrim came' (T), is born in the month of Dhū'lḥijja or when the pilgrims return from the *ḥajj* to Mecca.

Children born on the Prophet's birthday, *mīlād an-nabī*, on 12 Rabī' al-awwal, may be named *Maulūd* (*T Mevlût*), *Maulūdiyya, Miloud* (Tunis), and a birthday on the day of the Prophet's heavenly journey, *mi'rāj*, on 27 Rajab, can result in names like *Mi'rāj* (also transcribed *Mehraj*) or *Mi'rāj ad-dīn* (Pakistan). If the child is born in mid-Sha'bān, in the *laylat al-barā'a*, he may be called *Berat* (T), while the name *'Āshūr* (f. *'Āshūra Begum*) may indicate the birth on the tenth of Muharram, 'Āshūra day. Children born on the death anniversary of a saint, *'urs* (lit. 'marriage', viz. of the soul with God) appear sometimes as *'Urs* or *'Ursān*, and when the birth happened in a period when a certain shrine was visited, the child's name may be *Ziyārat*, 'Pious visit'. In areas under Persian influence, *Naurūz*, 'New Year', the vernal equinox, occurs frequently.

The days of the week can also be used as names: a child born on Friday may be called *Jum'a (Cuma)* or (P) *Ādīna*, while Thursday lends its name to *Khamīs, Khamīsū Khan, Khamsī* (Swahili) or, for a girl, *Khemisse (= khamīsa)*.[35] In Tashqurghan, on the other hand, Thursday is never used as a name as it implies bad luck.[36] Wednesday, *arba'a*, appears in North African names as *Raba'* or *Larbeh*, while Saturday's children can be *Sebti* or *Sabbati*. In Iran I found one *Pīr Yakshanbahī*, from *yakshanbah*, 'Sunday'.

It is even simpler to remember the season of the birth, especially in rural areas, as is evident from Enno Littmann's remark that a Bedouin boy by name of *Fallāḥ*, 'Fellah', was born when the fellahin were ploughing. [37] Already in ancient Arabia names like *Rabʿī* or *Ṣayfī*, 'Of the spring' or 'the summer' respectively, were used (always without the definite article), and among the names collected in Tunis all four seasons are represented: *Rabʿī*, *Ṣīfī* (from *ṣayf*, 'summer'), *Kharīfī* (autumn) and *Chatoui* (= *shitāwī*, from *shitā'*, 'winter'). *Maṭīr* is an Arab child born on a rainy day (from *maṭar*: rain) and Littmann found a number of names in the southern Hauran which recalled the rare event of snow: *Thalj, Thalīj, Thallāj, Thālij, Thalja.*[38] Again, some memorable event of the year can be preserved in a name: a child in the Punjab born during a famine may be called *Akālī*,[39] and a recent, more enjoyable occasion was the late Aga Khan's Diamond Jubilee, which resulted in numerous young Ismailis called *Diamond*; the same happened during his Platinum Jubilee, so that a number of *Platinum* are found in the Ismaili community.

In some countries, especially in India, children are sometimes named according to the astrological requirements of the hour of birth.[40] As each hour has a ruling planet the name should ideally begin with one of the planet's letters. If a boy is born in the hour ruled by the moon, *qamar*, he should be called *Qamar ad-dīn*, or else by using the last letter of *qamar*, names like *Raḥīm-bakhsh* can be constructed; if it is a girl, *Rābiʿa* or *Rāfiʿa* would be auspicious; for someone under the influence of Mars, *Mirrīkh*, appropriate names would be *Mīrānbakhsh, Maryam, Khayrullāh* and *Khadīja*, and so on. This tradition is still alive: a young Indian friend of mine, born on 7 Ṣafar, bears the name *Kāẓim*, as this is the day of Imam Mūsā al-Kāẓım, but he uses his astrological name *Ṭālib*. Another person's name was recently changed by his Sufi master into a lucky astrological name.[41].

A number of personal names have geographical connotations. The reason for calling a child by a geographical name is not always clear: is a *Mecca Beg* or *Madīna Khān* born in that place, or do the parents merely hope that he will reach the sacred place? *Mecca* as the surname of people who performed the pilgrimage, or underwent a miraculous adventure during their journey to the holy city, is attested from India. Names like *Dimishq Khān* or *Ghaznī Khān* seem to point out the native place, but the name *Najaf (Nazaf* in India) shows clearly that the person was the scion of a pious Shiite family who either had performed the pilgrimage to this sacred burial place of ʿAlī in Iraq, or hoped that their child might be blessed with such a visit. One finds *Ḥijāz Khān* and, among the Qarāqoyunlu Turcomans, *Miṣr*, 'Egypt' *Beg*. Connections with the birthplace are clear in the case of the Bedouin girl *Nfeyid*, 'little sand-desert', who was born in the Nefud desert.[42]. On the other hand, *Daryā Khān*, 'sea, big river', may have been called thus for his generosity or greatness.

It seems that geographical names are used more frequently for women than for men – perhaps because the Arabic *arḍ*, 'earth, ground' is a feminine word. As *Dunyā*, 'this world', *Kayhān* (P), 'world' and *Kishwar* (P) 'land' are used for women, the names of specific areas also occur: *Sīstān Khānim, Īrān, 'Irāq* or *Tūrān Khātun* are still found in the Middle East; and as in Iran a *Tehran Bībī* can be found, in Tunisia *Tūnis* and *Tourzeur* appear in women's names.[43] *Medina* has become a woman's name in Bengal because the heroine of a medieval romance is so called. In Turkey names of rivers are found: *Tuna*, 'Danube', *Dijla, Dicle*, 'Tigris' and *Idil*, 'Volga' were quite fashionable in the 1940s. In modern Iran one could even encounter girls by the name of *Amrīkā*, 'America'.

III

Help from God – Religious Name-Giving

One can imagine my shock when I read one morning in the *Pakistan Times* the headline: 'Nasrum Minallah dies in road mishap.' How could *Naṣrun min Allāh*, 'Help from God' (here spelled according to the Qur'anic pronunciation with an assimilated *m*) be connected with any mishap at all?

The poor man, so I understood then, was one of the numerous Muslims whose elders open the Qur'ān at random to select their child's name; and their eye had fallen on Sūra 61/13. This custom is widespread in the Indian subcontinent and in other, predominantly non-Arab, countries; and in many cases it leads to strange combinations, as the parents usually do not know enough Arabic to understand the implications of certain expressions. The biographer of the eighteenth-century Indian poet and scholar Azād Bilgrāmī tells us that one day someone knocked at Azād's door in Aurangabad and when asked his name, replied: *'Baʿdu bi'd-dīn'*, whereupon the scholar refused to talk to him because of the evil connotation of the words (Sura 95/7: 'And what makes you deny *after that the Judgment*?'). The hero of Sarshār's Urdū novel *Fasāna-i Azād* bears the name *Mirzā A-lam nashraḥ*, 'Did We not open [your breast]?' (Sūra 94/1), which may well have been taken from life; and a Turkish author's name is *Üzlifat*, 'brought near' (Sūra 81/13: 'When Paradise is brought near').

Names like *Shams wa'ḍ-ḍuḥā* 'Sun and morning-light' (Sūra 91/1), *an-najm ath-thāqib*, 'The radiant star' (Sūra 86/3) and *al ʿurwat al-wuthqā*, 'the firmest handle' (Sūra 2/157 and 37/21) occur; however, when *Ṣabrun jamīl*, 'Fine patience' (Sūra 12/59) is given to an Egyptian girl the implied meaning may also be that there are already too many daughters in the family.[1] Women with names like *Asrà*, 'He journeyed by night' (Sūra 17/1) or *Yusrà*, 'Ease' (Sūra 87/8, 92/7) can also be found. An interesting development is that of *Naṣūh*, derived from the Qur'ānic expression *taubatan naṣūḥan* 'sincere repentance' (Sūra 66/8) which appears already in Rūmī's *Mathnavi* as the name of the mischievous servant in the ladies' bath who then 'repented sincerely'.[2] People called *Aʿūdhu*, 'I seek refuge' exist, and *Qul huwa Allāh* 'Say: He is God' (Sūra 112/1) is the ancestor of a Shia *sayyid* family, while *Bismillāh* 'in the name of God', *Inshā Allāh* 'if God wills' and *Māshā' Allāh* (the latter, in Egypt, also feminine)[3] occur quite frequently among Pathans, but also now and then in other parts of the Muslim world – as in the case of the Jewish astromomer Manasseh who adopted, in the early

Middle Ages, the name *Māshā'Allāh.* Lately it has become fashionable in Egypt and probably in most Islamic countries to name children after concepts taken from the Qur'ān like *Rafraf* (Sūra 55/76), *Istabraq,* or *Sundus,* the 'brocade' mentioned in Sūra 76/21 and elsewhere: the latter name is, incidentally, also found in Anatolia.

There is still another method to avail oneself of the power of the Qur'ān to bless: instead of taking a word or sentence, one takes the first letter of the page opened to determine the child's name. The actual name is then often formed to constitute a sequence to the father's name; e.g., when the father is *Sharāfat 'Alī* and the first word on the page is *dhākirīn*, the letter *dh* determines the name, and the baby could be called *Dhahānat 'Alī* or some similar form. This method however can lead to the formation of meaningless names in a population of non-Arab background; verbs can even be used as nouns: as in a case in Hyderabad where one 'Abdun Na'īm took the Qur'ānic word *nuqīm*, 'We establish' (Sura 18/105) to form his son's name which he wanted to rhyme with *na'īm* – and the boy was called *'Abdun Nuqīm* 'the slave of We establish'. Qur'ānic expressions occur also in nicknames; the Persian Sufi Najm ad-dīn Kubrā obtained his soubriquet *Kubrā* from the expression *aṭ-ṭāmmat al-kubrā,* 'the greatest disaster' (Sura 79/34).

An often-quoted *ḥadīth* states that 'the names which God loves best are 'Abdullāh and 'Abdur Raḥmān'.[4] These two indeed occur very frequently in the Muslim world. The word *'abd* can be connected with any of the ninety-nine Most Beautiful Names of God, and the combination appears in transcription as 'Abdul-, 'Abdal, 'Abd al-, Abdel. In many cases, the ' (the Arabic letter *'ayn*) is not marked in the transliteration, and the rule that the l of the Arabic definite article should be assimilated to the so-called sun-letters (t, th, d, dh, r, z, s, sh, ṣ, ḍ, ṭ, ẓ, l and n) is often violated; the correct pronounciation is in such cases *'Abdur Raḥīm, 'Abduṣ Ṣabūr,* etc. Sometimes Divine names which are not given in the generally accepted lists printed at the beginning of modern copies of the Qur'ān can be found;[5] for example *'Abdul Jamīl,* relating to the *ḥadīth* that 'God is beautiful, *jamīl,* and loves beauty', or *'Abdul Akbar,* which points to the beginning of the call to prayer, *Allāhu akbar,* 'God is greater [than anything]'. Parents will, of course, ordinarily chose one of the *jamālī* or *luṭfī* Divine names, that is, one that expresses God's kindness and mercy (*laṭīf, raḥīm, wadūd*), forgiveness (*ghafūr, ghaffār*) or generosity (*karīm*). Thus, names like *'Abdul Laṭīf* or *'Abdul Ghaffār* by far outweigh the other combinations, although some *jalālī,* i.e. 'majestic' names like *jabbār* or *qahhār* are also commonly used. The name of the American basketball player *Karīm*

'Abdul Jabbār, is certainly fitting as it points both to his gigantic stature and his reliance on The Overpowering One. Another American convert, a painter, selected the name *'Abdul Muṣawwir*, 'slave of the One That Gives Forms'. But nobody would call his son *'Abdul Mumīt* or *-Khāfiḍ*, 'slave of Him Who Slays' or '– Who Lowers.'

As with other types of names, certain compounds are favoured in specific areas. Thus, *'Abdur Raqīb* and *'Abdul Kāfī* are frequent in modern Yemen. Sometimes the normal form of the Divine names is slightly changed so that *ḥāfiẓ* instead of the normal *ḥafīz*, *mājid* instead of *majīd* is found: e.g. *'Abdul Mājid*. Comparatively rare are combinations with more abstract Divine names, such as *Ạbduẓ Ẓāhir*, 'slave of the Outwardly Manifested', and even rarer still is its contrast *'Abdul Bāṭin*, '– of the Inner Hidden'. Likewise *'Abdul Awwal* (of the First) occurs at times, while *'Abdul Ākhir*, '– of the Last' is rarely, if ever, used. Emphasis is laid on God's unity and unicity, and the simple 'Abdullāh is separated into *'Abdul Ilāh*, 'slave of the God'. God's position as the only object of praise appears in names like *'Abdul Maḥmūd*, 'slave of the Praised One'. *'Abd rabbihi*, 'slave of his Lord' or even *'Abd rabb an-nabiy* '– of the Prophet's Lord' can be found. *'Abduhu*, 'His slave' is, however, generally accepted as being a name of the Prophet and therefore frequent (cf. Sūra 17/1, 53/9). (See p. 31.)

In the catagory called by Caetani 'pseudo-theophoric names'[6] the Divine name is replaced by an abstract noun: *'Abdus Subḥān*, derived from the exclamation *Subḥān Allāh!* 'Glorified be God!' belongs here and, even more, names like *'Abdud Dīn* or *'Abdul Burhān*, 'slave of the religion' or 'of the proof'; *'Abdul Fatḥ*, which occurred especially in Qajar Iran (1721-1925), may have the connotation of *fatḥun qarīb*, 'and near victory' (Sura 63/13) which is so often found in Shia inscriptions. That a contemporary Christian theologian who works for Christian-Muslim dialogue should have adopted the pseudonym *'Abd at-tafāhum*, 'Slave of mutual understanding', is highly fitting. (Incidentally, among Christians, names like *'Abdul Masīḥ* or *'Abduṣ Ṣalīb*, 'slave of Christ' or 'of the cross' are in quite frequent use.

These compounds which contain one of the Divine names are regarded as bearing a special sanctity: The Mughal emperor Humāyūn, who never uttered the name of God or the Prophet unless in a state of ritual purity, would address people by such names as 'Abdul to avoid a desecration of the Divine name.[7] *'Abdul* is nowdays frequently used among Muslims, even in the assimilated form: young 'Abduẓ Ẓāhir calls himself officially *'Abduẓ*. The sanctity of the names formed in this way is still very real in the Indian subcontinent where some people believe that prayer at the tombs of those called 'Abdur Raḥīm and similar combinations with 'Names of Mercy', as well as of those who bear one of the Prophet's names, is particularly efficacious.[8]

The diminutive of *'abd* is *'ubayd*; but it seems to be formed almost exclusively from 'Abdullāh – hence the numerous *'Ubaydullāh*s. Usually, it is the Divine name that undergoes a change for hypocoristic purposes, such as *Jabbūr* from 'Abdul Jabbār, *Ṣannū'* from 'Abduṣ Ṣāni'.[9] The feminine equivalent is *amat*, 'slave girl', like the frequent *Amatul Karīm*, often shortened to *Karīma* .

This kind of abbreviation corresponds to the tendency to leave out the *'abd* completely and to invent forms like *Ḥaqqī* from 'Abdul Ḥaqq, *'Abdī* from 'Abdullāh, or *Ḥamīd* from 'Abdul Ḥamīd. The witty journalist Shorish Kashmiri, seated during a conference in Lahore between Justice S. A. Raḥmān and Khwāja A. Raḥīm, joked about his good fortune to 'be placed between *Ar-Raḥmān* and *Ar-Raḥīm'*. It is nevertheless somewhat weird, and should shock every pious Muslim, to see in modern telephone directories so many Divine names appearing as family names, like Haq (Haque, Huq etc.), Wahid, Ghaffar etc, or to listen to a telephone conversation between *Qudrat-i-Khudā* (God's might) and *Ghulām Nabī* (servant of the Prophet) which begins with 'Khudā (God) speaking', and then 'Here is Nabī (the prophet) speaking. . .'.[10]

The word *'abd* should be used exclusively with Divine names. However, mainly in non-Arab countries, it has been and still is used with the names of the Prophet (e.g., like *'Abdur Rasūl, 'Abdun Nabī*), or the names of Shia imāms like *'Abdur Riḍā, 'Abdul Mahdī*. The Saudi authorities – so I have been told – will force pilgrims with such names to change them into combinations such as *'Abd rabb ar-Riḍā* which are theologically more acceptable forms. To express one's status as servant of the Prophet or the imām one should use either the Arabic *ghulām* 'servant', like *Ghulām Rasūl*, or a Persian or Turkish word like *banda, qul, quli* ('slave'). Interestingly, these latter words are also combined with Divine names in non-Arab areas. In pre-Safavid Iran, 'Abdullāh was changed in *Khudābanda*,[11] while the Turkish *qul* appears somewhat later to form names like *Allāhqulī, Raḥmānqulī, Qādirqulī* etc. In Central Asia one can even find *Maulānāqul*, 'slave of our Lord'.

Another *ḥadīth* urges the faithful: 'Call your children by the names of the prophets!';[12] and it goes on to state that the most disgraceful names for a believer are *Ḥarb*, 'War', and *Murra*, 'Bitterness' and that people named *Mālik* will have to suffer on Doomsday as there is no possessor, *mālik*, but God. Despite this wellknown tradition, the caliph 'Umar (634-44) opposed the use of prophets' names, perhaps out of fear lest they be disgraced by constant use; yet, many of the Prophet's companions called their sons by the names of messengers mentioned in the

Qur'ān. One can still find all the twenty-eight Qur'ānic prophets either with their full names or derivatives, although some of them, like *Hūd*, are now comparatively rare.

Thanks to the veneration due to Abraham (Ibrāhīm) as the ancestor of the Arabs and first builder of the Kaaba, his name is dear to the pious, and so is his surname *Khalīl Allāh*, 'God's Friend', often only *Khalīl*. (In the same way a common abbreviation of Ibrāhīm is *Ibish*, sometimes also *Ibbo*.) Abraham's sons *Ismāʿīl Dhabīḥ Allāh*, 'Slaughtered by God' and *Isḥāq* (Isaac) appear often, and so does *Yaʿqūb* (Jacob) and his son *Yūsuf* (Joseph), sometimes called *Kanʿān* (T *Kenan*), the epitome of beauty. *Mūsā*, the *Kalīm Allāh*, 'Addressed by God' is among the favourite names; his father-in-law *Shuʿayb* is also represented (especially in India) as are *Ayyūb* (Job), the patient sufferer, *Nūḥ* (Noah), *Dā'ūd* and *Sulaymān*. Thus, from *Adam* to *ʿĪsā* (Jesus, even with the appellation *Masīḥ*, 'Christ') and his relatives *Zakariyā* and *Yaḥyā* (John the Baptist) every prophet is found in Muslim nomenclature, including *Ilyās* and *Idrīs*, who are supposed to have entered Paradise alive. The mysterious prophet-saint *al-Khaḍir (Khiḍr, Khiżir, Hĭzĭr)*, the guide of the wayfarers and genius of greenery and rivers, also lends his name to boys. As in the Christian tradition names of angels are used, although there is a difference of opinion whether or not this is permissible. There are certainly people called after the archangels *Mikā'īl* (Michael) or *Jibrā'īl, Jibrīl* (Gabriel). In Persian the simple *Firishta*, 'angel', appears, and *Melek* (*mal'ak*) 'angel' is a common name for Turkish women. The gatekeeper of Paradise, *Riḍwān* (developed out of 'God's pleasure', *riḍwān*, without which no one can enter Paradise) gives his name to men and, with a feminine ending, to women: *Riḍwāna*.

If the names of earlier prophets are surrounded by an aura of blessing and protective power, how much more is the name of the final Prophet bound to bring blessing to those who bear it![13]

'Your name is beautiful, you yourself are beautiful, Muḥammad,' sings a medieval Turkish poet and expresses well the feeling inspired by this name. 'It would not hurt any of you if in his house were one or two Muḥammad',[14] said the Prophet himself; who also reportedly stated, 'If someone has four sons and does not call any of them by my name, he has wronged me.'[15] Did not a *ḥadīth qudsī*, an extra-Qur'ānic revelation, promise that everyone who is called Muḥammad will enter Paradise? And is it not said that angels come to the house in which a Muḥammad dwells? One expects the Prophet to be mysteriously connected with those who share his name. Būṣīrī, the thirteenth-century author of the *Burda*, the most famous Arabic encomium on the Prophet, expresses this idea when, smitten with illness, he says toward the end of his poem:

> For since I have been given the name of Muḥammad, he has for me an obligation,
> He, who is most perfect in fulfilling all his duties among the creatures.

For the Prophet would certainly help an ailing person who is named after him.

Besides this deep trust in the efficacy of the Prophet's name there was also a profound sense of awe and respect which induced some people never to pronounce the name of Muḥammad unless in a state of ritual purity. As the sixteenth-century Indo-Persian poet ʿUrfī sings:

> A thousand times I wash my mouth
> with musk and with rose water.
> And still, to speak your name
> is absolute impudence![16]

If a boy is called Muḥammad and has to be scolded, or if a grown-up Muḥammad is a liar or a thief, what is to be done lest the blessed name be polluted? One way out is to vocalize the consonants somewhat differently, e.g., as *Miḥammad, Maḥammad, Mūḥ* (mainly in North Africa) or *Mehmed* in Turkey, where the full name is reserved for 'our Lord the Prophet' (*peygamber efendimiz*). Forms like *Māmō* in West Africa, *Mēmō* among the Kurds or just a simple *Mīm* are also used.[17] The name of the Messenger, however, should never be mentioned without adding the formula of blessing or an honorific title to it.[18] In this connection it is revealing that the Bengali librarian Saif-ul-Islam remarks in his notes concerning the cataloguing of Muslim names that as 'most Muslims would object to an entry under the Prophet's name, the entry should be made under the element directly preceding it, e.g. under Nur Muhammad, Dewan Muhammad, etc.'[19] Such concern is apparently not felt when dealing with Divine names such as Ḥaq, Raḥmān etc., as we saw earlier.

It seems that in the course of time Muḥammad was generally augmented by other names, such as *Muḥammad Akhtar, Muḥammad Ḥamīdullāh*, etc., or used to form the second part of compounds as in *Adīna Muḥammad, Yār Muḥammad*, etc.[20]

There was also another way to secure the blessings of the Prophet's name, for Muḥammad was not his only name. The Muslims surround their beloved Prophet with numerous names, often ninety-nine as corresponding to the ninety-nine Divine Names, and these *asmā' sharīfa*, 'noble names', are nowadays often printed at the end of copies of the Qur'ān. Some authors enumerate more than two thousand names for the Prophet, many of which are developed out of Qur'ānic expressions.

The very root *ḥmd* with its connotation of laud and praise, which lies at the root of the word *Muḥammad*, 'the richly praised one', is thought to establish a special link between the Prophet and the Praised One, *al-maḥmūd*, that is God. *Maḥmūd* is however also understood as one of the names of the Prophet and can be used in its feminine form *Maḥmūda*, while *Muḥammad*, though a proper passive participle, occurs in the feminine, *Muḥammada*, only on some very early tombstones and then never again. In Indian Islam, however, a feminine *Muḥammadī* occurs.

From the same root *ḥmd* is derived *Aḥmad*, Muḥammad's eternal and heavenly name, by which he is mentioned in Sura 61/5 as the 'most praiseworthy' one who will complete the Divine revelation. It is this name *Aḥmad*, which led to daring mystical speculations: in an extra Qur'ānic word, God describes Himself as *Aḥmad bilā mīm*, 'Ahmad without the m' that is *Aḥad*, 'One'.

The root *ḥmd* belongs in general to the favourites in Arabic nomenclature. Besides the names just mentioned, one finds *ḥāmid*, 'praising', and its intensive *Ḥammād*, 'much praising'. *Al-Ḥamīd*, 'the Praised', belongs to the Divine Names and *'Abdul-Hamīd*, with its abbreviation *Ḥamīd*, is commonly used, along wih the feminine *Ḥamīda*. Out of these classical forms numerous derivations develop such as *Ḥammūd*, *Ḥammūda* or *Ḥammādī*, *Ḥamdī*, *Ḥamdān*, *Ḥamdūn*, and *Ḥamdīn*, the diminutive *Ḥumayd* and its enlargement *Ḥumaydān*, besides *Ḥamīdān* and *Ḥamdīs*; and in North Africa one finds *Ḥumaydūd*, *Ḥamdīd*, *Ḥamdūd* and *Ḥammādū*, to mention only the frequent forms.

The Prophet is mentioned as *'abduhu*, 'His slave' in the two important visionary accounts of Sura 17/1 and 53/10, and therefore, *'Abduhu*, *Abduh* has become a proper name. The mysterious letters at the beginning of Sura 20, *Ṭāhā*, and Sura 36, *Yāsīn*, are interpreted as Divine addresses to the Prophet and therefore used as names which are well-known even in the remotest areas of the Islamic world, be it in Gilgit or in the northern Deccan. Their first use as proper names may go back to non-Arab countries: *Yāsīn* occurs, to my knowledge, first in Herat in the tenth century. The letters *Ḥāmīm* at the beginning of Suras 40 to 46 are sometimes interpreted as *ḥabībī Muḥammad*, 'My beloved friend Muḥammad' and have therefore entered Muslim nomenclature, as have the Divine addresses at the beginning of Sura 73 and Sura 74: two Indian brothers by the names of *Muzzammil*, 'the wrapped one' and *Muddaththir*, 'the covered one' are Muslim theologians in the USA.

Muḥammad is called in the Qur'ān 'the one who brings good tidings' and 'the warner', *bashīr* and *nadhīr*: these two attributes are frequently used as proper names, sometimes expanded to *Bashīr Aḥmad* or *Nadhīr Aḥmad*. Out of his description as a 'shining lamp', *sirāj munīr*, the common *Munīr* (fem. *Munīra*) developed, as also the *laqab Munīr ad-dīn*, and the numerous compounds with *sirāj* 'lamp': *Sirāj ad-dīn, -al-ḥaqq, -al-islām*, 'Lamp of the religion', '– of the Divine Truth', '– of Islam', etc. As Muḥammad was known in Mecca as *al-amīn*, 'the trustworthy', *Amīn, Emin* or, in West Africa, *Lamine*, became favourite names along with the feminine *Amīna* (not to be confused with the name of the Prophet's mother, *Āmina*)

In a well-known tradition the Prophet's beauty is described by Umm Maʿshar whose barren sheep he had mysteriously milked, and the Persian poet Saʿdī has poetically transformed the qualities mentioned in her record in his famous line:

wasīmun qasīmun jasīmun nasīm
Elegant, well shaped, noble, and graceful.

These epithets can be found, though not too often, as proper names: *jasīm* forms the compound *Jasīm ad-dīn* (Bengal).[21]

In rare cases one finds *Rasūl, Resul*, 'Messenger', as a proper name; or even the somewhat daring combination *Muḥammad Rasūl Allāh* (Deccan).[22] In Bengal I encountered someone called, like the Prophet, *Khayrulbashar*, 'the best of mankind'. *Nūr al-hudā*, 'light of right guidance' occurs also, even – most surprisingly – as a woman's name. Shockingly enough, it was the Malaysian woman swimming champion who was called that![23]

Many believers have wanted to express their devotion to the Prophet by thanking him for the gift of a son: *Faḍl ar-rasūl* 'Kindness of the Messenger' or, in the East, *Rasūlbakhsh* 'gift of the Messenger', *Aḥmad-bakhsh, Nabībakhsh* 'gift of Aḥmad, of the Prophet'. And although the combination of *ʿabd* with any name but that of God is theologically objectionable, *ʿAbd an-nabī* and *ʿAbd ar-rasūl* occur, mainly in the East. But forms like *Ghulām Rasūl* 'servant of the Messenger', *Ghulām Yāsīn* '– of Yāsīn' or *Ghulām Sarwar* '– of the leader', are more common. Under Turkish influence, *Muḥammad-qulī* or *Peyghambar-qul* are not rare. In the Subcontinent the name *Ghulām ʿArabī* occurs, for *ʿArabī*, 'the Arab' is, like *Makkī, Madīnī, Hāshimī, Abṭaḥī*, a surname of the Prophet. The Arab background of Islam is particularly important for the Muslims in the Subcontinent, hence the use of combinations with these epithets.

As 'love of the Prophet flows in the veins of his community like blood',[24] as Iqbāl wrote, names expressing this love can also be found, again mainly in the eastern parts of the Muslim world: *Aḥmad-yār* or *Muḥammad-yār, Dōst-Muḥammad* or *Muḥammad-dōst*; but instead of these somewhat neutral words for 'friend' one encounters also *Muḥibb an-nabī* 'lover of the Prophet' and *ʿĀshiq Muḥammad*, 'infatuated with Muḥammad'. In the Subcontinent even more daring combinations are used, such as *Nūr an-nabī*, 'light of the Prophet' (a typical mystical combination), *Iqrār an-nabī*, or *Maḥmūd an-nabī*, 'affirmation of the Prophet' or 'praised by the Prophet'.[25]

As everything connected with the Prophet was regarded as filled with blessing it is not surprising that a man in the Middle Ages called his ten sons by the names of the *'ashara al-mubashshara*, the ten companions of the Prophet to whom Paradise was promised.[26]

In Sunni Islam, the first four caliphs and their names play a special role, while 'Alī and his descendants form the major part of Shia nomenclature. *Abū Bakr aṣ-ṣiddīq* appears in Turkey as *Bekir* and is likely to have as second name *Sĭtkĭ*, while *'Umar* (T *Ömer*) and his surname *al-Fārūq* go together; *Fārūq* can also be used independently and is found even in an Ismaili, that is Shia environment. *'Uthmān* (T *Osman*), who was married to two daughters of the Prophet, i.e. Umm Kulthūm and before that Ruqayya, is nicknamed *Dhū'n-nūrayn*, 'The one who possesses the two lights', which is often abbreviated to *Nūrī* or simply *Nūr*. The Shiites do not use the names of the first three caliphs, at least not after the mid-ninth century although two of 'Alī's own sons were called 'Umar and two 'Uthmān. Among Imām Ḥasan's sons, one 'Umar and one Abū Bakr are mentioned, and the tenth Imām, 'Ali an-naqī, had a daughter called 'Ā'isha (Abū Bakr's daughter and the wife of the Prophet).[27]

Names of other heroes from the early days of Islam are often found, be it the Prophet's uncles *Ḥamza* and *'Abbās* (this is particularly frequent among Shiites) or the name of his black muezzin *Bilāl*. This latter name became fashionable among Indian Muslims and in Pakistan owing to Iqbāl's two Urdu poems about this faithful companion of the Prophet.[28] It seems also that the name *Ṭāriq* became widely used in the same part of the world, after Ṭāriq's memory was evoked in one of Iqbāl's poems that celebrated the hero who crossed the straits of Gibraltar which still bear his name (*Jabal Ṭāriq*).[29] One may however also think in this connection of the beginning of Sura 86, where *ṭāriq* and *as-samā'* 'sky' are mentioned together – which induced an Arab friend of mine to call her granddaughter *Samā'*, the grandson being *Ṭāriq*. *Salmān* the Persian barber, who is the prototype of the Persians adopted into Muslim society, lends his name to quite a few boys although the word *salmān* in many idioms means simply 'barber' or some other lowly profession. A special sanctity surrounds *Uways al-Qaranī*, the Prophet's contemporary in Yemen, who became the model of those who find their way to God without a human guide. In the forms *Ways, Veysel, Oysul* (Kirgiz) his name is especially loved in Turkish areas. In Turkey itself even *Yemlikhā* appears, a name given to one of the Seven Sleepers.

The name of the Prophet's cousin and son-in-law *'Alī ibn Abī Ṭālib* is equally dear to Sunnis and Shiites, and tradition has it that Satan becomes angry when someone is called Muḥammad or 'Alī.[30] In the Shia tradition, 'the Prince of true men', *Shāh-i mardān* (hence *'Alī Mardān*) and his descendants through Fāṭima appear in rather variegated forms: 'Alī himself is called 'the lion of God', *Asadullāh*, for his mother had first called him *Ḥaydara*, 'lion' after his grandfather *Asad*, ('lion'); and thus names denoting 'lion' are frequently used in connection with him. Besides *Ḥaydar* and *Ghaḍanfar* one finds *Shīr* (P) and *Arslān* (T); all of them are used in compounds like *'Alī-Shīr*, *'Ali-Ḥaydar*. Since 'Alī is the 'commander of the faithful', *amīr al-mu'minīn*, and, according to legend, also 'the leader of the bees', *amīr an-naḥl*, names like *Amīr 'Alī*, *Mīr 'Alī*, *Amīr Aslān* or simply *Amīr* are well represented. Shia authors credit 'Alī with two hundred to a thousand names.[31] Famous is his surname *Abū Turāb*, 'father of dust', which was given to him, according to Shia tradition, by the Prophet who found him sleeping in the dust of the mosque, while the inimical tradition gives a different explanation and thinks this *kunya* was intended to be a curse: 'May his hands be in the dust!'[32] The name is quite common among Shiites, as is *Turāb 'Alī* (Dust of 'Alī). Among 'Alī's nicknames *Nūr Allāh* is most frequently used as a proper name, but *Yad Allāh* or *'Ayn Allāh* 'God's hand' or 'eye' appear too.[33]

Many names express the family's loving and devout relationship with the first imām or a sense that the child was born thanks to 'Alī's intercession. We may mention here *Luṭf 'Alī* 'grace of –', *Imdad* 'help of –',*Khayrāt* 'alms of –, *Minnat* 'gratitude owed to –', *Karam* 'generosity of –', *Yād* or *Yādgar* 'memory of –'. *Dād-'Alī*, *Bakhshish 'Alī* 'gift of 'Alī' occur in Iran; *Shāhwirdī*, 'the King ['Alī] has given' expresses the same idea with a Turkish verb. *Nawāz 'Alī* is 'cherished by 'Alī', while the love owed to the Imām is evident from *Muḥibb-*, *'Āshiq-*, or (with a Hindi word) *Piyār 'Alī*. *'Alī-Yār* or *Ḥaydar-dōst* are other common versions while *Yāvar 'Alī* is ''Alī's helper'.[34]

One may wish that the boy become a bearer of 'Alī's virtues or qualities, *Fażā'il* 'merits' or *Auṣāf 'Alī* 'good qualities'. His mysterious two-edged sword *Dhū'l-fiqār* is not only used as a proper name but also alluded to in compounds like *Qilich 'Alī* ''Alī's sword'; even *Panja 'Alī* ''Alī's fist' appears in Iran. Frequent also is the combination with *fatḥ*, 'victory': *Fatḥ 'Alī*. Persians and Central Asian Muslims like to connect the heroic first imām of the Shiites with the legendary hero of Iranian history, *Rustam*, to form the name *Rustam-'Alī*. The name can also be enlarged by endearing suffixes like *nūr*, 'light' or *gul*, 'rose': *'Alī-Nūr*, *'Alī-Gul*, and one sometimes has the feeling that it can be combined with almost every noun of positive meaning such as *Qand ʿAlī*, 'sugar of –'. *Ism ʿAlī*, 'ʿAlī's name' also occurs in Iran. ʿAlī's birthday is celebrated on 13 Rajab, hence one finds *Rajab ʿAlī* (combinations with other months occur also, though rarely).

As in the case of Muḥammad, the theologically incorrect form *ʿAbd ʿAlī* or *ʿAbdul Amīr* occurs, but more common are the Persian *banda* and the Turkish *qul*, as in *Banda ʿAlī*, *ʿAlīqul* or *Amīrqulī*, 'ʿAlī's servant, slave'. Even greater devotion to the beloved imām is expressed by *Qurbān ʿAlī*, 'sacrificed to –' and *Kalb ʿAlī*, 'ʿAlī's dog'. *Qoch ʿAlī*, his 'ram' (probably sacrificial) occurs, and in Mughal history one *Kafsh ʿAlī*, 'ʿAlī's shoe' is attested.[35]

The two sons of ʿAlī and Fāṭima, *Ḥasan* and *Ḥusayn*, have lent their names to innumerable boys in both Sunni and Shia circles.[36] Names like *Nūr al-Ḥasan*, 'light of Hasan', *Fayż al-Ḥasan*, 'gracious gift of –', *Alṭāf Ḥusayn*, 'kindnesses of –', *Irtiżā Ḥusayn*, 'approval of –', *Fidā Ḥusayn*, 'sacrificed to –' are used predominantly among Indo-Pakistani Muslims who also love combinations of Ḥusayn with nouns of the *tafaʿʿul* form such as *Tajammul-*, 'adornment –', *Taṣadduq*, 'donation of –' or *Tafażżul Ḥusayn*, 'favour of Ḥusayn'. Parallel to ʿAlī's names, *ʿAbdul Ḥusayn* and *Ḥusaynqulī* appear.

Sometimes, *Shabbīr* is substituted for Ḥusayn, as in *Ghulām Shabbīr*, for according to Shia tradition God ordered Gabriel to name ʿAlī's eldest son *Shibr*, (Arabic: Ḥasan) as ʿAlī's relation to Muḥammad resembled Aaron's relation to Moses, and Aaron's son was called Shibr. The younger one, then, became Shabbīr, and even the feminine form *Shabbīra* is sometimes used.[37] *Ḥasan* is also known as *Mujtabā*, *Ḥusayn* as *Murtażа*, and both can be called *Sibṭ*, 'grandson'. The second and third imām are sometimes combined as *Sayyidayn* to form names like *Ghulām(-i) Sayyidayn* 'servant of the two lords'. In other cases they are simply called 'the two Ḥasans', *Ḥasanayn*, as in *Ḥasanayn-nawāz*, 'cherished by –' or *Ḥasanayn-dōst*, 'friend of –'. A third son of ʿAlī and Fāṭima, who was prematurely born and did not live, was *Muḥsin* (derived from the same root *ḥsn*); his name too is dear to the Shia community.

In fact, all the names of the Imāms and their families are used, particularly in the Shia tradition, beginning from *ʿAlī Aṣghar*, the infant that was killed in Kerbela. The surname of the fourth imām, *Zayn al-ʿābidīn*, is sometimes ungrammatically split into two names, *Zaynal* and *ʿĀbidīn*. *Bāqir*, *Jaʿfar (aṣ-Ṣādiq)*, *Mūsā al Kāẓim*. *ʿAlī Riḍā (Rażā)*, *Muḥammad at-Taqī*, *ʿAlī an-Naqī* and *Ḥasan al-ʿAskarī* appear, as does the last one, the promised *Mahdī*. Generally these appear without the definite article: *Naqī*, *Ḥasan ʿAskarī*; and their names are, like those of their noble ancestors, combined with *ghulām* or *qulī: Ghulām Kāẓim, Ghulām Riżā, Mahdī-Qulī;* but again, combinations with *'abd* occu *'Abduṣ-Ṣādiq, 'Abd ur-Riḍā,'Abdul-Mahdī* etc.

Of course, 'Alī's father *Abū Ṭālib* also lent his name to Shia families and without the *Abū, Ṭālib,* another equivalent of 'Alī is formed. Often a family emphasizes its relation with the Prophet and the Imāms by calling their sons, for example, *Al-i Ḥaydar* 'family of Ḥaydar', *Sibt-i Ḥaydar, Sibṭ-i Ḥasan* 'grandson of –' as well as *'Iṭrat 'Alī, 'Iṭrat Ḥusayn* 'descendant of –'; *Aulād 'Alī* or – *Ḥaydar* 'children of –' also occurs. One may also simply refer to the Prophet as in *Āl-i Aḥmad, Āl-i nabī. Banī Fāṭimah,* however, occurs as a family name in Iran.

Sometimes the imām to whom one refers is not mentioned by name: one finds *Fakhr-i imām* and *Fażl-i imām* 'pride' and 'kindness of the imām', and the servitude owed to the imāms and even to the *sayyids,* Muḥammad's descendants, finds its expression in names like *Imām-qulī, 'Abd al-ā'imma* 'slave of the imāms' or *'Abd as-sādāt* 'slave of the sayyids'; and even *Kalb al-a'imma* 'dog of the imāms'. The name *Ma'ṣūm* reminds the reader of the fourteen 'innocent', *ma'ṣūm,* martyrs of Shia Islam; hence also the name *Ghulām Ma'ṣūm;* the feminine, *Ma'ṣūma,* however generally relates to Mūsā al-Kāẓim's daughter whose tomb in Qumm is a venerated place. The inventiveness of pious Indian Muslims seems to have no end: the practice of expressing dates by meaningful chronograms (by using the numerical value of the letters of the Arabic alphabet) can be seen in the name *Ghulām-i Āl-i Muḥammad* 'servant of Muḥammad's family', which yields the boy's date of birth, 1194AH / 1780 AD. (*gh* = 1000; *l* = 30; *a* = 1; *m* = 40; *a* = 1; *l* = 30; *m* = 40; *ḥ* = 8; *m* = 40; *d* = 8; the short vowels are not written).

As Qur'ānic phrases are sometimes transformed into proper names so one finds also – as early as 1581 in Bengal – one *Nād 'Alī Beg,* whose name refers to the invocation *Nādi 'Aliyyan* 'Call 'Alī, the manifester of miracles', which has been the most frequent invocation from Safavid times onward. *'Alī Madad* 'Help, 'Alī!' – a formula of greeting among the Ismailis – occurs also as a proper name.

For women, the Shia tradition carefully avoids *'A'isha* (the Prophet's young wife) as her relations with 'Alī and Fāṭima were somewhat strained, while *Khadīja,* Fāṭima's mother, is widely accepted. Fāṭima is the *Sayyidat an-nisā'* 'the mistress of women', *az-Zahrā* 'the radiant', *Batūl* 'virgin', *Kanīz* 'maiden', and male names like *'Abd az-zahrā* or *'Izz al-batūl* 'glory of the Virgin' can be found among pious Shiites.[38] Fāṭima is surrounded by still other names which are frequently found among Persian women, such as *Raḍiya* and *Marḍiya* 'content' and 'pleased', both derived from the description of the *nafs muṭma'inna,* the 'soul at peace' in Sura 89/27; further, *Ṭāhira* 'the Pure', *Mubāraka* 'blessed', *Zakiyya* 'pure, sinless' and *Muḥaddatha* 'she with whom [the angels] spoke'.

In Ankara in the 1950s I encountered some youngsters by the names *Ökkeş* and *Satïlmïş* and was curious to find the reasons for their names. The first was merely the Turkish version of the Prophet's companion *ʿUkkāsha,* who is buried near Islahiya close to the Syrian border and who is venerated as a saint by the local people. As for *Satïlmïş* (sold), and its feminine version *Satï,* the names pointed to a vow which the parents had made at a saint's tomb, promising that they would 'sell' the hoped-for child to the saint, that is, donate it or its services to the shrine.

To call a child after a local saint is a widespread custom in all religions, the most famous Muslim example being the emperor Akbar's son *Salīm,* later, as emperor, called Jahāngīr, who was named after Shaykh Salīm Chishtī, thanks to whose blessing he was born; although out of respect for the saint Akbar never actually addressed him by this name. In Tunis, *Chadli* (=*ash-Shādhilī*) is still frequent; around Kairouan one may find men called *ʿOqbī* after *Sīdī ʿUqba,* the conqueror of Tunisia, while in Gebes the name *ʿAbadi* is typical, remembering a local saint. Egypt has its *Dasūqī* (after the Sufi Ibrāhīm ad-Dasūqī), its *Aḥmad al-Badawī* (after the saint of Ṭanta whose fair is still attended by many), and *al-Mursī* (after the second master of the Shādhiliyya order in the thirteenth century), while among women, *Sitt Zaynab* and *Sitt Nafīsa,* both members of the Prophet's family, are much beloved and hence models for names. Whereas a pious mother in Istanbul may choose the name of the seventeenth-century mystical leader *Maḥmūd Hüdāyi* for her son, the villager near Ankara may call his son *Ḥüseyin Gazi* after the medieval warrior saint whose tomb stands on a hilltop overlooking the city. A Kashmiri may name a boy *Ghulām Hamadānī* to express his admiration for Sayyid ʿAlī Hamadhānī, to whom the Islamization of Kashmir in the fourteenth century is larged owed, while in Bihar one can expect names connected with *Sharafaddīn,* remembering Sharafaddīn Manērī (d. 1381), a mystical leader of great influence. Families may also call a child *Rifāʿī* or *Suhrawardī* in acknowledgment of their affiliation to this or that Ṣūfī order, and in many cases these attributions have turned lately into a kind of family name: *Muʿīnī* is the name of a family which claims descent from Khwāja *Muʿīnuddīn Chishtī* of Ajmer.

The names of Sufi masters and saints is an interesting chapter in itself. The spiritual leader, *Pīr* (P) and his descendants, *Pīrzāda,* are common in the eastern part of the Muslim world, and so is the *Murshid* (spiritual guide) and the *Makhdūm* (he who is served), whose descendants are known as *Makhdūmzāda*. Some saints are given surnames in the plural to emphasize their importance: for example, one finds Niẓāmaddīn *Auliyā* 'saints', and Ḥasan *Abdāl*, the *abdāl* being the hierarchy of forty invisible saints (in Turkey, the term is also used for members of a certain mystical tradition, like *Kayğusuz Abdal*). ʿUbaydullah *Aḥrār* 'free ones', but also *Evliya (=auliyā) Chelebi* belong here. The spiritual guide is, incidentally, always addressed and mentioned in the plural, and in Central Asia referred to as *īshān* (they).

Sometimes saints are referred to by nicknames that express their kindness towards their poor followers, such as *Pīr-i dastgīr*, 'who takes by the hand' (that is, ʿAbdul Qādir Jīlānī) or *Gharībnawāz, Bandanawāz*, 'who cherishes the poor', or 'the servants', nicknames of Muʿīn ad-dīn Chishti and Gēsūdarāz respectively. *Quṭb* (pole, axis) and *ghauth* (help) are titles for the highest members of the saintly hierarchy, and have often been arrogated by Sufis, for the saints are not exactly modest in their claims. Indian Sufism in particular has produced a long list of high-soaring epithets and nicknames for spiritual leaders – names that would shock any Wahhābī, and even any sober Arab Muslim. *Bāqī Billāh* (remaining in God) and *Fanā' fi'Llāh* (annihilation in God) are at least technical terms in Sufism, but *Rāz-i ilāhī* (Divine Mystery) is rather extravagant. *Tāj al-ʿāshiqīn* or – *al-ʿārifīn* ('crown of the lovers' or 'the gnostics') may be acceptable for a leading saint, but even our driver in Dehli, good Muslim but to my knowledge not a major saint, basks in the light of his name *Shams al-ʿārifīn* 'sun of the gnostics', abbreviated, for practical reasons, to *Shamshul*.

Many families with ties to Sufi orders or certain shrines reflect them, as mentioned above, in their nomenclature, be it the simple *Pīr-dād* (given by the Pir); *Pirden* (T) (from the Pir) or *Pir-nur* (T) 'Pir'[s] light' (all referring to Maulānā Rūmī); or a saint of yore like *Junayd, Ḥasan Baṣrī*, or *Jalāluddīn (Celâl*, in Turkey associated with Rūmī). The feminine name *Celâle*, although explicable as correct Arabic form was, in a particular case, indeed derived from Celâl[addīn Rūmī] as the parents were living in the compound of the shrine.

Possibly the most venerated saint in the Islamic world is ʿAbdul Qādir Gīlānī (Jīlānī, d. 1166). As he is *ghauth-i aʿẓam* 'the greatest Help' as well as *Muḥyī'ddīn* 'the reviver of the faith', numerous names with these ingredients point to him: addresses of thanks for granting a child, as in *Ghauth-bakhsh*, or, in India, *Ghauth-dinā*, as well as simple expressions of servitude: *Ghulām Ghauth, Ghulām Jīlānī, Ghulām Qādir* and the frequent *Ghulām Dastgīr*. In Tunis one can find *Djilani* or *Djelloli*.[39] In non-Arab countries, particularly in the Indian subcontinent, the lack of knowledge of Arabic grammar leads to constructions that sound impossible to an Arab ear. Who would expect that a woman could be called *Muḥyīaddīn un-Nisā Begum* or even *Ghulām Muḥyiaddīn un-nisā Begum!* (A lady of this name erected a well-known mosque in Hyderabad/Decann). One finds *Ghulām Ghauth Begum* and *Dastgīr Bī;* but more logical is *Jīlāni Begum* (a noted Urdu novelist). And while a man may be called *Muḥammad Ghauth* in deference to the 'greatest helper', a woman appears as *Ghauthiyya. Qādirī Begum* or *Baghdādi Begum* (after the last resting place of the saint in Baghdad) are not lacking either.

Similar names are formed in connection with the masters of other Sufi orders. The saints of the Chishti order, which in India is even more popular than the Qādiriyya, are remembered in names like *Ghulām Mu'īnuddīn* or *Ghulām Gharībnawāz;* and ladies can be named *Mu'īnuddīn an-nisā Begum, Chishtī an-nisā Begum,* but also simply *Mu'īna, Mu'īnī Begum. Quṭb un-nisā Begum* refers to Quṭb addīn Bakhtiyār Kākī of Mehrauli, *Ghulām Farīd ad dīn* and *Farīd un-nisā* to Farīduddīn Ganj-i Shakar of Pakpattan. Sometimes, a person is simply called *Ṣūfī* or *Ṣūfiyya;* and *Ghulām Murshid,* without specification of the spiritual guide's name, occurs also. To call one's son *Walī* (friend [of God]) can express a Sufi connection, as the word designates 'saint', but will be interpreted in Shia Islam as the *Walī Allāh* par excellence, that is 'Alī ibn Abī Ṭālib. *Walī Allāh* is also used, however, in a strictly Sunni environment, as the name of the great reformer *Shāh Walīullāh* of Dehli (d. 1762) shows. *Darwīsh (dervish)* is a good Sufi term and proper name, as is *Faqīr* and *Qalandar,* but the latter two are often used as a special designation of certain groups of Sufis, as *Allan Faqīr* or *Ḥusayn-bakhsh Qalandar.*

Allegiance

The further in time and space the Muslims moved from their origins the more they felt the need to identify themselves as members or even as descendants of the nucleus of the community of the faithful. People from the large Meccan clan of *Hāshim,* to which the Prophet belonged, distinguished themselves from their neighbours throughout the centuries, and are represented today in the Hāshimī kingdom of Jordan. Families related to the large unit of the Qurayshites appear now as *Qurashī* or, as this correct *nisba* was changed in many places later, as *Qurayshī (Qurēshi, Quraeshī* etc.) and thus maintain their original Arabic pedigree. Those whose ancestors belonged to the *anṣār,* Muḥammad's 'helpers' in Medina, call themselves *Anṣārī* while families tracing their lineage from the first caliph, Abū Bakr *aṣ-Ṣiddīq,* are known as *Ṣiddīqī,* and those connected with the second caliph, 'Umar *al-Fārūq,* as *Fārūqī (Faruki, Farooghi* etc.). Those Muslims in India who belonged to the *ashrāf,* the immigrant foreign Muslims, have especially emphasized their relations with the distant homeland of Islam.

A special place is occupied by the descendants of the Prophet through his daughter Fāṭima and her husband ʿAlī. They are known as the Fāṭimīs, or more generally as the ʿAlawīs (ʿAlvis). The members of the Prophet's family are called *sayyid* (pl. *sādāt*) or *sharīf* (pl. *ashrāf*). One distinguishes between the Ḥasanī and the Ḥusaynī *sayyids*, depending upon the ancestor: the family of Ḥusayn, the martyr of Kerbela, through whom the line of the Shia *imāms* continues, takes the place of honour. Some of them bear the simple *nisba 'al-Ḥusaynī'*; others trace their lineage back to one of the later *imāms*, such as *Mūsawī* or *Kāẓimī* from the seventh imām Mūsā al-Kāẓim, or *Riḍawī, Riżvi, Rażavī* from the eighth *imām* ʿAlī ar-Riḍā, *Naqwī* from ʿAlī an-Naqī. In order to make the pedigree look more correct some *sayyid* families, especially in Iran and even more in the Subcontinent, call themselves after the place where their ancestors settled or whence they migrated. The Shīrāzī *sayyids* and even more the influential Bukhārī *sayyids* in the Subcontinent are among such cases. Lakhiārī *sayyids* are those who settled close to the Lakhī range in Sind. Again, smaller factions in these *sayyid* families are called after a notable ancestor, for example the Shīrāzī *Shukrullāhī sayyids* or the *Qul Huwa Allāhī sayyids* in the Indus valley. A very important branch of the Ḥasanī sayyids are the *Ṭabāṭabā*, called after an early member of the family who, according to some sources, pronounced the word *qabā*, 'gown' as *ṭabā* due to a speech defect. In common parlance a Ṭabāṭabā belongs to the uppermost class of *sayyids*, the *sayyid as-sādāt*.

Sayyid families, who usually observe a number of special taboos and customs, generally prefix a title like *Mīr* or *Sulṭān* to their proper names, at least in the Eastern part of the Muslim world. Mīr-ʿAlī and Sultān-ʿAli, the two leading calligraphers in Herat around 1500, are typical examples. *Mīr* is thought to be derived from ʿAlī's title *Amīr*, 'prince [of the faithful]'. Sometimes one finds the title *khawāja*, especially in the East when the mother is a *sayyid* (although in general a *sayyid* girl would never marry beneath her status, and would remain single). The Urdu poet Khwāja Mīr of Dehli, known by his pen-name *Dard*, was given this double name as both of his parents were *sayyids* from different branches of the ʿAlawī family.[6] In the Subcontinent, the word *shāh* is often used after the given name of a *sayyid: Sayyid Ḥusayn Shāh Rāshdī, Sayyid Dhū'l-fiqār ʿAlī Shāh Bukhārī.*

In Iran, women express their relation to a *sayyid* family by *as-sādāt* (of the *sayyids*) with a preceding noun. One can understand names like *Iftikhār as-sādāt* 'Pride of –' or *Badr-, Akhtar-* 'full moon, star of –' and also the numerous superlatives like *Aqdas-, Akram-, Ashraf as-sādāt* 'most holy –, most noble –, most generous of –';[7] but the attested combination *ilāha as-sādāt*, 'goddess of the *sayyids*' does sound somewhat strange!

Finally, religious duties and objects form part of the nomenclature in traditional families: *jihād* 'Holy War' is a fairly widespread name, especially in Turkey *(Cihat)*; but one also finds *Ṣalāt* 'ritual prayer' and *Ṣadaqa* 'alms'. Again in Turkey one can encounter *Muṣḥaf* 'copy of the Qur'ān', *Ayet* 'verse of the Qur'ān' and *Gülbenk* (the Turkish prayer-formula used by the Bektashis). A Mevlevi family called their daughter *Semāʿ-nūr* 'mystical dance-light'. In Tunisia names like *Ḥasanāt* 'good actions', *Ḥerz, Ḥerouz* (= *ḥirz*) 'protecting prayer' and *Khatma* 'complete reading of the Qur'ān' are found, and even *Menāra* 'minaret', *Miḥrāb* 'prayer-niche' and *Zaouia* (= *zāwiya*) 'cell of a Sufi'.[40]

IV
'Mothers of the Faithful' – The Naming of Girls

The wish for a son is predominant in most cultures, and Islam is no exception. But what is to be done when Fate gives a family one daughter after another?[1] The fourth girl could simply be called *Rābi'a* 'fourth',and the following might also be numbered. But there are more eloquent expressions of disappointment: one may call a girl *Kifāya* 'Sufficience' (Yemen) or *Kāfī,* 'enough', *Khātima,* 'Finis!' (Tashqurghan), *Ḥaddī,* 'Stop!' (Tunis), *Seddenā,* 'may we be done [with the girls]'[2] (Bedouin); *Döne,* 'turn over [to sons]', *Gidi,* 'Off with you!' or *Yeter,*'Enough!' in Turkey. In the Egyptian countryside the eighth daughter of a family was called *'Udd wa'skut,* 'Count and be quiet!', and in a Persian tale the parents' sigh *Allāh bas,* 'God, [it is] enough' became the poor girl's name. *Dukhtarbas* 'enough daughters' or *Hamīn bas* 'enough of such ones' still occurs in Iran, as does *Nakh^{w}āsteh,* 'unwanted'. It seems, however, that this type of name is rare in the Indian subcontinent as families from both Sind and Bengal have assured me.[3]

Indeed, these unfriendly names reflect only one side of the coin, for there are a great number of lovely names to be given to girls. Many are simply feminine forms of male names, formed by adding the Arabic feminine ending – *a* (-*e*) to the male name – hence the numerous *Salīma (Selīme), Nazīha (Nezihe), Jamīla (Cemile)* (from names of the form *fa'īl*) or *Ṣābira, Shākira* (from the active participle *fā'il*). Often, the *fa'lā* form of adjectives denoting colours and defects appear, like *Samrā,* 'dark brown', from *asmar,* or *Wasmā* from *wasīm,* 'handsome'. Many other Arabic participles are used for girls both in the masculine and the feminine forms: *Maḥbūb, Maḥbūba, Munīr, Munīra.* The normal masculine comparative/superlative is also frequently used for women, especially in Iran, for example as *Ashraf,* 'nobler, most noble'.[4] In the same way verbal nouns (of the form *fa'āla*) are often used, such as *Malāha, Nabāha*; they appear in Turkish as *Melâhat, Nebahat, Necabet,* etc. A few names are formed from the verbal noun of the fifth form, *tafa''ul,* like *Tawaddud* from *wadd* 'love', or *Tabassum,* 'smile'. This latter name is, like a number of abstract nouns used for men and women.

Very often female names are formed from *nisbas* which, in turn, appear to be derived from *alqāb*: *Taqī ad-dīn* or *Nūr ad-dīn* become in common parlance *Taqī* and *Nūrī*, from which the female names *Taqiyya* and *Nūriyya* are derived. This type appears in dozens of Turkish and Arabic names. A very old example of this form – although of a different derivation – is *Baḥriyya*, which was given, according to tradition, to Asmā', the wife of ʿAlī's brother Jaʿfar ibn Abī Ṭālib, who went with him to Abyssinia, crossing the sea (*baḥr*).[5] In Arabic the ending – *a(tun)* is grammatically restricted to certain forms, but outside the Arab world it was apparently thought that any word could become feminine by the simple addition of this ending. That is especially true for Turkey where somewhat strange names for girls are sometimes encountered: abstract nouns like the Persian *jāvīd*, 'eternal' or the Arabic *tauḥīd* 'affirmation of God's unity', *taufīq* 'Divine support, success' and *taslīm* 'surrender' appear as *Cavide, Tevhide, Tevfika* or *Teslime*; likewise one can find *Eyyübe* from *Ayyūb, Imrana* from *ʿImrān*.

Early Arabic female names are sometimes nouns in the plural, like *Darāhim* and *Danānīr*, 'dirhams' and 'dinars', *Maṣābīḥ*, 'lamps', *Riyāḍ*, 'gardens' (now also used as a male name as in *Riyāż ul-Islām*), *Mulūk* (in Iran) 'kings' correspond to the *Salāṭīn* 'sultans' in an Eastern Anatolian village.[6] In Egypt and other Arab countries such plural forms are still in use: one finds *Azhār*, 'flowers', *Aḥlām* 'dreams', *Jawāhir* 'jewels' and *Jamālāt* 'beauties';[7] and a young friend of mine in Pakistan is called *ʿAnādil*, 'nightingales'. ʿAnādil's daughter bears the name *Lubnā* after the girl who inspired the ancient Arab poet Qays, for the women mentioned in classical Arabic love poetry are still favourites; thus *Salmā*, the most common name for the beloved, *Suʿād* (for whom Kaʿb ibn Zuhayr wrote his famous ode *Bānat Suʿād*, and especially *Laylā (Leyli)*, Majnūn's beloved. In Persian she was immortalized through Niẓāmī's epic, and so was *Shīrīn*, the Armenian princess who was the beloved of King Khusrau and of the stonemason Farhād: both names rank very high in the Persianate world. Somewhat rarer is *ʿAdhrā*, heroine of the love romance of Wāmiq and ʿAdhrā.

As men were and still are called by names drawn from Islamic history, women too can be given names with religious connotations; and a recent *fatwā* urged Indian Muslims to call their daughters after the 'mothers of the faithful', that is, the Prophet's wives. In the Qur'ān, only *Maryam*, Mary, is mentioned by name, but tradition knows *Āsiya*, Pharaoh's wife who saved little Moses from the river; *Zulaykhā*, famous for her love of Yūsuf (Joseph), and *Bilqīs*, the queen of Sheba are among traditional names. The name of the Prophet's mother, *Āmina*, is a favourite too, and so is that of his first wife, *Khadīja* (*Hatice* T), the 'best of women', *khayr un-nisā* (abbreviated *Khayriyya*). While *ʿA'isha* occurs only in Sunni circles her surname *Ḥumayrā* 'little red one' is also found in Shia Iran and India. *Fāṭima* is dear to all communities as is her epithet *Zahrā*; her surnames *Batūl* (virgin) and *Kanīz* (maiden) are rather restricted to Shia women. The names *Ruqayya, Zaynab,* and *Umm Kulthūm* refer to the daughters of the Prophet; but I suspect that nowadays Umm Kulthūm is more frequently used as a sign of admiration for the famous singer of that name. *Ḥafṣa,* one of the Prophet's wives, and *Nafīsa,* his saintly descendant, lend their names to a good number of girls, and *Rābiʿa,* originally a sigh at the birth of a 'fourth' daughter, has become fashionable because of the great medieval woman saint, Rābiʿa of Basra and, in Iran, in remembrance of the first Persian poetess, Rābiʿa of Quzdār.

As every man can be given a *kunya,* so too can every woman: *umm,* 'mother of –'. Again, as in male names, this can express a reference to a real son, like *Umm Fahd* or *Umm ʿAlī,* or a wish, as in *Umm al-banīn,* 'mother of sons', or appears in combination with a wished-for virtue, like *Umm Faḍl* (mother of merit). A number of women in Islamic history are known only by their *kunya,* such as *Umm Salāma* or *Umm Ḥākim*. Sometimes the combinations sound strange: as the name *Islām* has recently become more fashionable (although it is known from medieval history, as in *Islām Khān*), an Egyptian lady I know is addressed as *Umm Islām* 'mother of Islam'.

The male *ʿabd* is turned into *amat,* 'slave-girl', which, exactly like *ʿabd,* can be connected with every possible Divine name, from the frequent *Amat ul-karīm* to *Amat ul-Jāmiʿ*, 'slave-girl of the Most Comprehensive'. These names can then be abbreviated to *Karīma,* or *Jāmiʿa,* or *Ḥafīẓa* from *Amat ul-Ḥafīẓ*. However, the feminine *ʿAbda* also occurs, but never with a Divine Name, as it usually designates a black slave-girl. As with boys, religious names often serve as 'umbilical names' for girls and are generally followed by the 'real' name by which the child is called. Among these, flowers and beautiful natural objects abound. Beginning with *Būstān* 'garden', one finds in all languages *Lāle* 'tulip', *Nīlufar* 'lotus-flower', *Yāsmīn* 'jasmine', *Nargis,* 'narcissus', *Rīḥāna* 'sweet-basil', and more detailed or unusual designations such as *Nabāt* 'sugarcane', *Shakūfa* (P) 'opening bud'; in Turkey one encounters *Çiğdem,* 'crocus', *Demet,* 'bouquet of flowers', and *Jāle* 'dew-drop'.

As in the West, the rose is very prominent in women's names all over the Islamic world, particularly in the Persian-Turkish areas. Names with *gul* (T pronunciation *gül,* modern Persian *gol,* which now denotes 'flower' in general) abound. Among the Mughal ladies of sixteenth-century India one finds *Gulbadan* 'rose-body', *Gulrukh, Gulrū, Gulʿadhār,* 'rose-face', *Gulbarg,* 'rose-petal', *Gulrang,* 'rose-coloured', *Gulshan* and *Gulistān* 'rosegarden', *Gul-i raʿnā,* 'lovely rose'. Among modern Turks we encounter, besides the names just mentioned, *Gül-*

dalĭ, 'rose-twig', *Gülfiliz*, 'rose sprout', *Gülseren*, 'spreading roses', *Gülçīn*, 'gathering roses', *Gülbahār*, 'rose-spring', *Gülbün*, 'rose root', *Gülperi*, 'rose fairy' and even *Özgül*, 'the self [is] a rose'. Charming also are *Baghda gül*, 'rose in the garden' and *Yurdagül*, 'a rose for the country'. Traditional Muslim names are combined with *gül*, like *Ayşegül* or *Gülfatma*. This use of *gul* as an expression of tenderness is also common in the Persian world, especially in Afghanistan. Alongside all these flowers it is not surprising that *Bahār*, 'spring' or *Bahār Bānū* 'lady Spring' appear among women's names.

Another favourite word is *nūr* 'light', which occurs alone and in numerous combinations, such as *Nūr un-nisā*, 'light of the women'. In Turkey girls can be called *Nurten*, 'body of light', *Nurhan*, 'prince of light', *Binnur*, 'a thousand lights', *Ilknur*, 'first light', or *Yurdanur*, 'light for the country'. Iran excels in combinations with *mihr*, 'sun'; the Arabic *shams* 'sun' (grammatically feminine!) is 'feminized' as *Shamsa, Shamsha* (thus in India). Luminous heavenly objects are frequently used as names for girls, from *Āsumān* (P) and *Falak* (A) 'sky' to the Arabic *Najma*, 'star', with its Persian and Turkish equivalents *Akhtar* and *Yĭldĭz*; *Thāqiba*, derived from the Qur'ānic *najmun thāqib*, 'shining star', appears as do the names of the Pleiades: *Thurayyā (Soraya, Süreyya*, in T also a male name), *Parvīn* (P) and (T) *Ülker*. *Nāhīd* (P) and *Zuhra* (A), 'Venus' is also common.

Just as the rose is predominant among the flowers so the moon, the heavenly body closely connected with Islam and with Turkish folklore, appears in various names. The full moon, *badr*, has always been a metaphor for perfect beauty which is why Arab ladies are called *Badr al-budūr*, 'Full moon of the full moons', or *Sitt al-budūr*, 'Lady of the full moons' as well as (P) *Mahsatī*, 'Moon lady' (today used with the pronunciation *Mahāstī*, approximately, 'you are a moon'). The Persian *māh*, 'moon' (also with a short a) appears alone or as *Māham*, 'My moon', and in numerous combinations such as *Māhpeykar*, 'moon figure', *Mahliqā* (T *Mehlika*), 'moon-like', *Māhrukh*, 'moon cheek', *Māhpāra*, 'moon-piece', *Māhdukht*, 'moon daughter' and *Mahtāb*, 'moonlight'. *Māhīn* is 'related to the moon.' In purely Turkish names *ay*, 'moon' occurs very often, as in *Ayperi*, 'moon fairy', *Aymelek*, 'moon angel', *Şenay*, 'happy moon', *Ayĭşĭk*, 'moon-light' (which reminds one of the classical name *'A'isha*, T *Ayşe*); *Aysel*, 'moonlike',[8] *Ayten*, 'moon-body', to mention only a few. *Hilāl*, 'crescent moon' is used for both sexes. And when the Persian-Ottoman tradition calls a beautiful woman *Mihrimāh*, 'Sun-moon', then the modern Turk calls her, with the same meaning, *Günay*.

Although names of animals and birds are common for men, they seem to be less frequently used for women. Of course, nightingales appear already in ancient Arabia: *Bulbula, Hazār* (P), as do gazelles, *Ghazāla*, and in T *Meral, Ceyhan*, and *Geyik*. Even *Keçi*, 'goat', has been recorded as a woman's name in Eastern Anatolia. The mythological bird *Humā* appears in Iran and Turkey, and Turks sometimes call their daughters *Kumru*, 'grey dove', *Suna* or *Ördek*, 'duck', *Güvercin*, 'dove'. *Tadhrū*, 'partridge', occurs in Iran and in Pakistan. *Shāhīn*, 'falcon' may be inspired by Iqbāl's praise for the high-soaring bird. But unusual is the name of the daughter of the Seljukid ruler *Chaghri Beg*, 'Lord Hawk' who was called *Aslān Khātūn*, 'Lady Lion'.

Parents like to give names of precious stones and jewels to girls although this, like many names of flowers, was previously done for slave-girls rather than for free women. Now these names are freely used: *Almās*, 'diamond', *Gauhar*, 'jewel or pearl', *Shajarat ad-durr*, 'pearl-tree' (the slave who became Egypt's ruler in 1246), *Durrdāna*, 'pearl', *Durrishahwār*, 'royal pearl', *Lu'lu'a* (A) and *Inci* (T) for 'pearl' are equally common.

Sometimes the 'delicately walking girl', *Ghāda*, is compared to an idol, *Ṣanam*, or a fairy; *Parīkhān*, 'fairy queen', *Parīzād*, 'fairy-born', *Parījān* 'fairy-soul' and *Parīsīmā*, 'fairy-face' are also found in the Persianate tradition. She could be *Raushanjabīn*, 'of radiant forehead', and make every one happy – hence the numerous compounds with the P-*shād*, 'happy', like *Dil-shād* 'of happy heart', *Daulatshād* or *Gauhar shād, daulat* being happiness and reign. Modern Turks will call girls *Sevil*, 'be loved!', *Sevin*, 'enjoy, be happy', *Gülümser*, 'smiling', *Hepşen*, 'always cheerful', or *Sevinç*, 'joy'. On the other hand, the girls' alleged charming coquetry is alluded to in compounds with the Persian *nāz*, 'coquetry', such as *Māhnāz*, 'moon –', *Binnāz* (T), 'a thousand blandishments', *Ismināz* (T), 'her name is. . .' ', *Shakarnāz*, 'sugar –', further *Nāzlī* or *Nāzī* 'coquettish'. They can also be an (all too lovable) 'affliction', *Fitna* or *Āfet*. And as women are supposed to be decorative, names with the ending – *ārā*, 'adorning' are not rare in the Persianate world, such as *Anjuman-ārā*, 'adorning the assembly', *ʿĀlam-ārā* or the more famous *Jahān-ārā*, 'world adorning'. According to a recent Indian publication, *ārā* can be added to almost every noun to form an elegant female name. *Jahān*, 'world', again occurs alone and in numerous compounds, from *Nūr-jahān* to *Raunaq-jahān* or *Khurshīd-jahān*, 'lustre' or 'sun of the world'. *Ashraf-jahān*, 'the noblest of the world' occurs as well.

Women are supposed to be dreamlike, hence names like *Ru'yā*, *Ḥulyā*, 'dream', and *Sarāb*, 'mirage' can be found; and their 'incomparable' beauty is expressed by *Farīda* (A) and *Yegāne* (P), 'unique', and the Turkish *Birsen*, 'you are one', as well as *Nādīda* and *Bēnaẓīr* (both P), 'the like of whom was never seen'. Noble qualities like *Mürüvvet (muruwwa)*, 'manly virtue' serve as girls' names, as does *Fazilet (faḍīla)* and its Turkish equivalent *Ertem*, 'virtue', or *ʿAdalet*, 'justice'.

In Iran, romantic names with a lively lilt are – or were recently – favourites such as *Afsāna*, 'tale', *Parvāna*, 'butterfly', *Paymāna*, 'goblet' or *Tarāna*, 'melody'. One should also not forget the poetical names used in the Arab world, like *Munyat al-munā*, 'wish of wishes', *Qurrat ul-ʿayn*, 'cooling of the eye, darling', a name still very common in the Muslim world, *Nūr ʿaynī*, 'light of my eye', *ʿAyn al-ḥayāt*, 'fountain of life', *Qūt al-qulūb*, 'nourishment of the hearts' or *Mā' as-samā*, 'water from heaven' (which occurs also as a male nickname).

Sometimes parents in upper-class families in Turkey and Indo-Pakistan, where the use of Arabic and Persian names is always much more frequent than among the lower classes or in the rural areas, select high-sounding religious names for their daughters. Thus *Sidra*, the Lote-tree at the farthest border of Paradise (Sura 53/10) and *Ṭūbā*, the beautiful paradisiacal tree, are found and someone called his two daughters *Tasnīma* and *Kauthar*, the two waters of Paradise (cf. *Tasnīm* and *Kauthar* for men). *Firdaus, (Firdevs)* and *Jannat* (in T. *Cennet*, also male), both names for Paradise, appear among women's names, and so does *Iram*, the famous garden of Shaddād mentioned in the Qur'ān (Sura 89/6). No wonder that one finds *Malak (Melek)*, *Firishta*, 'angel' and even the plural, *Malā'ika*, 'angels', as well as *Ḥūriye*, 'houri-like'. The fountain in Mecca, *Zamzam*, lends its name to Ms *Zamzama* (unless one interprets it as 'murmur'). Among women in the area around Erzerum in north-eastern Anatolia, *Tevrat* and *Incil*, 'Tora' and 'Gospel', are found. That *Dunyā*, 'world' is used, is not surprising as the material world (as opposed to the spiritual sphere) was always identified with women, and is, besides, grammatically feminine.[9] In Persian, *Gītī* and *Kayhān*, 'world' occur; but it is somewhat surprising to encounter in Istanbul a *Kā'ināt Hanïm*, 'Lady Universe' and *Ezel (azal)* 'pre-eternity', or to meet Persian students named *Hastī*, 'existence' and, shocking enough, *Elāhe*, 'goddess'.[10] Compared to these names, a woman in Dhaka called *Layl u nahār*, 'Night and day', has an almost modest name. And one is relieved to find in rural areas, or among Bedouins, girls called after household goods: *Bunna*, 'coffee bean'; among Egyptian fallahs, *Tamra*, 'date', *Finjān* 'cup'; or *Kishmish* (P), 'dried raisins', in Turkey; and *Turunj*, *Portakal* and *Nāranj*, the three citrus fruits, in Iran. Indian Muslims tend to accumulate as many names as possible, and we can feel for the gentleman in Hyderabad who, on learning that his future wife's name was *Amat al-jāmiʿ Juwayriya Jawāhir Jasmine*, asked in despair whether this was a name or a prescription for some exotic drug. Otherwise one finds a tendency in India to invent feminine forms by adding the Hindi suffix -ī to any name: ʿAbbās becomes *ʿAbbāsī*; Akbar, *Akbarī*, Anwar, *Anwarī* and the Persian *-zād*, 'born' is changed into *zādī*, like *Shahzādī*, 'princess'.

New names are constantly invented – sometimes meaningful, sometimes – as it seems – mainly for the sake of euphony. *Muzhgān*, 'eyelashes', may be explained by the look of the newborn girl but is now quite frequent in Iran and also in Turkey. A girl in Egypt was recently called *Tuhādā*, 'fit to be given as a present', and I also met one *Hamasa*, 'whisper'. A Yugoslav Muslim woman called *Tājīde* told me that she was, of course, expected to be a boy and to be called after her uncle Tāj ad-dīn, but the parents then invented the form Tājīde, which nicely fits into the pattern of many Turkish names of Persian origin, such as *Güzide* 'chosen'.

Many women's names are formed with words denoting 'woman, lady', such as the Persian *bānū: Mihrbānū, Māhbānū* etc. Likewise, *dukht*, 'daughter', appears as part of the name, such as *Tājdukht*, 'crown-daughter' or the well known *Tūrāndukht*, 'Turanian daughter', our Turandot. Even the Arabic *sittī* (from *sayyidatī*) is found in Persian names, such as *Māhsitti* or *Zarsitti*, 'gold-lady'.[11] *Sitt*, on the other hand is used in Egypt mainly among the peasants, and is now regarded as somewhat old fashioned: but names like *Sitt il-Ahle*, 'lady of the family', *Sitt il-Beit*, ' – of the house', and even *Sittuhum*, 'their lady', have been used.[12]

Another way of naming girls is to use the combination of *un-nisā*, 'of the women', as second part of a compound. These names are very frequent in the Indian subcontinent where – parallel to the names with *ad-dīn* – almost every noun can precede the genitive. *Sayyid an-nisā, Sulṭān an-nisā, Amīr an-nisā* determine the woman as ruler among her peers, *Zēb un-nisā* and *Zīnat an-nisā* 'ornament of the women', were two of the Mughal emperor Aurangzēb's daughters. One can also understand *Zubdat un-nisā*, 'cream of the women', while *Jannat un-nisā*, 'Paradise of the women' is somewhat more exotic. These names, which became very fashionable in upper-class families (and whose second part is often left out in common parlance) were sometimes apparently substitutes for a name which a hoped-for son would have received: this is the case for *Iqbāl un-nisā* or *Masʿūd un-nisā* and similar compounds.[13] Strange combinations connected with saints' names, such as *Junayd un-nisā*, have been mentioned earlier. The word *khānum* (T *hanĭm*) sometimes forms part of a name (similar to *bānū): Nargiskhanum*; *Begum* even occurs alone as a proper name. Here again fashions change: the women of the first generations of Ismailis in East Africa had mainly Persian names with an added *khānum*; now, this suffix is barely used, and 'modern' names have become fashionable.

Often it is not thought appropriate to mention a woman's name at all, and therefore the Bedouins may refer to a woman as *mastūra*, 'the veiled one'.[14] This word is generally used when talking politely about women, and occurs also as a proper name (as in Pakistan). *Mastūra* belonged also to the official forms of address for ladies in medieval correspondence; while other terms of address were *al-maḥrūsa*, 'the protected one', *al-maṣūna*, 'the sheltered, chaste one', *ad-dār*, 'the house', *al-jihat*, 'the direction' etc. which were then enlarged with titles according to the addressee's rank, such as *al-jihat ash-sharīfa* 'the noble direction' or *ad-dār al-ʿāliyya*, 'the lofty house'.[15]

A study of the forms of address for Muslim women in various parts of the world would be most welcome; it should range from the expressions just mentioned in medieval Arabic society to the change of emphasis in Turkish titles which extend over Iran and India as well. *Khānim, Begum,* and even *sulṭān, sulṭāna* are used – always after the proper name: *Parihan Hanım, Zubayda Begum, Cemile Sultan*. Like many other titles they have now lost their aristocratic value and have become quite common whereas their use was formerly restricted to certain well defined social strata. The same is true for the Indian *Bībī, Būbū, Bīwī,* which usually precede the name: *Bībī Fāṭima, Būbū Rāstī,* and *Bī,* which often follows it as in *Maryam Bī*. The North African *lāla, lalla* belongs to the category of honorific addresses, as in *Lalla Mīmūna*, 'Lady Maymūna', (= 'the happy one').

Courtesans in India were given the surname *-jān,* like the heroine of Ruswā's famous Lucknow novel *Umrao Jān Adā*; in the Deccan around 1800, they were called by names with *-bakhsh,* like *Parī-bakhsh* or *Ḥayāt-bakhsh*.

V

'Lions, Moons and Roses'
The Nickname or Laqab

One of the basic functions of the *laqab* (nickname, pl. *alqāb*) is to distinguish people of the same name from each other. This may be done simply by using words denoting the 'elder' and the 'younger', as in *Ḥasan al-kabīr* and *Ḥasan as-ṣaghīr*, 'the great' and 'the little Ḥasan'. In Persian, *kālān* and *kūchik* can be used for the same purpose, and Turkish uses *büyük* and *küçük* or *qōja (koca)*. Sometimes, the comparative/superlative *al-akbar* and *al-aṣghar* or, in the case of women, their feminine form *al-kubrā* and *aṣ-ṣughrā* are found, as in *Khadījat al-kubrā* and *Zaynab aṣ-ṣughrā*. If there were more than two persons with the same name, the second was known as *al-ausaṭ*, 'the middle one'. Formerly, distinctions like *al-khayr*, 'the good one' and *ash-sharr*, 'the bad one' occurred as well.[11] Another distinction, used especially in Turkish areas, is that of colour: *aq (ak)* 'white, noble' and *qarā (kara)* 'black', also 'lowly' often serve to distinguish between individuals and tribal confederations, as with the Turcomans of the White Sheep and the Black Sheep, *Aqqōyūnlū* and *Qaṛāqōyūnlū*.

Soubriquets like *uzun* (T) in *Uzun Ḥasan*, (the fifteenth century Turcoman ruler) reproduced in Arabic as *Ḥasan aṭ-ṭawīl*, 'the tall Ḥasan', belong already to the category of bodily characteristics, and it is indeed here that languages have developed their most colourful nicknames. In the West one need only think of Notker *Balbulus* (stutterer), the ninth century Carolingian hymn-writer. Although Muslims are warned in the Qur'ān not to use nasty nicknames and, in subsequent tradition, not to address any with a *laqab* he dislikes, a great number of bodily peculiarities and defects are expressed in *alqāb*. That is all the easier as Arabic has a special grammatical form to denote such characteristics, (i.e. *afʿal*, fem. *faʿlà*.) A peep into the telephone directory of the Yemen – to give only one example – shows that such names are as common today as they were throughout Islamic history, and many of them apparently have turned into proper family names. One finds, to mention only a few examples, *al-aṣamm* 'the deaf', *al-aʿraj* 'lame', *al-akwaʿ* 'he with protruding elbows', *al-ashʿath* 'the unkempt one'. Numerous adjectives point out a defect in sight: *al-aḥwal* 'squint-eyed', *al-aʿshā* 'night-blind', *al-aʿwar* 'one-eyed', *al-aʿmash* 'blear-eyed', *al-aʿmā* 'blind' – to which one can add *ḍarīr*, 'blind', as well. However, in the case of blind people euphemisms are often used, such

[redacted]

as *baṣīr*, 'seeing'; or a blind scholar was given the *kunya Abū'l-ʿaynā'*, 'father of the large-eyed woman'.[2] This grammatical model can be emphasised by a different vocalization: *al-utrūsh* 'stone deaf', *al-uʿrūj*, 'very lame'. Among the feminine *alqāb* of this type the most famous is that of the pre-Islamic poetess Tumāḍir, famed for her threnodies, who was known as *al-Khansā'*, 'the pug-nosed woman'.

In North Africa such adjectives tend to merge with the article: *al-azhar*, 'the radiant or blond one' is contracted into *Lazaar*; *al-azraq*, 'blue' becomes *Lazreg*, *al-aswad*, 'black', *Lassoued*.

The same tendency to point out bodily defects is of course found among non-Arabs: here *Timur-i lang*, 'limping Timur' (hence our *Tamerlane*) is the best-known example. *Qizil (kĭzĭl)* 'red' is quite frequent among Persians and Turks; someone with a mole would be called in Turkish *mingli* (as in *Mingli Aḥmad)* or, in the Ottoman form, *benli*. As can be seen from this example, such *alqāb* precede the proper name: *Bĭyĭklĭ Muṣṭafā*, 'Muṣṭafā with moustaches', *Boynueğri Meḥmet*, 'Mehmet with the bent neck'. There are, as in Arabic, innumerable nicknames of this kind, from *boynu-baziq*, 'with a thick neck' to *qaraqaş* 'with black eyebrows', *burunsuz* 'without a nose', *qabāqulāq*, 'with thick ears' , *Yesārī*, 'left-handed' etc. Many of these developed into actual family names, as in Arabic: *Gözübüyükzade*, 'son of the one with large eyes'. The Arabic historian Ibn Taghrībirdī in the fifteenth century explains that the Turkish name *ūshqūlāq* means *üç kulak*, 'with three ears', for such nicknames were very common in his time among the Mamluks in Egypt and Syria who were, after all, largely of Turkish origin. Individuals with six fingers are known from Persian, *shash angusht*, and Turkish, *altĭ parmak*, and not a few people were known as *deli*, *teli* (T) or *diwāna* (P) 'mad', like *Deli Hüseyin Paşa* as contrasted to *Küçük* (little) *Hüseyin Paşa*.

Contrary to the tendency to highlight people's defects, one may use positive *alqāb* for them. This is certainly the case in areas of Iran such as Azerbaijan, where a blind person may be called *chashm-i ʿAlī*, ''Alī's eye', and a bald one, *zulf-i ʿAlī*, ''Alī's tresses'.

It seems that everywhere animal names are used as *alqāb*, whether it be *ḥimār* (donkey), *timsāḥ* (crocodile), *al-fahd* (the cheetah), *al-jamal* (the camel), *al-jāmūs* (the water buffalo), or *zurāfa* (giraffe – which still occurs in Ṣanʿā). In Persian one may find *Zhinda Pīl* (living elephant) or *pīltan* (of elephant's size). In Turkish *börü* (wolf) or *kökbörü* (grey wolf), *tilkī* (fox) and many more appear not only as proper names but also as nicknames.

Such *alqāb* offered excellent opportunities for satirists, as when the two secretaries of a Mamluk amīr were distinguished by the nicknames *ḥimār*, 'donkey' and *thaur*, 'bull'![3] Perhaps worse was the situation in the Persian city of Abivard in the twelfth century where all the civil servants bore animal nicknames so that a poet, Bābā Saudā'ī, stated in his verse:

The superintendent is a *dog* (Ṣadr ad-dīn *sag*)
The revenue collector is a *camel* (Jalāl ad-dīn *Istarjānī* Qurbān)
The tax collector is a *cow* (Muḥammad Kala *gāw)*
And the qāḍī is a *donkey* (Abū Sa'īd *khar*).
What then is the villager's fate due to them?
To be kicked, to have to count money, and beating. . .[4]

People with feline characteristics might be called *al-quṭayṭ*, 'little tom-cat', or *Mashīsh*, 'cat'; elegant and flighty ones, *farṭūṭ* or *farfūr*, 'butterfly'. Sometimes we are informed about the reason for a specific *laqab*: the *māliki* jurist in 'Cairouan (d. 240/854) was called *Saḥnūn*, i.e. a sharp-eyed bird. *Babbaghā* 'parrot' is a fitting surname for a poet; in Delhi, the poet Amīr Khusrau (d. 1325) was tenderly called *ṭūṭī-yi Hind*, 'India's parrot' (for parrots, contrary to Western understanding, are connected in the eastern Islamic world with sugar, sweet speech, and wisdom). The *laqab* of the noted Egyptian politician, *Zaghlūl*, means 'squab'.

To call a successful merchant in Tunisia *fār adh-dhahab*, 'gold mouse' is certainly a good idea; but why, one asks oneself, was someone nicknamed *kurā' an-naml*, 'ant's trotter'? 'Alī ibn Abī Ṭālib appears sometimes as *ya'sūb*, 'King of the bees', owing to his leadership and his legendary relation with bees. The wellknown author *Dīk al-jinn* is 'rooster of the jinns', so called because he was ugly and had green eyes, and the leader of the White Sheep Turcomans, *Qarāyelek* (T) is 'black leech'. Of a more honorific nature are the soubriquets from the animal world given to Sufis, such as *al-bāz al-ashhab*, 'the white falcon' for 'Abdul Qādir Gīlānī, or *Shahbāz*, 'royal falcon', for Lāl Shahbāz Qalandar in Sind.

Nicknames formed from plants are equally common: *al-ward*, 'the rose', *falāfil*, 'pepper', *az-zabīb*, 'raisin' are still in use *(bū zbīb*, 'father of raisins' means, however, in Tunisian parlance, someone with pimples). *Baṣl*, 'onion' and *biṭṭīkh*, 'water melon' are known from the Middle Ages, and a man of yellowish complexion could fittingly be called *utturuja*, 'lemon'.[5] Edibles – besides the vegetables just mentioned – are also used to form nicknames. A tenth-century scribe is known by the Persian soubriquet *khushknānja*, which goes back to *khushknān*, 'dry bread'.[6] In the case of the Arab poet *Farazdaq* (flat piece of bread) his actual name was soon forgotten as a consequence of his nickname, and the same 'flatness of the face' which is alluded to in his case is expressed, in modern Tunisia, by the *laqab Bū khobza*, 'father of flat bread'. One can also understand why a sweet-tongued scholar became known as *ziqq al-ʿasal* 'leather bag for honey'. The person nicknamed *qaṣab as-sukkar* 'sugar cane' may have been either of sweet character or very generous unless the name, as Goitein has pointed out for similar 'sweet' names, is antiphrastic and is used to satirize a very unpleasant individual. He mentions in this connection *qaṭā'if*, a very sweet pastry.[7] It is not always easy to explain such soubriquets unless the story behind it (or perhaps invented to explain a peculiar name) is known, as in the case of the great Indo-Muslim ascetic Farīd ad-dīn *Ganj-i shakar*, 'sugar treasure', who was so abstemious that as a reward for his asceticism pebbles turned into candy. But what is the story of *Daqīq al-ʿīd*, 'flour of the Feast', whose descendant was a well known author in Egypt in the late thirteenth century? And why did *As-sukkar wa'l-līmūn*, another Egyptian from Mamluk times, receive his nickname 'Mr Sugar and Lemon'?

A common way of distinguishing people is to call them by one of their favourite expressions. Thus the Ṭabāṭabā *sayyids* are so-called, according to the usual explanation, because their ancestor pronounced the word *qabā*, 'gown' as *ṭabā*.[8] The poet *Ḥayṣa Bayṣa* used to repeat these two obsolete words with the meaning 'in dire straits', and a Persian bears the nickname *Khush Khush*, which may be rendered 'Mr OK'.[9] A Moroccan leader who liked to interrupt other people by inserting 'just two words', *jūj kelmāt*, became known by this expression; another by his constant use of *hākadhā*, 'thus', and a merchant who pointed to his merchandise with the French expression *celui-là* was called *swēlā*.[10] Other customs are also immortalized in nicknames: a historian who constantly plucked hairs from his beard while lecturing was nicknamed *al-mantūf*, 'plucked out'.[11] But much more important is *al-Muqannaʿ*, 'the veiled' prophet of Khurasan in the eight century.

People's imagination in inventing colourful *alqāb* is apparently without limit, and although al-Nawawī devotes a whole chapter of his book to warning his readers not to designate people by nasty *alqāb*, especially not such as pertain to physical ailments,[12] his compatriots rarely heeded this advice. It is understandable that a hairy person might be not only *shaʿrānī* or *shaʿrāwī* (both meaning 'hairy') but also *ra's al-ghāba* 'forest head'; worse is the *laqab laṭīm ash-shayṭān*, 'smitten by Satan', for a poor creature with a misshapen face. And who would like to be called *rijl aṭ-ṭā'ūs*, 'peacock's foot', which is the ugliest part of a beautiful bird, or *udhn al-ḥimār*, 'donkey's ear'? *Layl ash-shitā'*, 'winter night' for a very long, gloomy individual would be preferable.[13] To call a very short man *al-ḥuṭay'a*, 'the dwarf', is as natural as is *al-ghūl*, 'frightening ghost' for someone of terrifying ugliness. When a disgusting governor of Yemen was called, because of his looks, *ʿajūz al-yaman*, 'the old crone of the Yemen', it makes some sense, as does the soubriquet *ẓill ash-shayṭān*, 'Satan's shadow', for a rebel – probably to contrast him with the legitimate caliph who was God's shadow on earth. And it must have been a rather untidy *qāḍī* in Bursa (he died in 1574) who was known as *kül kedisi*, 'cat living in the ashes',[14] although long before his time a Qarmathian agitator in the tenth century was known as *Ibn Hirrat ar-ramād*, 'son of the ash-cat'.[15]

The Arabic litterateur al-Thaʿālibī relishes the enumeration of such nicknames from Baghdad and Nishapur, some of which are rather eccentric. But he cannot tell us why someone was called *ṣūf al-kalb*, 'dog's wool', *sarāwīl al-baʿīr*, 'camel's pants' (reminiscent of 'the cat's pyjamas') or *niqāb al-ʿanaz*, 'goat's belly' (resembling German family names like *Ziegenbalg* or *Ziegenspeck*). *Liḥyat at-tays*, 'buck's beard, goatee' is explicable, but why was one of the caliph al-Muʿtamid's eunuchs called *ʿaraq al-maut*,'sweat of death'?

The use of such nicknames is still common, as recent studies from North Africa show:[16] *wajh al-kabsh*, 'ram's face', for example ; and while a tiny individual can be called *kallāshay'*, 'like nothing', an extremely tall and skinny one was named *khayṭ al-bāṭil*, the long thin gossamer that sometimes floats in the air. A great liar in Tunis became known as *gharbāl lekdūb (ghirbāl al-kadhūb)*, 'sieve for lies', a vain, silly person appears as *qonṣol al-kilāb*, 'the dogs' consul', and a tall, haughty man was known as *Degōl*, 'De Gaulle',[17] while his counterpart in medieval Arabia bore the nickname *ʿadīd al-alf*, 'counted for a thousand'.[18]

As decent women are rarely seen outside their homes there was no reason to give them *alqāb*; prostitutes, however, can be called by nicknames which, judging by the material from North Africa, are quite outspoken, such as *kāmyō*, 'truck' for a brutal woman of this type. If the intention was to hurt the family's honour one could address a person as *Ibn al-badhrā'*, 'son of one with a large clitoris'.[19]

As people are quicker to recognize defects in others than to acknowledge their beauty or kindness, the number of ugly and nasty *alqāb* by far outweighs those which are pleasant and laudatory. However, among the qualities most highly praised is generosity: *Mā' as-samā'*, 'water from heaven', or *qātil al-jūʿ*, 'he who kills hunger', are among the soubriquets given to generous people.

A beautiful person could be called *dībāja*, 'brocade', and one of the Egyptian Mamluks was surnamed *khawand*, 'princess', owing to his stunning beauty. Likewise the young mystical poet Ibn ʿAfīf ad-dīn at-Tilimsānī became known as *ash-shābb aẓ-ẓarīf*, 'the elegant youth'. Some *alqāb* point also to wealth and ease, such as the Persian *hazār asp*, 'a thousand horses' or *shasht kalla*, 'sixty herds of cattle', as a Seljuq poet was known.

In certain circumstances, *alqāb* were given to people to attract good fortune, especially by associating them with a famous person of the past. We find this custom especially in the Eastern part of the Islamic world where forms like *Dārā-Shikōh*, 'with the glory of Darius', are common, particularly in high-ranking families. One of Dārā-Shikōh's sons was *Sulaymān-Shikōh*, 'with the glory of Solomon'. *Yūsuf-jamāl* or *Yūsuf-shamā'il* appear as well, wishing the person 'Joseph's beauty' and 'Joseph's noble qualities'. One of my young Indian friends is *Kulthūm-shamā'il*, 'a girl with the noble qualities of Umm Kulthūm' (the Prophet's daughter).

Other *alqāb* of this auspicious character are *Nīkū Siyar* and *Farrukh Siyar*, 'of good life' and 'of happy life', or *Raushan Akhtar* and *Farkhunda Akhtar*, 'radiant star' and 'lucky star'. This kind of *laqab* however, borders on the official regnal surnames by which caliphs and sultans called themselves and which cannot be discussed in detail here.[20] We mention only one very typical example, that of the ʿAbbasid caliph al-Muqtafī (who ruled from 1135-1159): he chose his regnal title because the Prophet had appeared to him in a dream and told him:

> This affair will reach you – so follow (*fa'qtafi*) God's command!

Such cases are quite frequently attested for poets, who may be named after a particularly striking line from their verse.[21] Perhaps the most amusing example is that of the poet *ʿA'id al-kalb*, 'he who visits the dog' who complained that nobody looked after him during his illness:

> And I even visit your dogs when they are sick;
> but you do not visit me!

Sometimes poets are named as a consequence of some adventure, as in the case of *Ta'abbaṭa Sharran*, 'he carried something evil under the arm pit', or else because of some pretention as with *al-Mutanabbī*, 'the pretender to prophethood', who perhaps owed his name to some early connection with ultra-Shiite groups in ʿIraq.

One special case of *alqāb* has to be mentioned here which occurs in the classical period of Arabic, that is a genitive relationship between the proper name and an object or person: *Kuthayyir ʿAzza* was called after his beloved ʿAzza, and one Umayya who was constantly engaged in ritual prayer, *ṣalāt*, became known as *Umayyat aṣ-ṣalāt*. The relation to a specific tribe or family can also be expressed in such a *laqab*: *Aʿshā banī Asad*, 'Aʿshā who belongs to the tribe Banu Asad'.

As in other cultures, a person's profession would often provide a *laqab*. Many of these nouns have the same word pattern in Arabic such as *al-khayyāṭ*, 'the tailor', *al-warrāq*, 'the papermaker' or 'copyist', *al-*

ḥaddād, 'the blacksmith', *al-jarrāḥ*, 'the surgeon', *al-bannā'*, 'the mason', *al-khayyām*, 'the tent-maker', *al-ḥallāj*, 'the cotton-carder', and infinitely more. Many were taken over into other Islamic languages and usually lost the definite article *al-*. It should not be, however, assumed that they all indicate an individual's present profession; the professional *laqab* of an ancestor is often used for generations and merely becomes a family name.[22]

As well as the frequent use of the word pattern just mentioned, one can also find professional names derived, as a *nisba*, from a plural: *al-qalānisī*, 'the hat-maker' (who produces the high hats typical of medieval scholars, the *qalansuwa*), *ath-tha'ālibī*, 'the dealer in fox furs', *al-qawārīrī*, 'maker of glass bottles', or *as-sa'ātī*, 'clock maker'. Others are not distinguished by a special form, like *aṣ-ṣayrafī*, 'the money-changer', 'banker', *al-bayṭār*, 'the vet' or *al-mustaufī*, 'the paymaster'

In Persian no special forms are used to define professions but professional *alqāb* are, of course, also frequent, be it *pūstīndūz*, 'he who stitches fur coats', *bāzargān*, 'merchant', *isfahsālār*, 'commander', or *kamāngar*, 'bow-maker'. Some Arabic titles are much more used in the Persianate world than among Arabs; a good example is *munshī*, 'the secretary', which is a *laqab* often found among the clerical class in Iran and India.[23]

Sometimes the Turkish suffix *-ji* is found in Persian (and even Arabic) professional *alqāb*. In Turkish a person's profession is generally given by adding the suffix *-ji (ci,çi)* to the object of his or her work: *ekmek*, 'bread' = *ekmekçi*, 'baker'; *halĭ*, 'rug' = *halĭcĭ*, 'rug-maker, rug-dealer', *çorba*, 'soup', *çorbaçĭ*, 'the person in charge of the soup' (an important office in military circles as well as among the dervishes). In India one can add the suffix *-wālā* (fem.*-wālī*) to a noun and thus produce a *laqab* indicating the profession: *sōdāwāterwālā* is someone who sells soda-water.

As we have already seen, many of these *alqāb* have developed into regular family names. This is also true of the numerous nouns in Indo-Muslim names which appear time and again and are likely to confuse the reader who does not understand why there are so many *Chaudhry* (spelled in a dozen different ways). *Chaudhry* corresponds exactly to the German *Schulze* (the headman of a village), which is equally frequent – and also differently spelled – in Germany. The same is true for *malik*, which in the Subcontinent means the owner of a village, and the somewhat rarer *arbāb*, 'lord', the chief of an area (mainly in Iran and the North West frontier). *Mīrzā* is used among the Turco-Persian aristocracy; *nawāb* (hence our nabob) is member of a ruling family. *Sēthī* means a wholesale merchant.

In the Turkish areas one finds *bey*, which traditionally should be the address for descendants of a high-ranking official, a *pāshā*, but has turned into a general address which is placed behind the proper name: Osman Bey. The well-known *Efendi* was formerly restricted to people with higher education; now it ranks below Bey.[24] *Çelebi*, 'nobleman', is the official title of the descendants of the great mystical poet Maulānā Jalāl ad-dīn Rūmī, (d. 1273) but is also found among other families (in Arabic it appears as *Shalabī*). Many of these time-honoured titles, including those denoting military ranks, have degenerated into proper names, like *lasker* (Tunis = *al-ʿaskar*, 'the soldier') or the frequent *bāshā*, 'Pasha'.[25] Both in areas under former Ottoman rule and in Iran one finds *alqāb* (again turning into proper names) with the suffixed *-aqasī*, 'master of' like *kĭzlar ağasĭ*, 'the master of the girls', i.e. the head eunuch, or with *-bāshī*, 'head of-' like *bostancĭbaşĭ*, 'head-gardener'.[26]

Professional names could sometimes be given as a nickname just to tease the bearer: Ibn Taghrībirdī mentions a Mamluk nicknamed *al-fahlawān*, 'the hero', but 'he was not known for any art or craft, and was called that only metaphorically'[27] – something that is certainly behind many a strange professional *laqab*.

Closely related to professional *alqāb* and in part a subgroup of them are those with a religious connotation. We need not mention the innumerable *ḥājjī*, who have performed the *ḥajj*, the pilgrimage to Mecca; nor the *qāḍī*, 'the religious judge', and *muftī*, 'who gives legal opinions'. In the Subcontinent such designations precede the proper name: *Mufti Jamāl ad-dīn*. *Muqri'* or *qāri'*, 'he who recites the Qur'ān' belong here, as does *ākhūnd*, 'religious teacher' (often Shiite), *imām* 'leader of prayer' and *ḥāfiẓ*, 'he who knows the Qur'ān by heart'. The frequently mentioned *molla* or *maulwī* has had a somewhat chequered history: the classical Arabic meaning of *maulā* is both 'client' and 'master'; the title *maulā amīr al-mu'minīn*, 'the client of the Commander of the faithful' was given in 'Abbāsid times to rulers who were semi-independent. As *mūlāy*, it constitutes part of the title of the Moroccan sultans, such as *Mūlāy Idrīs*, and as *maulānā*, 'our lord' (T pronounciation *Mevlâna*) it becomes the honorific title of religious scholars in the Middle Ages. As such it is still used. *Maulwī* now often designates someone who has obtained the degree of *maulwī fāżil or maulwī kāmil* (comparable to a BA or MA in secular institutions) from a theological seminary (*madrasa*), i.e. the traditional theologian. In its abbreviation *mullā, mollā*, it has assumed a rather negative connotation among liberals.

Sometimes the religious office is even more specific as in *imām al-ḥaramayn*, 'the *imām* of the two sacred places, i.e. Mecca and

Medina', or *qayyim al-jauziyya*, 'the custodian of the Jauziyya mosque'. *Shaykh al-islām*, formerly merely an honorific title, developed into the highest religious office in Ottoman Turkey. Great admiration for a person's learning is expressed by calling him *'allāma*, 'most learned', as in the case of the Shiite theologian Ibn Muṭahhar al-Ḥillī (d. 1326) and, in our own century, Dr Muḥammad Iqbāl (d. 1938). In the Shia world the title *mujtahid*, 'who independently interprets the Divinely inspired law', is traditional for the leading theologian; *āyatullāh*, 'God's sign' is of more recent origin, from Qajar times. *Ḥujjat al-islām*, 'proof of Islam', formerly reserved for the greatest theologians of their epoch, has become our day merely a title for a preacher or a theological teacher in Iran.

Sufi connections are also clearly marked in the *alqāb*: an early ascetic might be known as *al-bakkā'*, 'he who weeps much'; *shaykh* and *murshid*, 'spiritual guide' in the Arab world (*shaykh* has a different connotation in the Subcontinent), or the Persian *pīr* for the same high rank are traditional. A *majdhūb* is someone who has become demented under the attraction, *jadhba*, of an overwhelming religious experience, and *faqīr*, 'poor' occurs nowadays often in names of people attached to a Sufi shrine, like *Allan Faqīr*, a singer in Pakistan. In Turkey, *akhī (ahĭ)*, the member of a religious organisation in the Middle Ages, appears in names like *Ibn Akhī Turk*, and *ghāzī*, 'the fighter for the faith', can also be used as the *laqab* for a hero. Bābur, the founder of the Mughal empire in India, expresses, in a little poem, his happiness that he can now truly be called *ghāzī*.

At times, family relationships also appear in the *laqab*, like *dāmād*, son-in-law, in a number of Turkish names, e.g., Dāmād Ibrāhīm Pāshā, who was related to the sultan. Such titles – like the Indian *kōkā*, 'foster-brother', or *angā*, 'wet-nurse' – are frequent in Mughal India and help in sorting out the complicated family patterns of the members of the ruling aristocracy.

Still another type of *alqāb* are those given by rulers to great artists, scholars, or physicians.[28] They proliferated in the course of time and sometimes became quite cumbersome. Poets would usually become *malik ash-shu'arā'*, 'prince of poets', or, in Arabic countries *amīr ash-shu'arā'*. One can also find a *tāj ash-shu'arā*, 'crown of poets'. Painters and calligraphers could be surnamed *zarrīn qalam*, 'golden pen', *jawāhir raqam*, 'jewel letters', *'ambarīn qalam*, 'ambergris pen', or could simply be styled *nādir al-'aṣr* or – *az-zamān*, 'the rarity of the age' or 'of the time'. Their profession could be preceded by *sharaf*, 'honour of –', for example *sharaf al-udabā'*, 'honour of the literati', – *al-ḥukamā*, ' – of the physicians', or by *iftikhār*, 'pride of –', like *iftikhār al-ḥukamā'*.

It is regrettable that a physician in the late sixteenth century was nicknamed *sayf al-mulk*, 'sword of the kingdom', because most of his patients died from his treatment.[29] Very often, however, physicians are connected with Jesus, *'Īsā al-masiḥ*, (Jesus, the Messiah) whose breath revived the dead, or with Galen, the model of ancient medical knowledge: thus one finds *masīḥ az-zamān*, 'the Messiah of the age' or *Jālīnūs az-zamān*, 'the Galen of the age'.

Sometimes the honorific *laqab* was fitted to the person's proper name or, in the case of a poet, to his pen-name. Thus, the poet *Falakī*, 'connected with the sky, *falak*', was named *shams ash-shu'arā*, 'sun of the poets', while one *Faḍl Muḥammad* became *afḍal ash-shu'arā*, 'the noblest of the poets'. An outstanding scholar was sometimes famed as *Baḥr al-'ulūm*, 'the ocean of sciences', which was replaced in British India by the title *Shams al-'ulamā'*, 'sun of the scholars'.

A *laqab* could also be bestowed posthumously. Just as the Prophet called Ḥanzala, who was slain in the battle of Uḥud, *ghasīl al-malā'ika*, 'washed by the angels',[30] so too his cousin Ja'far bore the *laqab aṭ-ṭayyār*, 'the flying one', because after his hands and feet had been cut off he 'flew' as it were to paradise. In general, those who are slain in the Path of God, in religious war, or die because of other specified causes (for instance during pilgrimage) are honoured by the *laqab shahīd*, 'martyr'. People killed for other reasons appear – sometimes – as *maqtūl*, 'killed'. Thus, the founder of the illuminist, *ishrāqī*, school of Sufism, Suhrawardī, who was killed in 1191, is still remembered as *Suhrawardī al-maqtūl* to distinguish him from the two other famous Sufis with the same *nisba*. A scholar who drowned during a flood in Mecca in 842AH/1439 became known as *al-gharīq*, 'the drowned one', and some unlucky individual who was flayed alive is remembered as *al-maslūkh*, 'the flayed one'.

Finally, one should always add the words *al-marḥūm* 'the one to whom mercy has been shown', or rather 'will hopefully have been shown', or *al-maghfūr*, 'the one who is – or hopefully will be – forgiven' when talking about a deceased person. The Mughal emperor Jahāngīr distinguished his two younger brothers who had predeceased him, Murād and Danyāl, as *al-marḥūm* and *al-maghfūr*. The Mughal emperors themselves are referred to after their death by special titles: Bābur is *firdaus makān*, 'whose place is paradise', Humāyūn is *jannat āshiyānī*, 'he whose nest is in Paradise', Akbar is *'arsh āshiyānī*, 'he whose nest is on the Divine Throne', and Jahāngīr is *jannat makān*, 'he whose place is paradise'.

Among the *alqāb* one finds one group that developed into a real *ism*, (proper name) and is used today, especially in the Subcontinent, very frequently. This is the group constituted by a noun plus *ad-dīn*, 'of the religion', such as *Badr ad-dīn*, 'full moon of religion', *Ḥusām ad-dīn*, 'sword of religion'. These *alqāb* precede the proper name: *Shihāb ad-dīn Aḥmad.*[31]

This type of name has developed out of the official honorary titles, the *khiṭāb*, which were given to leading men of state and religion to emphasize their rank and dignity. Originally they were composed of an impressive noun plus *ad-daula*, 'the state', which could then be enlarged to – *ad-daula wa'd-dīn*, like *'Izz ad-daula wa'd-dīn*, 'Glory of state and religion'. During the days of the Buwayhid sultans such titles were bestowed upon ministers and political leaders by the caliph, and the Būyids were all known by honorifics, e.g. *'Aḍud ad-daula*, 'pillar of the state'. Besides *ad-daula, al-mulk* was also used, according to Niẓām ul-Mulk's *Siyāsatnāma* mainly for governors[32] e.g. *Sayf al-mulk*, 'sword of the kingdom'. Soon titles composed only with *ad-dīn* were bestowed upon civil functionaries, scholars, judges, and other primarily religious officials.

It seems that the Ghaznawid ruler Sebuktīgīn (d. 997) was the first to bear the double title *Nāṣir ad-daula wa'd-dīn*, 'helper of state and religion'. Already at that time the use of honorific *alqāb* must have been frequent enough to inspire al-Khwārizmī, a somewhat rebellious poet, to write:

> What do I care that the 'Abbasids have thrown open the gates
> of *kunya*s and *alqāb*?
> They have conferred honorifics on a man whom their ancestors
> would not have made doorkeeper of their privy!
> This caliph of ours has few dirhams in his hands –
> So he lavishes honorifics on people![33]

After 1200, compounds with *ad-dīn* became part and parcel of the name, the person's qualities or rank notwithstanding. This custom, however, developed primarily in the Eastern part of the Muslim world. Kramers suggested Persian antecedents for this and tried to establish possible connections between Islamic names like *Farīd ad-dīn, Bahā' ad-dīn* or *Ghiyāth ad-dīn* and the Persian names *Farīdūn, Behdīn,* and *Kāmdēn* respectively.[34] This may or may not be correct; in any case, indulgence in *alqāb* of all sorts soon became typical of the eastern part of Islam while in the West – perhaps as a reaction against the flood of honorifics used by the 'Abbasids and Fatimids – such *alqāb* were given only rarely. One of the few, and in this case wellchosen, *alqāb* in Spain is that of the eloquent vizier and author Ibn al-Khaṭīb who was known as *Lisān ad-dīn*, 'tongue of religion'. Otherwise, one has the feeling that the use of royal or lofty epithets for people without the proper rank was not considered fitting, as the Spanish poet Ibn Rashīq sighs:

Royal epithets not in their proper place –
Like a cat that by puffing itself up imitates the lion.[35]

It is significant that already in the early eleventh century al-Bīrūnī mentions, in his *al-Āthār al-bāqiyya*, the nonsensical use of pompous epithets which have become 'clumsy to the highest degree, so that he who mentions them gets tired before he has hardly begun; he who writes them loses his time in writing, and he who addresses (people) with them runs the risk of missing the time for prayer'.[36] This is especially true for the Indian subcontinent where many of those honorifics were and still are used as personal names, often in highly surprising combinations which sometimes run counter to grammar and logic. But the use of names with *ad-dīn* very soon became a custom in the Middle East as well, as a look at biographical dictionaries shows; and when Ibn Maymūn (d. 917/1511) reached Egypt from his Moroccan homeland he complained that people had exchanged good Sunni names like Muḥammad or ʿUmar for Shams ad-dīn or Zayn ad-dīn respectively, thus introducing a *bidʿa*, a heretical innovation, and 'have changed the Prophet's *sunna* and exchanged it for a devilish innovation.'[37]

The development was irreversible, and soon elegant relations between *ism, kunya,* and *laqab* appear: a *Naṣr Allāh* would be nicknamed *Nāṣir ad-dīn*, a *Saʿd, Saʿd ad-dīn*. *Muḥammad* is combined frequently with *Shams ad-dīn*, 'sun of religion', *Aḥmad* with *shihāb–*, *taqī–*, and *tāj ad-dīn*, 'radiance', 'the devout' and 'crown of religion'. *Yūsuf* is often connected with *Jamāl ad-dīn*, 'beauty of religion', owing to the fame of the Qur'ānic Yūsuf (Joseph) as paragon of beauty, and he may be given the appropriate *kunya, Abū'l-maḥāsin*, 'father of good, beautiful qualities'. Ibrāhīm was sometimes combined with *burhān*, 'proof', perhaps because of the similarity of the root consonants *b.r.h.* And when *Maḥmūd* is combined, as happens often, with *Naṣīr ad-dīn*, one can find the reason for this in the Qur'ānic verse Sūra 17/81-82: 'God will perhaps send you to a praiseworthy (*maḥmūd)*, place. . . and say. . . and grant me helping strength, *sulṭānan naṣīran*'.[38] Turkish and Persian names were of course included in this process, and one finds *Ḥusām ad-dīn Lājīn* or *Jamāl ad-dīn Aqqūsh*, as in fact in the Mamluk army where each name of a Turkish or Circassian officer was mechanically combined with an *ad-dīn laqab*.

Most of the nouns preceding *ad-dīn* point to power, radiance, strength: *nāṣir*, 'helper', *badr*, 'full moon', *nūr*, 'light', *shams*, 'sun', *najm*, 'star', *ʿaḍud*, 'pillar, strength', *ghāzī*, 'victorious', *ṣadr*, 'breast, uppermost part', *asad* or *ḍirghām*, 'lion' and so on. One has the feeling that in the eastern part of the Muslim world almost any noun could be combined with *ad-dīn*, and the useful list compiled by Dietrich[39] can be extended by quite a number of strange combinations – from the Bengali *Mafīz* (= *muḥāfiẓ*, 'preserver') *ad-dīn* to *samā' ad-dīn*, 'heaven of religion'. The traveller Ibn Baṭṭūṭa in the fourteenth century mentions *sayyidnā fulān ad-dīn*, 'our lord so-and-so of religion', and although this is probably only a kind of abbreviation, people have continued to invent combinations which make an Arab (and an Arabist) shudder. Thus, one can find Persian nouns preceding the *ad-dīn*, such as *āftāb ad-dīn* 'sun of religion', *mahtāb* 'moonlight' – and what about *nāyāb ad-dīn*, 'the rare one of religion'? In the Subcontinent one can sometimes trace a development from the popular *chirāgh dīn*, 'lamp of religion', to *chirāgh ad-dīn* and finally to the correct, fully Arabic, *sirāj ad-dīn*. The *i* of *iżāfet*, showing the genitive relation, which would be required for a correct Persian construction imitating the Arabic form, is often left out, and instead of *fērōz-i dīn*, 'splendour of religion', the person is simply called *Fērōz Dīn*. *Alif dīn*, 'the *alif* (the first letter of the alphabet) of religion', is attested and gave the satirist Akbar Allahābādī the chance to congratulate the bearer of this name, author of a religious treatise, that he was not *bē-dīn*, 'without religion' (or 'the *bā*',' the second letter in the Arabic alphabet, 'of religion.'). Combinations like *faqīr ad-dīn* 'the poor one of religion' or *shafī' ad-dīn*, 'intercessor of religion' sound strange to an Arab, but among the compositions with Persian nouns, *aghāz ad-dīn* 'beginning of religion' is attested as early as the beginning of the fourteenth century in the biography of Niẓām ad-dīn Auliyā of Dehli. People also tended, and still do, in India and Pakistan, to extend any *ism* by adding *ad-dīn*, thus *'Umar ad-dīn*, *Manṣūr ad-dīn* etc. In recent times veneration for the poet-philosopher Iqbāl is reflected in names like *Iqbāl ad-dīn*. In Indonesia, *mās* or *almās ad-dīn*, *dhahab ad-dīn* and *'aqīq ad-dīn* are found: 'diamond', 'gold', and 'agate of religion'. And the reason why a poor Bengali bore the incredible name *Peynir ad-dīn*, 'cheese of religion', was, so I was told, that the boy's father had informed his Hindu landlord of the child's birth and asked for a name, and the latter who was just eating his breakfast, suggested 'cheese' which the Muslim villager then islamicized by adding *ad-dīn*. On the other hand, Indo-Pakistani Muslims delight in highsounding combinations of Arabic terms with *ad-dīn*, such as *Iḥtishām ad-dīn* or *Tamyīz ad-dīn*, 'decency' or 'distinction of religion'. *Islām ad-dīn* is also attested, and even recommended; and it seems typical that the Egyptian poet *Ṣalāḥ 'Abd aṣ-ṣabūr* called the mild mystical guide in one of his poems *Bassām ad-dīn*, 'the one that constantly smiles. . .'.[40] A variant of names with *-dīn* are forms like *Dīnyār*, *Dīndōst*, 'friend of religion', which occur in Iran.

Many of these colourful names are in practice somewhat too cumbersome for daily use, and thus several ways of abbreviating them were invented. One is to use the noun preceding *ad-dīn* with the article and call a *Nāṣir ad-dīn* simply *an-Nāṣir*. In this case the actual *ism* can precede the abbreviation: instead of *Badr ad-dīn Maḥmūd* one may write *Maḥmūd al-Badr*, or *al-Badr Maḥmūd*.[41] In other cases a long ī, that is a *nisba* ending is added to the noun so that *Jamāl ad-dīn Yūsuf* becomes *al-Jamālī Yūsuf*; *Zayn ad-dīn* 'ornament of religion' appears as *az-Zaynī*, etc. The *ad-dīn* may also be omitted completely and the person called simply *Nūr* instead of *Nūr ad-din* or *Kamāl* instead of *Kamāl ad-dīn*. In Turkey both forms are used side by side: *Seyfettin* (= *sayf ad-dīn*) becomes *Seyfi, Bahāettin, Baha*. Many of the 'secondary *nisba*s' like *Fetḥī* (from *Fatḥ Allāh*) or *Nūrī* have then again entered Arabic nomenclature through the Ottoman medium, and a good number of them produce feminine forms, like *Fethiye, Nuriye*, etc.

In Iran and India another change occured around 1600: names with *ad-dīn* were abridged by adding a long *ā* to the governing noun: *Taqī ad-dīn* became *Taqīyā*; the famous philosopher *Mollā Ṣadrā* (d. 1640) was originally *Ṣadr ad-dīn*, the calligrapher *Rashīdā, Rashīd ad-dīn*. Thus names like *Amīnā, Kamālā, Jalālā, Sirājā, Ruknā or Shujāʿā* developed and typically Indian names like *Taʿẓīm ad-dīn*, 'glorification of religion', appeared as *Taʿẓīmā*. Sometimes, the ending was enlarged to *-ay*: *Mukhliṣāy*.

Special *'ad-dīn' alqāb* were given to slaves and eunuchs, and their use especially in Mamluk Egypt is well documented – a slave *ʿAmbar* 'ambergris' would be called *Shujāʿ ad-dīn*, a *Muḥsin* became *Jamāl ad-dīn*.[42] Occasionally ladies of note were given a name with *ad-dīn*, such as *Ṣafwat ad-dīn* or *Ṣafiyat ad-dīn*, from the root *ṣafiya*, 'to be pure'.

Besides the *alqāb* formed with *ad-dīn* related names with *al-islām, al-milla*, 'the religious community' or *ash-sharīʿa*, 'the religious law' are known from classical times as honorifics so that great scholars could be addressed as *ṣadr* or *tāj ash-sharīʿa*, 'noblest part' or 'crown of the religious law'. Again mainly in the eastern part of the Islamic world, such titles, especially those with *al-islām*, were turned into proper names, and one encounters *Saʿādat al-islām, Farīd al-islām, Rafīq al-islām, Nadīm al-islām, Nadhr al-islām, Riyāż al-islām*, that is 'Felicity', 'the unique', 'the companion', 'the intimate friend', 'the vow', 'the gardens of Islam' respectively. Even *Ẓuhūr al-islām*, 'the appearance of Islam', *Kayf al-islām, Firdaus al-islām* and *Sāqī al-islām* can be found in Indo-Pakistan and Iran, meaning 'condition, good mood', 'Paradise' and 'cupbearer of Islam'. Combinations with Persian nouns occur in this case as with *ad-dīn*: *Khurshīd al-islām*, 'the sun of Islam'. Sometimes other religious concepts are used in Pakistan: I met one *Qayṣar al-hudā*, 'the emperor of right guidance' as well as *Asrār al-īmān* 'mysteries of the faith'.

A related feature of all this is the formation of *alqāb* with *az-zamān* 'of the time'[43] They are found as honorifics from the Middle Ages onwards, as for example the noted 'Abbasid author *Badīʻ az-zamān Hamadhānī*, or the poet *'Ayn az-zamān*, pointing to the assumption that the writer was 'the unprecedented master' or 'the essence (or eye) of his time'. Others were called *Auḥad az-zamān*, 'the unique in his time'. In Mughal India such titles were given to famous painters like *Nādir az-zamān*, 'rarity of his time', but eventually these too were used as proper names. The governing noun it always one of praise and should be translated as a superlative: *Khayr az-zamān*, 'the best of his time', *Ḥamīd*, 'the most praiseworthy', *Maḥbūb*, 'the beloved', *Khalīq*, 'most qualified', *Sa'īd*, 'the luckiest', *Arshad*, 'the best-guided', *Salīm*, 'the soundest', *Rafīʻ*, 'the most sublime' or *Munīr az-zamān*, 'the most brilliant of his time'. As early as Qalqashandī's handbook for chancelleries one finds someone surnamed *ghurrat az-zamān*, 'the prime of his time',[44] and in the East, the Persian *āftāb* (sun) is connected with *az-zamān*.

There are related combinations with *al-'ālam*, 'the world'; and besides the typical Sufi appellation *quṭb al-'ālam*, 'the pole, or axis, of the world' one encounters *Badr al-'ālam* (or in Persian construction, *Badr-i 'ālam*), 'full moon of the world', *ṣabīḥ* or *badīʻ al-'ālam*, 'the handsome or unprecendented-one of the world'.

In connection with names that express gratitude for the birth of a child we have already mentioned *'Aṭā Allāh* or *Hibat Allāh*, 'God's gift'. But other combinations of *Allāh* with a preceding noun – besides *'Abdullāh* – are also used in amazing variety. They may have developed out of the nicknames given to some prophets in the Qur'ān, like *Khalīl Allāh*, 'God's friend' for Abraham. Later, Noah was known as *Najiy Allāh*, 'saved by God', Adam as *Ṣafīy Allāh*, 'God's sincere friend' and Idrīs as *Rafīʻ Allāh*, 'uplifted by God'. The first caliph Abū Bakr became known as *'Atīq Allāh*, 'freed by God', because God had freed him from Hellfire,[45] and among 'Alī's surnames one finds the high-sounding *Yad Allāh*, 'God's hand' and *'Ayn Allāh* 'God's eye'. One of the most famous heroes of early Islamic history, Khālid ibn al-Walīd, was praised as *Sayf Allāh*, 'God's sword'. The surname *Jār Allāh*, 'God's neighbour' is attested for the famous commentator on the Qur'ān, az-Zamakhsharī, who spent many years in Mecca, being 'close' to God. In modern times the Tatar reformer Mūsā Jārullāh is the best-known bearer of this name. The Turkish designation *Bayt Allāh*, 'God's house', may also refer to someone who stayed near the Ka'ba for a long time.

Many of the compounds with *Allāh* expressed bravery in God's service, beginning with 'Alī's surname *Asad Allāh*, 'God's lion', to *Fatḥ Allāh* or *Ẓafar Allāh* (*Ẓafrullāh*), 'Help' or 'victory of God'. Often a feeling of trust and reliance on God's strength and help is expressed in such names, as in the nouns *satr* 'covering', *ḍayf* 'host', *ḥifẓ* 'preservation', *rāḥat* 'rest', *sa'd* 'felicity', *amān* 'safety' or *qudrat Allāh* 'God's power'. The quite common *Raḥmat Allāh*, 'God's mercy' appears in the Indian subcontinent often as *Rahimtolla*. Sometimes religious expressions are turned into names of this kind, from *Ayat Allāh*, 'God's sign' (not only as title but as name!) and the Qur'ānic *Ṣibghat Allāh* (Sura 2/138), 'the colouring of God', to expressions of constant gratitude like *Ḥamd Allāh* or *Shukr Allāh*, 'Praise to God', or 'Thanks to God'.

One can also find *Nūr Allāh* 'God's light', *Żiyā' Allāh* 'God's radiance', *Ṣun' Allāh* 'God's work', *Rizq Allāh* 'God's nourishment', *Ḥizb Allāh*, 'God's party'; and even *Rūḥ Allāh* 'God's spirit' – the Qur'ānic designation for Jesus – turns up. And someone in the rural areas of Iraq called his son *chelb* (= *kalb*) *Allāh*, 'God's dog', 'so that he may be faithful like a dog to God'. On the other hand, there is *'Āshiq Allāh*, 'he who is an ardent lover of God'.

Many of the names are difficult to explain, and it seems that a tendency set in to form compounds with *Allāh* and most of the Divine names known from the type *'abd* +, and thus, instead of *'Abdur Raḥīm*, *'Abdus Salām* one encounters *Raḥīm Allāh, Salām Allāh, Ḥamīd Allāh* (which is a surname of the Prophet, 'praised by God' and may have triggered off this development).[46] There are similar combinations of a Divine name with *ad-dīn: Raḥīm ad-dīn, Ḥamīd ad-dīn* etc.

The imagination of Indian Muslims did not stop there. Often the word *Allāh* was replaced by one of the Divine names among which *al-ḥaqq*, 'the Divine Truth' (a typical Sufi designation for God) appears most frequently, along with *ar-raḥmān*, 'the Merciful'. A few examples from recent Indo-Pakistani nomenclature include: *Asad ar-raḥmān*, 'lion of the Merciful'; *Ẓill ar-raḥmān*, 'shadow of the 'Merciful'; *Sājid* –, 'he who prostrates himself'; *Mīzān* –, 'scales of – '; *Faṣīḥ* –, 'eloquent – '; *Mumtāz*, 'chosen, elect – '; *Mustafīz* –, 'favoured by the Merciful', and so on. *Badhl ar-raḥmān*,'offering of the Merciful', occurs besides *Sayf ar-raḥmān*, 'sword of the Merciful', which may strike us as somewhat incongruous, and even *Tanzīl ar-raḥmān*, 'sending-down by the Merciful' appears although this is a designation of the Qur'ān.

Al-Ḥaqq appears in *Iḥsān al-ḥaqq*, 'benificence of the Divine Truth'; *Żiyā' al- ḥaqq*, 'radiance of –'; *Niẓām* –, 'order –'; *I'jāz* –, 'non-imitable miracle –'; *Nasīm* –, 'breeze –'; *Hidāyat* –, 'right guidance', or *Sha'n al-Ḥaqq*, 'matter, prestige, rank –'. Again, one feels that almost any noun with a positive value can be combined with these Divine names.

Among the other Divine names that are used in combinations *Karīm*, 'the Benificent', appears several times, as *Anwār al-karīm*, 'lights of the Beneficient', *Rajā'* – and *Miṣbāḥ* –, 'hope' and 'lamp of the Beneficient'. One can also find *'Azīz aṣ-ṣamad*, 'he who is dear to the Eternal, Incomparable', *Sirāj al-maulā*, 'Lamp of the Lord', *Nūr al-bāqī*,'Light of the Everlasting', *Najm al-ghanī*, 'star of the Rich', *Khalīq as-subḥān*, 'worthy of the Highly Praised'. Even the term *kibriyā'*, 'Divine Grandeur' is found in names like *'Ināyat-i kibriyā*, 'Kindness of the Grandeur' or *Ghulām-i Kibriyā*, 'servant of the Grandeur' (in both cases, however, with the Persian construction, not with the Arabic genitive),

A century ago, Garcin de Tassy remarked that this type of high-flown name is generally used in Indian *sayyid* families;[47] but it has apparently proliferated in other circles as well. A glance at a Pakistani newspaper or the Lahore or Dhaka telephone-directory reveals many more such combinations which sound strange, even impious, to Arabs. But in the Subcontinent, and to a certain extent in Iran too, they are considered perfectly normal, and some recently published lists of Islamic Names from Iran and India list and recommend them.

Finally, one may ask in what relation a name like *Ḥabīb Allāh*, 'God's friend' (one of the Prophet's surnames) stands to Persian names often found in the Afghan areas such as *Khudāyār, Khudādōst, Yazdānyār* or *Allāhyār*, all with the meaning 'God's friend'. But here much more research remains to be done.

We have already mentioned that in many cases a grammatical *kunya* – *Abū x* – may assume the function of a *laqab* because this construction frequently points to some physical or psychological abnormality: *Abū sinna*, 'Father of one tooth', *Abū shāma*, 'Father of a mole', *Abū rujayla*, 'Father of the little (deformed) foot', etc.[48]

A related form used in *alqāb* is constructed with *dhū*, fem. *dhāt*, 'owner, possessor of – '; *Dhū'n-nūn*, 'the possessor of the fish' is the *laqab* of Jonah (Yūnus) who was swallowed by the fish; the poet *Dhu'r-rumma* is 'possessor of an old piece of rope'.[49] *Dhū* often occurs with a following dual as in *Dhū'l-qarnayn*, 'possessor of the two horns', an epithet usually taken as referring to Alexander the Great. Someone 'with two left hands' is *Dhū'sh-shamālayn*, while a dexterous and successful official could become known as *Dhū'l-yamīnayn*, 'the one with two right hands'. Such forms appear in official titles in 'Abbasid times where one finds the *dhū'l-wizāratayn*, 'he who was vizier twice', or *dhū'r-riyāsatayn*, who was administering 'two leading positions'.[50]

Finally, the racial or family background of a person can also often form a *laqab*. This is particularly so in non-Arab areas with their widely differing tribes, races, and clans whose names were not, as with the early Arabs, expressed by a *nisba*. Such *alqāb* – many of which are now used as family names – include the following. Among the Turkish peoples: *Tatar, Chaghatay, (Chughtay), Qibchaq, Moghul,* and among the great Turcoman federations: *Barlas, Bahārlū, Shāmlū* etc. Among the Iranians are found *Afshār, Zand, Qājār, Kurd* or the Kurdish *Ardalān,* while among the Pathans the *Bangash, Lodi, Khilji (Ghilzay), Durrānī* and *Khaṭak* are well-known; here many names are formed by adding *-zay* or *khēl* (family of –) to the tribal name: *Yūsufzay, Kakākhēl.* The *Awān, Tiwāna, Kanbōh, Nūn, Lund, Chima and Siāl* are usually related to the Punjab, the *Batt* and *Dār* to Kashmir. The *Balōch* and their tribes – like *Leghārī, Talpur* – occur, as do the Sindhi *Sumroo, Agro* etc. In the names of Central Asians, Pathans and Balochs who have settled in Iran or Indo-Pakistan throughout the centuries, the word *Khān* is used before the tribal name: *Khushḥāl Khān Khaṭak, Muḥammad Khān Jamālī, Nabībakhsh Khān Balōch, Karīm Khān Zand* and many more. Lately many families have dropped these tribal *alqāb,* which explains the enormous number of people with the family name *Khān.*

VI

'A Name too Heavy to Bear' *Change and Transformation of Names*

Endearment

Beautiful and highsounding as many Islamic names are, they could hardly be used in the family. On the one hand one must avoid the desecration of the names of prophets or names connected with religious values by all too frequent use. On the other hand – and this is perhaps even more important – it was, and still is, considered improper to address respected members of the family and society at large by personal name. In early Islam, to address someone with his or her full name was regarded as highly formal and official, and to call a woman *Yā Ḥafṣa bint 'Umar!* (O Ḥafṣa, daughter of 'Umar) would create an atmosphere of respect. The use of the *kunya* for such purposes has already been mentioned (p. 00 above). Other ways of expressing respect toward an elder member of the family, or even of a large circle of acquaintances, is to revert to terms of relationship such as *abla, apa* (T) 'elder sister' (either alone or with the preceding name: *Maryam apa*) 'uncle', 'aunt' (differentiated according to the paternal or maternal line) and many more.

In the Subcontinent *miyān* is a respectful but loving way to address a venerable elderly man: Quṭb ad-dīn will thus be called *Quṭub Miyān*. Likewise, the suffix *-jee* is often used to imply a kind of good wish, as in *apa-jee*, 'dear elder sister'; among the Bohora community it often forms family names: *Ṣāliḥjī*. The use of such forms of address is very extensively developed in Muslim societies and would deserve a special study.

Besides these, many forms of endearment have been invented for children and family members, and the *'urf*, the name by which a person is known in the family, is often completely different from his or her given name.

One way to express endearment is by the use of the diminutive. However, diminutive forms can also be used for invective, and the Prophet expressly warned his followers to use them for deprecative purposes, *taḥqīr*.[1]

The Arabic diminutive is formed by changing the vocalization of the noun: that is, the first consonant is pronounced with a short u, the second one with an ay: *Faḍl* becomes *Fuḍayl; 'abd, 'ubayd*, and *Ṭalḥa, Ṭulayḥa*; the same is true for the feminine: *Ḥafṣa* becomes *Ḥufayṣa, Jamīla, Jumayla*. Names with a long *ā* in the first syllable change this into an *uway: Khālid* becomes *Khuwaylid; Ḥārith, Ḥuwayrith.* And when a word had a form like *ṣaghīr*, 'small', one can also say *ṣughayyir*, 'very, very small', or *kuthayyir*, 'a little bit more' from *kathīr*. Elatives follow the same rules, as in *Uzayriq*, 'the little blue one'. Such diminutives appear sometimes in nicknames: a poetaster might be called *shuway'ir*, from *shā'ir*, 'poet', and a satirist by the name of Ja'far was known as *Ja'far Ju'ayfirān*. Interestingly, words with a feminine ending can be changed into masculine forms in case of endearment: the Prophet called 'Ā'isha, *Yā 'A'ish*, Abū Hurayra, *Yā Abā Hirr*, and Usāma, *Yā Usaym*.[2]

Besides these regular forms, Arabic has a number of hypocoristic forms like *Fayṭama* from Fāṭima.[3] In the case of names consisting of *'abd* and a Divine name the *'abd* is put in the diminutive only rarely, as in *'Ubayd Allāh* whereas usually the divine name undergoes a change. Thus 'Abdul Fattāḥ may appear as *Futaytiḥ*, 'Abdul Qādir becomes a soft *Quwaydir* or a more forceful *Qaddūr*. 'Abdul 'Aẓīm, 'Abdul 'Azīz or 'Abdus Salām can be reduced to *'Azzūz* (also 'Azzūj) and *Sallūm*. A long *ū* in the last syllable seems to be typical for many of the hypocoristic forms, and at times the last consonant of the name is duplicated: 'Ā'isha becomes *'Iyūsha* or *'Ayshūsha*; Fāṭima, *Fuṭayṭūm*, Aḥmad and Ḥāmid turn into *Ḥammūd, Ḥammūda*, Sulaymān into *Sallūm*, Ḥasan into *Ḥassūna*. This latter form again can be abbreviated so that *Ḥassūn* becomes *Ḥassū, Ḥassō*. Forms ending in *-ō* are very frequent in Anatolia. The ending *-ūna*, incidentally, is also used for the masculine, while some feminines lose their final -a: Fāṭima can become *Faṭṭūm (Pattūm* in South India)

Another frequent ending for endearment is the syllable *-ūsh*, like *Faṭṭūsh, (Fattōsh)* from Fāṭima, *'Allūsh* or *'Aliyūsh* from 'Alī, or *'Abdūsh* from any *'abd* +. The *-sh* alone is found in common abbreviations like *Memish* from Mehmet (Muḥammad), *Ibish* from Ibrāhīm. Such diminutives are not lacking in Persian and in Turkish either. Persian forms them by adding *-k* to a noun: *Ḥusāmak*, 'little Ḥusām'. But it seems that these forms are more commonly used for deprecative purposes: *Ḥāfiẓak* can be translated as 'shabby little Ḥāfiẓ', *ṣūfīyak*, 'miserable Sufi', or *muṣannifak*, 'worthless author'. For a satirical poet the nickname *kāfirak*, 'little infidel' was quite appropriate. Turkish uses *jik, juq (cik, cuk)* for diminutives, and the Mamluk historian Ibn Taghrībirdī is at pains to explain the name *'Alījiq* by stating 'and *jiq* is a diminutive in Turkish'.[4] However, here the endearment is probably as strong as, if not stronger, than the negative connotation of the diminutive.

As for proper nicknames, they often differ so much from the original name that the non-initiated will have difficulty in recognizing them (as happens in the West as well). Attempts are made to invent forms that are easy to pronounce; and especially in the Subcontinent where complicated Arabo-Persian compounds prevail, the name is often shortened: Ṣalāḥ ad-dīn becomes *Ṣally*, Iftikhār ad-dīn, *Iffī*, Badr ad-dīn, *Baddū*, or Shihāb ad-dīn, *Shabban* etc. Even simple names are still more simplified in family usage: Maḥmūd becomes *Moodi*, Murtażā turns into *Muzhan*, Fāṭima appears as *Fōtī* or *Fōtō*, 'Affāf as *Fifi*.

In *sayyid* families where children are given a long list of official names the '*urf* by which they are known in the family can be completely unrelated, and one may discover that an 'Ādil or Sulaymān is really called Pir Sayyid Mīrān Shāh. Often the nicknames are taken from the common language of the environment: in the Subcontinent one finds Hindi, Sindhi, Pashto or Bengali nicknames for children;[5] they can thus be better integrated with the surrounding society. The same is the case for boys and girls who study in British or French schools and are then called *Lily* or *Ruby* instead of Mumtāz or Rukhshāna – despite their unchanging Muslim loyalties. This tendency becomes even stronger in Muslim families settled in the West, where a Jamshīd may appear as *Jimmy*.

A special way of abbreviating a name is to use only the initial – *Mīm Nūn* may be the name under which some Muḥammad, or Muṣṭafā, Nāṣir is known, and the Indian author *Zoe* (= *ẓ*) *Ansari* is officially called *Ẓill ur-raḥmān*. This type of abbreviation seems to be more common in Turkey (such as *Mim Kemal*, from Mustafa Kemal) and India than among the Arabs.

Slaves and Mamluks

It was an old rule among the Arabs to give their sons ugly and frightening names 'as a bad omen for the enemy', while slaves were given attractive names which could be appreciated at home.[8] There were, however, a few names which could not be used for slaves, as the Prophet had recommended that slaves should not be called *Yasār*, 'comfort, prosperity', *Najāh*, 'Success', *Baraka*, 'Blessing' and similar positive nouns. It would be a bad omen if one were to ask; 'Is *Najāḥ* there?' and a negative answer was given: one could understand that as 'success has left the house'![9] On the other hand, names of flowers, gems and precious substances were usually given to slaves, both male and female, and they could be called *Mabrūk, Mabrūka* 'blessed', *Mas'ūd*, 'happy', *Umm al-khayr*, 'mother of good things' or *Marḥabā* 'welcome' – names which could be found till recently among the descendants of slaves in Tunisia.[10] *Lu'lu'a* 'pearl', *Marjān* 'coral', were also typical for slaves.

In later times, especially among military slaves, certain rules were applied for the naming of eunuchs:[11] Abyssinian eunuchs were to be called *Mithqāl*, 'a unit of weight', *Jauhar*, 'jewel' or *Yāqūt* 'ruby, garnet': those from Byzantium were given the Persian name *Khushqadam* 'welcome', *Fīrūz* 'turquois' or *Kāfūr* 'camphor'. But the rules were apparently flexible as *Kāfūr* also occurs for black slaves (camphor being white!) and *Yāqūt* the calligrapher was a Byzantine slave. Qalqashandi even enumerates the *alqāb* which were assigned to eunuchs: a *Marjān* should be called *Zayn ad-dīn* 'beauty of religion', a *Mithqāl, Sābiq ad-din* 'preceding in religion', etc.

Even more interesting is the way in which normal Mamluks were named after being imported from South Russia or the Caucasus to Egypt where they were sold to the sultan and the amīrs. Each amīr had a certain number of military slaves at his disposal; according to his rank their number varied between ten and a hundred. At times the original names of the Mamluks were kept, although (especially in the case of Caucasian slaves) they barely resembled any Georgian or Circassian word as the Arabs' pronunciation changed them so much that 'some Turks and non-Arabs do not understand them when they hear them, or only after a great effort', as Ibn Taghrībirdī, himself a member of the Turkish establishment in Egypt, rightly complained. A typical case is the name of Sultan *Barqūq* whom everyone would read happily as the Arabic *barqūq* (apricot), but Ibn Taghrībirdī explains it as an arabicized form of the Circassian *mallī khūq*, which means 'shepherd'.[12]

An early Mamluk source tells how the Mongol conqueror Ghāzān Khan asked a Mamluk why he had three names,[13] and the answer was: the first is the proper name such as *Ināl* (from the root *inan*, to believe), *Jaqmaq* 'firestone', *Tengiz* 'ocean', *Yāghmūr* 'rain'; then came the *nisba*, relating to the person who had bought and manumitted him. Thus, if the first owner was one Mujīr ad-dīn, the Mamluk would be *Jaqmaq al-Mujīrī*. If the purchaser was the sultan himself, the *nisba* would be formed from his throne-name: the Mamluks of al-Ashraf Qaytbay were the *Ashrafī*. If there were several rulers with the same regnal name in a short space of time, as often happened in Mamluk Egypt, the *nisba* would be enlarged by the ruler's names: *Jaqmaq al-Ashrafī Qaytbay* (or even *al-Qaytbāhī*), *Ināl al-ashrafī Ṭūmān Bay*, etc. The third kind of name appeared when a Mamluk was first bought by an amīr, or civil servant, and then sold to the sultan. In this case, the first owner's name was connected by *min* (from) with the Mamluk's proper name. Thus one finds *Malbay min Ṭarabay al-ashrafī, Özbek min Ṭuṭukh* (the founder of the Ezbekiyye in Cairo) and many more.

The Mamluks were apparently often given new names; otherwise the great number of the same name at certain points in history would be difficult to explain. There are whole clusters of *Qoṣrauh*, of

Qanṣauh, etc. The name *Qanṣauh*, incidentally, should correctly be pronounced *Qaniṣauh*, 'his blood is healthy', *ṣauh* being the Central-Asian equivalent of the Ottoman *ṣāğ*.[14]. A similar correspondence can be found in the name *Aqṭauh*, which is Ottoman *Aqdāgh*, 'white mountain'.

Often, a Mamluk had a special *laqab*, pertaining to some of his qualities, or to his price: *al-Alfī* was someone whose price had been 'a thousand' dīnārs and *Qanṣauh Khamsmi'ah* (500) was bought for 'five hundred' dīnārs. Sometimes the Mamluk's origin was indicated, as in *Abāẓa*, *Rūs*, or *Mughal*, or he was distinguished according to his work in the barracks: *etmekji* 'baker', *al-jashnagīr*, 'he who tries the food', *ad-dawādār* 'the inkpot holder, i.e. secretary', etc. Special features were also expressed by *alqāb*, partly in Arabic, like *al-afram* 'toothless' or in Turkish, like *qiziljā* 'reddish' or *qarāgöz* 'black eye'. A Mamluk's Turkish *laqab anālī* is correctly explained by Ibn Taghrībirdī as 'he has a mother' – perhaps the mother had been sold along with her son?

With their advancement up the military ladder the Mamluks acquired official *alqāb* by which they had to be addressed in correspondence. The luckiest one might become *atābeg*, the commander-in-chief, and perhaps sultan, and then be surrounded by a long list of high-sounding titles, many of which still adorn metal and glass objects produced in the fifteenth and early sixteenth centuries.[15]

Change of name

Since a name carries a strong *baraka*, it may have to be changed if some misfortune befalls the child because its name 'is too heavy' for it, or does not agree with its disposition or with the astrological requirements of the hour of birth. The name can be changed, too, if the family experiences bad luck after the child's birth. Even at a later stage it can be changed as a consequence of a major event in the individual's life.

The Prophet himself changed the names of several of his followers, for he did not want opprobrious names used in the young Muslim community.[16] Thus one *Shihāb*, 'quick flame' was called *Hāshim*; a man by the name of *Ḥarb*, 'war', became *Silm* 'peace'; and the clan of the *Banū Mughwiya*, 'sons of Error', became *Banū ar-Rushda*, 'sons of right guidance'. A family whose name was changed by the Prophet became known as *Banū Muḥawwala*, 'the sons of the one who was changed'.[17]

As the name shows one's identity, the adoption of a new name is part and parcel of the process of conversion, although not by formal baptism as in Christianity. Sometimes the new name shows joy that the person is now a member of the community that is saved – therefore *Munji'a*, 'the saved one' is typical of women converts in Tunisia.[18] In other cases – thus Jews in North Africa – one would adopt the name of the person who had shown the way into Islam.[19]

It often happens that the new name resembles the old one in form or sound: when the Jewish astronomer *Manasse* became a Muslim he was called *Mā shā' Allāh*[20] – a name that agrees with the sound of his original name and also conveys the feeling of happy admiration. Snouck Hurgronje has given interesting examples of the changes of strange-sounding names of Muslim pilgrims from Java during their stay in Mecca where they were given 'real' Muslim names.[21] The maintenance of sound pattern or meaning can also be observed in the case of Western converts to Islam: one Wilfried calls himself *Murād* (= 'will') *Farīd*. *Farīd* and *Farīda* occur also in other cases where the German name contains the syllable *-fried*. A James can easily become *Ya'qūb*, and a Victoria may reappear as *Viqār an-nisā'*. The change of name was common in the case of slaves who were given beautiful names of good augury. The Mamluks too were often given new names after being imported from Central Asia to Egypt (s.p.) as Ibn Taghrībirdī states: 'Inal's name was not *Īnāl*, but it was established as Inal.'[22]

Similarly in the case of adoption a good augury was sometimes sought: an Indian boy who greeted Akbar's commander-in-chief with the words *Fatḥ mubārak*, 'congratulations for the victory!' was adopted by him and became known as *Fatḥ Mubārak*.[23] Similar cases can be found in various periods of Islamic history. But a *Laqīṭ(a)* would always be reminded by his name, whether used as *ism* or as *laqab*, that he was a 'foundling'.

A problem arises today over the change of Arabic names into European ones, as in the case of Tunisians or Algerians who want to conform to French custom and therefore adopt names that are similar in sound to the original, like *Belli* for *Ben 'Alī*, *Raymond* for *Raḥmān*, or are approximate translations of the Arabic meaning as in the case of *Lucien* for *Munīr*, both from the root 'light', *lux* and *nūr* respectively.[24] The tendency of Muslims in anglophone countries to replace *ad-dīn* by *Dean* is part of this trend.

The Pen-name, takhalluṣ

In addition to the types of names mentioned so far, a special name is used by writers. This is the pen-name, *takhalluṣ*, by which a poet identifies himself in a clever pun in the last line of his poem. This custom developed in Iran in the early Middle Ages and remained in use through the centuries. The *takhalluṣ* was sometimes chosen by the poet himself, sometimes by his patron, and frequently by his *ustād*, his teacher of poetics; or if he was a member of a Sufi fraternity his spiritual guide might select a fitting name. Pen-names can reflect something about the writer's personality or family: the great Persian poet *'Urfī* in Akbar's India chose this name because his father was a judge both in *shar'ī*, religious, and *'urfī*, customary, law. *Ḥāfiẓ* simply pointed to his skill as someone who knew the Qur'ān by heart, while Rashīd ad-dīn *Waṭwāṭ*, 'the bat' was so-called because of his small, ugly frame. Rather different is the case of Muṣliḥ ad-dīn *Sa'dī*, who chose his pen-name to express his relationship with the Shirazi prince Sa'd-i Zangī. Some poets even used a *takhalluṣ* that would shock pious Muslims, such as *Kufrī* 'connected with *kufr*, infidelity', a name against which the reformer Aḥmad Sirhindi protested energetically.[25] For a lady, who should be decently hidden, *Makhfī*, 'concealed' was a good *takhalluṣ*. (She was in fact Zēb un-nisā, emperor Aurangzēb's daughter).

Pen-names can also reflect the poet's aspirations, such as the Persian *Khushgū*, 'speaking well', or *Anwarī*, derived from *anwar*, 'most radiant'. The Indian poet Walī Deccanī has written a charming little Urdu poem about his beloved's beauty, in which he uses exclusively the pen-names of famous poets:

> Your face is like sunrise (*Mashriqī*), your beauty most radiant (*Anwarī*), your manifestation that of divine beauty (*Jamālī*); your eye is cuplike (*Jāmī*), your forehead paradisiacal (*Firdausī*), your eyebrows crescent-like (*Hilālī*). Walī is longing for (*Shauqī*) and inclined toward (*Mā'il*) your figure and eyebrows, so that every verse of his is sublime (*'Ālī*), and every hemistich imaginative (*Khayālī*).

Sometimes the *takhalluṣ* is derived from the poet's proper name, like Khalīl Allāh *Khalīlī*; at other times it wittily contrasts with the given name: one Muḥammad 'Āqil, 'intelligent', adopted the pen-name *Nādān*, 'ignorant', while Badr-ad-din, 'the full moon of religion', called himself *Hilālī*, 'connected with the new moon' (*hilāl*). For someone called Asad Allāh, *Ghālib* is an appropriate pen-name, as both point to 'Alī ibn Abī Ṭālib. Some Indian poets by the name of Shirāj ad-din, 'lamp of religion', called themselves *Chirāgh*, 'candle' (P), or else *Parwāna*, 'moth, butterfly', as the moth immolates itself in the candle. In later times, especially in the Indian subcontinent, poets preferred melancholy names which reflected the whole atmosphere of those times: *Bēdil*, 'weak' (lit. 'without a heart'), *Bēkas*, 'lonely', *Bēkhud*, 'without one's own self'. A typical example of a chain of poetical names belongs to a line of Sufi poets in eighteenth-century Dehli: the Naqshbandi master 'Abdul Aḥad *Gul*, 'Rose', gave his favourite disciple the name *'Andalīb*, 'nightingale', and as the nightingale in Persian poetry always laments, full of pain, longing for the rose, 'Andalīb's elder son was given the *takhalluṣ Dard*, 'Pain', while the younger one was called *Athar*, 'Result' – in the hope that the nightingale's painful complaint would finally 'result' in happiness. Dard gave his own son the pen-name *Alam*, 'Pain', and a later member of this family is known as *Firāq*, 'Separation'. The pen-names thus tell a whole romance.

In periods when artificiality was highly praised and the art of *mu'ammā*, 'name puzzles', was practised even by major poets, one might insert a riddle into the pen-name, as did the fifteenth-century Persian writer Sībak, 'little Apple', who translated his name into Arabic, *tuffāḥ*, changed the sequence of the letters and became famous as *Fattāḥī*.

The custom of using pen-names or pseudonyms continues to our day although it is now usually journalists and professional writers who use them to express their ideologies. Arab writers take names of famous classical authors such as *Abū Firās* or *al-Jāḥiẓ*, or else allude to them, like the woman traveller 'Iṣmat Khānim, who writes as *Bint Baṭṭūṭa*, referring to the medieval traveller Ibn Baṭṭūṭa. The pseudonym can refer to a whole literary programme, as in the case of the Lebanese writer *Adonis*, whose imagery, like that of some of his contemporaries, harks back in part to the mythology of the Ancient Near East. *Abū Ya'rab* for a Saudi, *Abū Furāt* for an Iraqi writer are quite typical, while a Tunisian artist calls himself – not very modestly – *Ḥayāt al-qulūb*, 'Life of the hearts'.[26] A musical critic in Pakistan is *Mausiqār*, while another journalist in the same country expresses his sceptical views under the name of *Zeno*. And amusing is the *takhalluṣ* of an Egyptian satirist, *Khonfashār*, in which the Persian word *khunfashār*, 'blood-shedding', is cleverly hidden.[27]

Regional variants and non-Arab formations

Stefan Wild has argued that certain Arabic names bear a kind of regional flavour, such as *'Abduṣ Ṣabūr* or *'Abdul Mu'ṭī* which sound, to the Arabs 'Egyptian', or *'Abdul Mu'min*, which has a North African sound.[28] It is natural that specific names are favourites in certain countries; besides, a number of grammatical forms seem to be related to specific areas. One of these forms, which has long attracted the interest of Orientalists, is the ending *-ūn* which is frequently found in North Africa and medieval Spain: there we find numerous *Ḥamdūn, Khaldūn, Ḥafṣūn, 'Allūn, Farḥūn, Baḥrūn* and so on. They can be extended by an additional *-a*, as in *Ḥamdūna* or *Raḥmūna*, an abbreviation of *'Abdur Raḥmān*. The similarity of this ending to the Spanish ending *-on*, the Italian one *-one* has been discussed especially by Dozy.[29]

Another ending that is widespread in Arabic names but abounds in Yemen is *-ān*. Everyone is familiar with the good old Arabic names like *'Adnān* and *Qaḥṭān*, but a glance through the telephone directory of Yemen yields about a hundred different names ending in *-ān*, among them *Jahlān, Ja'shān, Ḥauthān, Khayrān, Daḥmān, Dhībān, Zaydān, Radmān, Sarḥān, Shamsān, Ṣab'ān, 'Adhbān, 'Aqlān, Ghamdān, Farwān, Qamḥān, Kaḥlān, Nūrān* and *Ḥīlān*. It is possible that here a memory of the ancient south Arabian definite article, a suffixed *-ān*, survives. Particularly interesting are *fu'aylān* forms like *'Usayrān* and *Nuqaybān*. The ending *-ān* occurs also frequently in the Najd, as Hess has shown for Bedouin names. Remarkable, too, are the number of names with the ending *-ūh* in Hodaida, such as *Muḥammadūh, Qādirūh, 'Adarūh, 'Āsūh* etc.; this may be a specifically Tihāma variant.

The change from *k* to *ch*, and from *q* through *g* to *j* (mainly before *a, e,* and *i*) in dialects of Iraq and Arab Khuzistan, produces forms not always easy to identify, like *chelab* from *kalb*, 'dog', *Jāsim* from *Qāsim*.

Even greater are the changes which Arabic names underwent in non-Arab environments. In early Iran one can find forms like *'Alkā* and *Ḥaskā* for *'Alī* and *Ḥasan* in the city of Rayy; in Hamadan the suffix *-lā* was used, as in *Aḥmadlā*, while in Sava an *-ān* was often added: *Ja'farān*.[30] The difficulty of pronouncing the Arabic *ḍ* correctly led everywhere to its replacement by *z*: *Murtaḍā* becomes *Murtażā, gharaḍ* (aim), is transformed into *gharaż* and becomes in India (with a typical change from z to j) *gharaj, gharja*. This change z-j is particularly strong in Bengal and Gujarat where additionally the exchange between *s* and *sh* can be observed. I often wondered why someone was called *Shīrāz ad-dīn* until I discovered that he was really a *Sirāj ad-dīn. Zayn ad-dīn* appears as *Joyn ad-dīn*, and some names, especially in Bengal, are barely recognisable. I suppose that also the name of the Arabic poet *Kushājim*, whose grandfather was from Sind, may be a 'sindhicized' pronunciation of *Kāẓim: Kush* representing the *ksh, j* the *ẓ*.

Another feature of Muslim names in India, especially in the north, is the acquisition of an additional long *ā*, sometimes slightly nasalised: *Raḥīm* (= 'Abdur Raḥīm) becomes *Rahimāṅ, 'Ā'isha, Aishāṅ, Iḥsān* appears sometimes as *Aḥsānā*. In Telugu-speaking areas in southern India, Muslims often add *ayya* or *-lū* to proper names, so that one finds *Ḥusaynayya* or *Ḥasanlū*, while among the Canarese-speaking population the ending is more frequently *-appa*, like *Ḥusaynappa*. Often the *f* is changed into *p* , so that *Fāṭima* may appear as *Pattumappa*. And the transcription of Arabic names into the alphabets of South India poses additional problems: 'Abdur Raḥmān will appear as *Abdul regman*.[31] One should also remember that in many names and titles, which would grammatically require a clear genitive construction, such as *Āftāb ad-dīn* or *Khurshid-i dīn*, 'sun of the religion', the short *i* of the *iżāfet* is generally left out so that *Āftāb dīn, Khurshīd dīn* appear. Purists, of course, pronounce the name *Jānjānān*, 'darling', 'soul of souls', as *Jān-i jānān*, and the title *Khānkhānān* as *khān-i khānān*.

Even farther removed from classical pronunciation are Muslim names in Indonesia, and Snouck Hurgronje has given a number of favourite names borne by Javanese Muslims who came to Mecca and who loved to be called by the names of great Muslims sages and scholars like *Shāfi'ī* or *Ghazālī*, which were pronounced as *Sapingi, Sapi'i* and *Gadjali* respectively.[32] The Arabic *ḍ* often appears in Indonesia as *dl*, and in some areas of South India as well as in West Africa it is changed into a deep *l*; *Murtaḍā* becomes *Murtala.*

To return to the western part of the Muslim world, one may remember that among the Berbers the circumfix *t* is often added to Arabic names and nouns: *Manṣūr* grows into *Tamansurt*, *'Azza* into *Taazait*, and the famous reformer *Ibn Tumart* is 'the son of little 'Umar'.[33] In West Africa, *Muḥammad* can become *Mamadou*, and *Aḥmad*, *Amadou.* A survey of names in Guinea shows *Muḥammad* as *Māmādī*, *'Abdallāh* as *Būrlay*, *Sa'īd* as *Sédou*, *al-Ḥasan* as *Lansiné*, *Khadīja* as *Kediā*, and the title *shaykh* as *sékou.*[34]

Further problems are encountered in Russia, and the names of Muslims in the Tatar, Uzbek, Tajik and Kazak areas can be studied fairly well thanks to the comparatively large literary output from those areas. Generally, the Russian ending *-ov, -ev, -yev* is added to the Muslim name; *'Abdus Sattār* becomes *Sattarov*; *'Umar*, *Umarov*, *'Alī Muḥammad* is *Alimukhamedov*, though *Magomedov* occurs also as a derivation from *Muḥammad.* The composer *Raḥmaninoff* seems to carry a derivation of an ancestral *'Abdur Raḥmān.* *'Abdul Ghafūr* appears as *Gafurov* or *Gapurov*, and *Jum'a*, 'Friday' turns into *Dzumaev.* The Tajik transcription of the long *ā* as *o* produces forms like *Dodikhudaev*, from *Dād-i khudā*, 'God's gift'.

Arab-Turkish compounds abound, naturally enough, in Central Asia where one is likely to find some *Alaverdiev* = *Allahverdi* 'God has given', *Rahmanqulov* = *Raḥmān-Quli* 'slave of the Merciful'. Among the Turkmens, *Muḥammad 'Ali* is changed into *Mambetaliev* and *Uwaysberdī*, 'Uways has given' becomes *Ovezberdiev*. Purely Turkish names like *Esengeldiev*, from *esen*, 'healthy' (or transformation of *ḥasan*) plus *geldi*, 'he came', or *Sarymsakov*, from *sarĭmsak* (garlic), are worthy of mention as examples; and certainly remarkable is the variant of *'Ubaydullāh* as *Gubaidullin* with the feminine *Gubaidullina*.

These are only a few hints – anyone who has looked in the index volume of the *Revue du Monde Musulman* will agree that the possibilities of rendering Islamic names seem to be unlimited!

When non-Arabs joined the Muslim community new forms of names appeared, especially during the supremacy of the Persian Buwayhids. It is significant that two of the leading proponents of Arabic grammar were both Persians and bore Persian names or nicknames: *Sībawayh* and *Nafṭawayh*. Persian names of this type ending in *-oy* or, in Arabic transcription, *-way*, *-wayhi*, are quite common in the early period: *Sībawayh* would thus be 'like an apple' (*sīb*), while apparently his colleague *Nafṭawayh* received his name because of his dirty appearance and foul smell – he resembled *nafṭ*, black odorous bitumen. In this category names like *Durustawayh, Shīrawayh, Miskawayh, Khiḍrawayh, Khumārawayh* appear in the first centuries of Islam.

They slowly disappeared, but other Persian names emerged to take pride of place in all areas under Persian cultural influence from Turkey to India; some of them were also integrated into Arabic nomenclature. It shows the prestige of such names that the Turkish rulers of Delhi in the thirteenth century, though boasting of their Turkish origin, still chose the names of Persian heroes for their sons. The mythical kings of Iran as they had been immortalized by Firdausī in his *Shāhnāma* at the beginning of the eleventh century became fashionable, and thus one meets today numerous *Khusrau* (T *Hüsrev*, in Tunisia *Khosrof*), *Farīdūn, Hoshang, Kayqōbād, Iraj, Tahmurath, Siyāwush, Isfandiyār, Parvīz* and so on. The name of the Iranian super-hero, *Rustam*, is sometimes combined with that of ʿAlī. *Dārā*, 'Darius' and *Iskandar*, 'Alexander' appear as models of greatness, and even the name of *Afrāsiyāb*, the ruler of Turan, is used. Girls were, and still are, called after *Tahmīna*, (Rustam's wife), *Manēzha* or *Rukhshāna* 'Roxane'. *Pūrān-dukht*, the daughter of Khusrau Parvīz has given her name to women, as has *Shahrbānū*, Yazdagard's III daughter, the mother of the fourth Shiite imām, Zayn al ʿĀbidīn. *Shīrīn*, the 'sweet' heroine of Niẓāmi's epic poem, has lent her name to innumerable girls.

Although many of the Turkish Central-Asian tribes adopted Arabic and Persian names when they entered the stage of Islamic history, a good number of original names survived. Among them are the numerous names combined with *alp*, 'hero', *tigīn, tekīn*, 'prince', *arslān, aslān*, 'lion', which remained in use throughout the centuries, as did the names of birds of prey (*sonqor, lājīn, sanjar, tughrūl* etc.) and names connected with *demir, timur*, 'iron'. Some of them appear in Arabic in the late Middle Ages, such as *Aydemir*, 'moon-iron', *Ibn Qutlūbughā*, 'son of the Lucky Steer', *Ibn Duqmāq*, 'son of the Hammer', or *Ibn Taghrībirdī*, 'son of the God-Given'.

Among the Ottomans the emphasis shifted to Arabic or Persian names, with Turkish expressions used more as nicknames. This is true at least for the upper classes where Persian names (as in India) were always cherished. Unfortunately there exists no study of the nomenclature in rural areas in earlier times. Many Arabic words were used by the Ottomans in a peculiar way and then came back to the Arabs as verbal nouns: *Iḥsān* 'beneficence', *Servet* (= Arab. *tharwat*) 'wealth' or *nisba*-forms from composite names, like *Ḥaqqī (T Hakkĭ)* from *'Abdul Ḥaqq* 'Slave of God' etc. With the emergence of modern Turkey the renewed interest in Turkish mythology and history became evident both in personal names and, after 1934, in the newly created family names. The legendary *Oghuz Khan* and his sons; the heroes *Dede Korkut, Temuçin* and *Çingiz* all appear again, as does the ancestor of the Ottoman house, *Orhan*, and the nicknames of Sultan Selīm I (*Yāvūz*, 'grim'), Bāyezīd I (*Yĭldĭrĭm*, 'lightning') as well as figures from cultural history such as *Sinān* 'spearhead' (A), the leading architect of the sixteenth century. The change from religiously oriented names to modern ones has been studied several times recently,[35] and names like *Bentūrk*, 'I am a Turk', or *Türksen*, 'You Turk', attest to the feeling of pride among Turks.

Appendix
Some Notes on Turkish family names

During the last century several Islamic countries have introduced laws for the adoption of family names. In Algiers this dates back to 1882, Tunisia demanded family names in 1925,[1] Iran promulgated a law in 1932, and the Egyptian Civil Code of 1970 introduced them in Sections 38 and 39. In Turkey the Civil Code of 1926 stipulated that 'names', meaning family names, should be used. In fact several families had been known by the same name through the centuries, such as the *Köprülüzade* and the *Evrenosoğullarĭ*, and these names used to precede the given name: *Fĭndĭkoğlu Fahrettin* (Fakhr ad-dīn). But the *Soyadĭ kanunu* of 1934 ordered that everyone should have a family name in the Western sense. This resulted in a complete change in the naming patterns[2] and the results were all the more remarkable as the law was passed only six years after the adoption of the Roman instead of the Arabic script. It has been estimated that some 75% of the new names were fabricated according to personal predilections so that the lineage was completely broken and even siblings did not necessarily use the same new family name. Thus, nobody could guess whether some *Mehmet Akyürek* (= 'white heart') or *Ali Önder* (= 'leader') were related to any other family named Akyürek or Önder, or whether in fact they were brothers. The first to receive one of the new family names was *Mustafa Kemal* himself, who was acclaimed on November 1934 as *Atatürk*, which was intended to mean 'Father of the Turks'; and his descendants were to bear the name *Atadan*, 'From the father'. Atatürk himself selected a number of family names for his close friends, sometimes changing them several times.

There was no limit to people's imagination when choosing their names. Some of them were certainly selected for reasons of euphony, without any deeper meaning; but certain ideals become clear even from a superficial survey. There were those who kept their old family names ending with *-oghlū* (son), like *Bĭyĭklĭoğlu*, 'son of someone with a moustache', or *Yenişehirlioğlu*, 'son of an inhabitant of Yenişehir'. Others, like the *Köprülü*, cast off the time-honoured *-zāde*. Others again chose the ending *-soy*, 'family, clan', as in *Yazansoy*, 'family of the one that writes', which happens to be the surname of a calligrapher. Someone with the name *Şemsi* (from *Shams ad-dīn*, 'sun of religion') took the family name *Güneşsoy*, 'Sun family'; many *-oğlu* chose instead the suffix *-gil*, and so on. The longest Turkish family name, developed out of a nickname, is *Uzunağacaltĭndayataruyaroğlu*, 'Son of the one who lays and sleeps under the big tree'.

Often a hankering after ancient Turkish ideals and the names of heroes was expressed in the new names. Names combined with *gök*, 'blue, heaven', are reminiscent of the Siberian ancestors, the *Göktürk* and this name actually occurs. A good number of family (and also first) names can be traced back to the mythological *Oğuz Khan* and his six sons *Gün* 'sun', *Ay* 'moon', *Yĭldĭz* 'star', *Kök* 'heaven', *Tağ* (= *dağ*) 'mountain' and *Tengiz* (= *deniz*) 'ocean'. These concepts are found in a considerable proportion of names in varying combinations. Titles of heroes appear likewise, such as *alp*, 'hero', and *tīgīn, tekin*, 'prince'; they can also be found in combination, from *Alptegin* to *Tökin*.

It is hardly surprising that the ancient Turkish tribes like *Çağatay* or *Selcuk* lent their names to quite a few families, and the same is true of the alleged predecessors of the Turks, the Hittites – *Eti* – and Sumerians, *Sümer*, who also provide the name *Lugal*, 'King'. The homeland of the Turks, *Turan*, also provided a meaningful surname. The great rivers important for Turkish history turn up too, from *Araz*, 'Araxes' to *Tuna*, 'Danube'. Animal names long since used as first names, were transferred to family names, and there are many *Doğan*, 'falcon', *Ertuğrul*, 'male hawk' (also the name of an early Turkish hero), *Kartal*, 'eagle', often specified as *ak* 'white', *kara* 'black', or by similar adjectives. Predatory animals like *Arslan*, 'lion', and *Kaplan*, 'tiger' can be found alone or in combinations, and the percentage of wolves, *börü* or *kurt*, is considerable, as the grey wolf, *bozkurt*, is a symbol of Central Asian Turks.

A favourite compound is *ak*, 'white', which also has the meaning of 'pure, noble, wealthy', as in *Akkuzu*, 'white lamb', *Aküzüm*, 'white grape', *Akbulut*, 'white cloud' or *Akzanbak*, 'white lily'. Very frequent as a strengthening element is *öz*, 'self', which often serves to emphasize a certain aspect of the person's body or character. *Özdil*, as our teacher of Qur'ānic recitation was called, points to his pure, beautiful tongue or speech, *dil*; *Özkan* emphasizes the 'blood', *kan*; *Öztürk* is the quintessential Turk, and if someone is called *Öztemiz* it means absolute purity (*temiz*, 'pure'). We had a milkman by the name of *Özsüt*, *süt* being 'milk', and there is the corresponding name *Paksüt* 'pure milk'. *Ün*, 'honour' is another favourite in family names: *Ünver*, 'give honour', *Ünsev*, 'love honour', *Üner*, 'honour-man', and the *er*, 'man', leads to the innumerable names in which this word appears, like '*Erol*, 'be a man', *Erdal*, 'man-branch', *Özer*, 'real man' or *Gençer*, 'young man'. As the arrow, *ok*, plays an important role in ancient Turkish history, (for example the *on-ok*, 'ten arrows', a Uygur tribe) the word has also often been used to form family names, such as *Üçok*, 'three arrows'.

Names that point to the bearer's – real or hoped for – heroism and bravery are quite common: *Güvendik*, 'we have trusted', *Güçbilmez*, 'he who knows no difficulties'. *Güçüyener*, 'he who overcomes difficulties', *Arslankorkut*, 'lion-frightener', *Sönmez*, 'inextinguishable'. *Demir, temir*, 'iron' and *taş*, 'stone' serve to form names alone or in combinations, be it *Demirdağ*, 'iron mountain' or *Denktaş*, 'equal to a stone'. And of course ancient *alqāb* were, as might be expected, transformed into family names such as *Akkaş*, 'with white eyebrows', *Samurkaş*, 'with eyebrows like sable' or *Ağzĭbüyük*, 'with a large mouth'.

Political ideas feature prominently in family names. The Secretary General of the Millet Partisi in the 1950s bore the belligerent name *Tahtakĭlĭc*, 'sword against the throne',[36] while other, more mellow, have styled themselves *Vatansever*, 'he who loves his fatherland', or *Yurdakul*, 'servant of the country', as the famous nationalist poet Mehmet Emin called himself. Names like *Yurdatap*, 'worship the fatherland', or *Yurdaydĭn*, 'homeland-radiant', belong to this category; and in general terms, an idealist might call himself *Ülkütaşĭr*, 'he who carries an ideal'.

In many cases, Arabic or Persian concepts were changed into the related Turkish ones or at least into words that sounded more Turkish: many people by the name of *Amīn, Emin* changed their names into *Inal* or *Inan* because the Turkish root *inan* corresponds to the Arabic *amina* 'to believe'. The historian *Ibnülemin Inal* is a good example of this trend, while the poet Yahya Kemal alluded to the *Şehsüvaroğlu* family of his ancestors by taking the family name *Beyatlĭ*: *şeh* = *bey*, 'lord', *süvar* = *atlĭ*, 'riding, with a horse'. Mixtures of Turkish and European syllables occur too: the most famous example is the art historian *Celāl Arseven*, the first syllable of whose family name is nothing but the transcription of the French *'art'* to which *seven*, 'loving, lover' is cleverly added: he is the true 'art lover'.

Many of the old professional *alqāb* in *-ci* survived, as in *Demirci*, 'blacksmith' or *Mumcu*, 'candle maker', but new professional names were also invented. When a farmer called himself *Sürerçeker*, 'he ploughs', it makes as much sense as when physicians chose names like *Yaşat*, 'Make alive!' or *Kurtaran*, 'who saves, rescues', or *Sağlam*, 'whole and healthy'. The same is true for the cobbler *Gezdiren*, 'he who makes (people) walk' and the merchant *Binbirçeşit*, 'thousand-and-one-kinds'. Goldsmiths by the names *Altĭnören*, 'gold weaving', or *Altĭnbaş*, 'gold head' were common in the 1950s in Ankara, and dentists liked the name *Altĭndiş*, 'gold tooth', while an ophtamologist was known as *Gözdüren*, 'he who makes (people) see'. One of my favourites was the owner of the Karadeniz restaurant, who selected the name *Açkurt*, 'hungry wolf'; but a photographer *Nuri Gölge*, whom I encountered somewhere in Central Anatolia, also showed good taste as his name *Nuri*, derived from *nūr*, 'light', was complemented by the family name *Gölge*, 'shadow'. Less appealing was the sweetmeat-vendor *Ramazan Sa'im*, in whose name and family name 'fasting' and the month of fasting, Ramadan, were combined; or a boy with the family name *Dümdüz*, 'absolutely straight, plain' whose parents had absurdly called him *Kaya*, 'rock'.

A particularly interesting assortment of family names was found in the 1950s among the physicians of Konya. Among them were Dr *Demirağ*, 'iron net', a specialist in bone-setting, and *Sa'im Săg*, 'fasting – healthy'; the gynaecologist Dr *Genç*, 'Young' and the bacteriologist Dr *Doğru*, 'right, correct'; Dr *Boğazgören*, 'he who sees the throat' was most fitting for an ear-nose-and-throat specialist, and who could fail to trust an urologist with the family name *Gürpĭnar*, 'powerful fountain'?

Today family names no longer tell such stories as they did at a time when people still remembered why they, or their father, selected them, and which stories were connected with them. But even today many Turkish family names reflect the ideals that were uppermost in the minds of people half a century ago, and provide a clue to the Turkish mentality.

Notes

INTRODUCTION

1 In R. Brünnow and A. Fischer, *Arabische Chrestomathie aus Prosaschriftstellern*, Leipzig 1935, p. 3.

2 Cf. J. Frazer, *The Golden Bough*, II, chapter IV §1, 'Personal Names tabooed', and the relevant chapters in G. van der Leeuw, *Phenomenology of Religion*, and F. Heiler, *Erscheinungsformen und Wesen der Religion*, Stuttgart 1961.

3 Leone Caetani and Guiseppe Gabrieli, *Onomasticon Arabicum*, Rome 1915, p. 59 n. 2.

4 J. H. Garcin de Tassy, 'Mémoire sur les noms propres et sur les titres musulmans', *JA* sér. 5, III (1854), p. 422.

CHAPTER I

1 *Encyclopedia of Islam*, new ed. (1954-), vol. IV, pp. 179-81, s.v. *ism*.

2 About the inflection of proper names see Wolfdietrich Fischer, *Grammatik des klassischen Arabisch*, Wiesbaden 2nd.ed. 1986, §141,1; §153: the correct form is *Maliku'bnu Sa'di'bni Muḥammadin*. For the formation of plurals see Caetani, *op. cit.*, p. 55: the *Talḥas: at-talḥāt*, the *Muḥammads*: *al-muḥammadūn*; the *'Abdallāhs*: *al-'Abādila*; the *Fāṭimas*: *al-Fawāṭīm*. Often, the dual is used to unite two people by the same or similar names: *Al-Ḥasanān* are *Ḥasan* and *Ḥusayn*; this form then can be used as a proper name as well, and appears especially in Persianate areas among Shiites in combinations like *Ghulām-i Ḥasanayn* or *Ghulām (-i) Sayyidayn*, 'the servant of the two Ḥasans' or 'of the two lords' (again, Ḥasan and Ḥusayn). A list of feminine forms for males may be found in Werner Caskel, *Ǧamharat an-nasab*, Leiden 1965, Vol. I, pp 45-50. Stefan Wild suggests that these names may have an apotropaeic meaning, e.g., to hide a male child by a female name in order to confuse the evil spirits. 'Arabische Eigennamen' in *Grundriß der Arabischen Philologie* I, Wiesbaden 1982, p. 157.

4 For a survey of animal names cf. Ibn Qutayba, *Adab al-kātib*, Cairo 4th ed. 1963, p. 63ff; the names of birds, *ibid*,. p. 56ff. Caetani, *op. cit.*, p. 78, gives a long list of animal names, mainly based on this work. Animal names are frequent in the Punjab too, and a number of popular verses deal with the qualities of people bearing this or that name, as for *Billā*, 'tom cat':

Billā nām us mard kā jā sāda ghāṭ men hoi
Jahān dekhan māren us sē aur pálen nahin sab koi.
'Cat' is the man who is always on the watch;
Where men see him they kill him, and none cherish him.

R. Temple, *Proper Names of Punjabis*, ?, p. 168.

4 There is a list of plants in Ibn Qutayba, *op. cit.*, p. 54ff.

5 P. Marty, 'Folklore Tunisien', *REI* 10 (1936), esp. 389, 396. Many attempts to explain the meaning of Islamic names for modern parents who live in the West show how wrong and misleading the explanations can be.

6 See Caskel, *op. cit.*, I, p. 49.

7 See Caetani, *op. cit.*, p. 53-4, and Theodor Nöldeke, 'Bemerkungen über hebräische and arabische Eigennamen' *ZDMG* 15 (1851), p. 807.

8 Garcin de Tassy, *op. cit.*, p. 451.

9 In the useful lists of Dr 'Abdul Karīm Bihniyā, *Nām*, Ahwaz 1981, which contains an analysis of some 3000 names borne by almost 38,000 individuals, only 233 double names are found. A special type of double name can be found in the Indian subcontinent where children from Muslim-Hindu marriages bear names pointing to both traditions, such as *Khadīja Srinavas* or *Enamulkabir (= In 'ām al-kabīr) Brahma.* It is said that the son of the leading Muslim Bengali poet Nadhr ul-Islām, whose wife was Hindu, bore the name *Muḥammad Krishna*, but was generally known as *Bulbul* (Nightingale); see Afia Dil, 'A comparative study of the personal names and nicknames of the Bengali speaking Hindus and Muslims' in *Studies on Bengal*, East Lansing 1976, p. 70.

10 *Encylopedia of Islam*, 2nd ed. Vol. V, 395-6 s.v. *kunya*; also *ibid.*, Vol. I, 828; *Bā*; Caetani, *op. cit.*, pp. 132-33 gives a long bibliography. The first study is J. F. D. Kosegarten, 'Über den Vornamen oder die Kunje der Araber', *ZfKM* 1 (1837), 297-312; further Ignaz Goldziher, 'Gesetzliche Bestimmungen über *kunja*-Namen in Islam', *ZDMG* 51 (1897), 256-66, and the same, 'Der Gebrauch der *Kunja* als Ehrenbezeichnung' in *Muhammedanische Studien* Vol. I, 267. Some interesting material is to be found in Barbara Stowasser-Freyer, 'Formen des geselligen Umgangs und Eigentümlichkeiten des Sprachgebrauchs in der frühislamischen städtischen Gesellschaft Arabiens', *Der Islam* 42 (1965), 25-57; Anton Spitaler, 'Beiträge zur Kenntnis der *kunya*-Namengebung', in *Festschrift W. Caskel*, Leiden 1968, pp. 336-50; Albert Dietrich, 'Das *kunya*-Wörterbuch des Muslim ibn al-Ḥağğāğ' (which contains more than 4000 *kunyas*), in *Festschrift W. Caskel*, pp. 43-52.

11 See August Fischer, 'Vergöttlichung und Tabuisierung der Namen Muhammads bei den Muslimen', R. Hartmann and H. Scheel (eds), *Beiträge zur Arabistik, Semitistik und Islamwissenschaft*, Leipzig 1943, p. 316 n.

12 According to some sources, the Prophet himself prohibited the use of the *kunya Abū 'Īsā*,, see Ḥusayn Nūrbakhsh, *Farhang-i nām*, Tehran 1981, p. 16.

13 Yaḥyā ibn Sharaf an-Nawawī, *Kitāb al-adhkār*, Cairo 1312/1894-5, p. 378-9. Spitaler, *op. cit.* p. 327 n 2. I am told that nowadays in the Yemen, one can tease a man by calling him by a *kunya* such as *Abū Fāṭima*.

14 Kosegarten, *op. cit., passim*; Caskel, *op. cit.*, I p. 48.

15 I. Goldziher, in *Muhammedanische Studien* I 267

16 Stowasser-Freyer, *op. cit.*, p. 32 n.

17 Nawawī, *op. cit.*, p. 375-76.

18 Thus in Kosegarten, *op. cit.*

19 Kosegarten, *op. cit.* p. 502 after Ibn Khallikān (whose work is his main source)

20 Caskel, *op. cit.*, I p. 48.

21 However, *ibn al-* can also be pronounced *bel* so that misunderstandings are possible.

22 Nawawī, *op. cit.*, p. 374; Theodor Nöldeke, 'Zur tendenziösen Gestaltung der Urgeschichte des Islam', *ZDMG* 52 (1898) p. 30.

23 Marty, *op. cit.*, pp. 399-401.

24 On the confusion between *laqab* and *kunya* see Heinrich Freiherr von Maltzan, 'Über Beinamen bei den Arabern des Magrib', *ZDMG* 24 (1870), pp. 617-23, and Stowasser-Freyer, *op. cit.*, p. 31, n 31.

25 Caetani, *op. cit.*, p. 104. Abū 'Aṣīda died in 694/1295.

26 Richard T. Antoun, 'On the significance of names in an Arab Village' *Ethnology* 7 (1968), p. 158.

26 Example from Garcin de Tassy, *op. cit.* p. 441.

27 Naimur Rehman, 'The *kunya* names in Arabic', *Allahabad University Studies 5* (1929), 6 (1930). A modern example is the *kunya* given to the Mercedes car in Saudi Arabia: *Abū Najma*, 'father of the star'.
29 See August Fischer, 'Vergöttlichung', p. 315.
30 Caetani, *op. cit.*, pp. 138-39.
31 G. Levi della Vida, 'Matronymics among Arab poets', *JAOS 62* (1942), 156-171, based on Muḥammad ibn Ḥabīb's 'Matronymics of Poets', *kitāb man nusiba ilā ummihi min ash-shuʿarā'*.
32 For the irregular *nisbas* see Wright, *Arabic Grammar*, 3 ed., Vol 1 §249.
33 Marty, *op. cit.*, p. 371.
34 Rudolf Sellheim, '"Familiennamen" im islamischen Mittelalter', in *On the Dignity of Man, Oriental Studies in Honour of Frithjof Rundgren*. Stockholm 1986, pp. 375-84.
35 S. D. Goitein, 'Nicknames as family names', *JAOS* 90 (1970), 517-24.
36 *Encyclopedia of Islam*, 2nd ed., Vol. V 618-31, s.v. *laḳab*. Caetani, *op. cit.*, p. 144 ff. A good survey is A. C. Barbier de Meynard, 'Surnoms et sobriquets dans la littérature arabe', *JA* 10ᵉsér. 9 (1907) 173-244, 365-428; 10 (1908) 55-118, 193-273.
37 Barbier de Meynard, *op. cit.*, *JA* 10, p. 112.
38 al-Ḥallāj' was called *ḥallāj al-asrār* in Khuzistan, *al-Mughīth* in India, *al-Muqīt, al-Mumayyiz* in Khurasan, *Abū ʿAbdallāh az-zāhid* in Fars, *al-Mustalim* in Baghdad and *al-Muhayyar* in Basra.
38 Sellheim, *op. cit.* p. 381

CHAPTER II

1 Nawawī, *op. cit.*, p. 368; M. J. Kister, *'Call yourselves by graceful names'*, Jerusalem 1970. A special custom of the Prophet Muḥammad is mentioned in the *ḥadīth* s.v. *taḥnīk*: the Prophet put some of his saliva into the baby's mouth and called him Ibrāhīm.
2 Nūrbakhsh, *op. cit.*, p. 5.
3 That this name was not rare, perhaps as a nickname, is proved by the *nasab Ibn Qunfudh*, the Algerian jurist and historian (d. 1406 or 1407).
4 J. J. Hess, *Beduinennamen aus Zentralarabien*, Heidelberg 1912.
5 CF. Abū'l-Fażl, *A'in-i Akbarī*, transl. Blochmann and Jarrett, Calcutta 1868, Vol. I p. 558; Marty, *op. cit.*, p. 409.
6 Ibn Qutayba, *op. cit.*, p. 57.
7 Snouck Hurgronje, *Mekka*, transl. J. H. Monaha, Leiden 1931, p. 110, where the formula used is 'I name thee as God has named thee'. It has to be remembered that according to Shiite tradition ʿAlī's name was also given by God.
8 Pierre Centlivres, 'Noms, surnoms et termes d'addresse dans le Nord Afghan' *Studia Iranica I* (1972), p. 93.
9 Nawawī, *op. cit.*, p. 365.
10 Badaoni, *Muntakhab at-tawārīkh*, transl. vol. II. W. H. Lowe, p. 259.
11 Abū'l-Fażl, *Akbarnāma*, transl. H. Beveridge, Calcutta 1897-1921, Vol. III, p. 582.
12 Nūrbakhsh, *op. cit.*, p. 17.
13 Indian Muslims apparently have a tendency to amass names and titles. A typical example is that of Khwāja Mīr Dard, the mystical author of Delhi (d. 1785). In his comprehensive Persian *ʿIlm ul-kitāb*, Delhi 1310H/1892-3, p. 62, he describes more than 100 names and surnames by which God had honoured him. His father, the mystic Nāṣir Muḥammad ʿAndalīb (d. 1758)

surrounded the heroes of his mystical 'novel' *Nāla-i 'Andalīb*, (Bhopal 1309 H/1891-2), with whole clusters of high sounding names – one wonders whether this custom reflects the search for identity: who is the real *Dard* under this plethora of names? Cf. A. Schimmel, *Pain and Grace*, Leiden 1976, pp. 83-84.

14 Cf. C. E. Bosworth, transl. *The Laṭā'if al-Ma'ārif of Tha'ālibī; The Book of Curious and Entertaining Information.* Edinburgh 1968, p. 86 for an *'ayn* son of *'ayn* son of *'ayn* who killed a *mīm* son of *mīm* son of mīm.

15 Dr Ülkü Toksöz, *Anne ve çocuk*, Ankara 1968; pp. 261-73: *Çocuğumuza ne isim koyalim?*

16 Marty, *op. cit.*, p. 409.

17 Ibrāhīm as-Samarrā'ī, *Al-a'lām al-'arabiyya*, Baghdad 1964, p. 12.

18 Cf. Bihniyā, *Nām*, p. 35, about the change the name *Rachel* underwent in Iran, where it was transcribed, according to French pronunciation, *Rākhel*, then *Rāshel*, then changed into *lāsher* which finally resulted in *lāshe*, 'carcase'.

19 In Iran the name *Anaverdī*, 'mother has given', is known. One may also think of the name of the famous geographer *Ibn Khurdadhbih*, 'Gift of the excellent sun'.

20 Albert Socin, 'Die arabischen Eigennamen in Algier', *ZDMG* 51 (1897) p. 500.

21 E. de Zambaur, *Manuel de généalogie et de chronologie. . .* , Hannover 1927, p. 179.

22 Kirzioğlu M. Fahrettin, 'Kuzeydoğu Anadolu'da kullanilan Türkçe erkek adlari' *TFAD* 5 (1949).p.76.

23 Temple, *op. cit.*, p. 30.

24 Z. Dalboy, 'Konya'da adlarla ilgili gelenek ve i nanmalar', *TFAD* 80 (1956), 2280-82.

25 Marty, *op. cit.*, 394.

26 Dalboy, *op. cit.*, p. 2280.

27 Temple, *op. cit.*, pp. 23-30.

28 Bihniyā, *Nām*, p. 36.

29 Cf. Jalāl ad-dīn Rūmī, *Mathnawī-yi ma'navī*, ed. Reynold A. Nicholson, 8 vols., London-Leiden 1925-40, Vol. II line 1743:
'Fāṭima is praise for women,
If you call a man [like that] it hurts like a spear.'

30 Marty, *op. cit.*, p. 376.

31 Centlivres, *op. cit.*, p. 91.

32 Marty, *op. cit.*, p. 375.

33 Kadriye Ilgaz, 'Istanbul'da doğum ve çocukla ilgili adetler ve inanmalar', *TFAD* 93 (1957), pp. 1481-82.

34 According to H. Storey, *Persian Literature, A biblio-biographical survey*, he died in 1359.

35 Marty, *op. cit.*, p. 394.

36 Centlivres, *op. cit.*, p. 91. Marty enumerates a number of names derived from *khamīs* or *khams*, 'five', and mentions the magic properties of the number five which is often used in curses. Should the Afghan aversion to the *khamīs* be related to these beliefs?

37 E. Littmann, 'Leben und Arbeit', *Oriens*, 29-30, p. 64.

38 E. Littmann, 'Beduinen- und Drusen namen aus dem Hauran-Gebiet'. *Abh. Gesellschaft der Wissenschaften*, Göttingen 1920; cf. Hess, *Beduinennamen*, for the problem, esp. p. 113.

39 Samarrā'ī, *op. cit.*, p. 20, quotes the case of a woman *Kīluwwah* in Upper

Egypt who was born when the kilogram was introduced as weight.

40 Temple, *op. cit.*, p. 80; Ja'far Sharif, *Islam in India*, transl, G. A. Herklots, ed. William Croke, Oxford 1921, esp. pp. 30-34.

41 Muẓaffar ad-dīn Aḥmad, *Islāmī Nām*, Delhi n.d., mentions, e.g., for a boy born on Tuesday in day-time: *'Abdul Qādir, 'Abdus Sattār, 'Alī, Yūsuf, Ya'qūb, Qādir, Sa'īd, Ḥasan, Ḥusayn, Abū Bakr, 'Umar, 'Uthmān.* A girl born on Friday night should be called *Najm as-nisā, Jamīla, 'Ābida, Āmina, Khadīja, Ḥalīma* or *Fāṭima.*

42 Hess, *op. cit.*, p. 50.

43 Marty, *op. cit.*, p. 404.

CHAPTER III

1 E. Littmann, 'Eigennamen der heutigen Ägypter', *Studii Orientalistici*, Rome 1956, p. 89.

2 Jalāl ad-dīn Rūmī, *Mathnawī*, Vol. V, 2227 ff. The name *Naṣūḥ* is also found in aṣ-Ṣafadī, and in modern India *Taubat an-naṣūḥ* is attested as a woman's name in Muẓaffar ad-din Aḥmad, *Islāmī Nām*.

3 In the Subcontinent such names can become feminine by adding *Begum, Khanim* or similar feminine addresses to them: *Bismillāh Begum*.

4 Bihniyā, *Nām*, p. 368.

5 Caetani, *op. cit.*, pp. 87-79 gives a list of 113 Divine names which are used in compounds.

6 Caetani, *op. cit.*, p.90.

7 Badāonī, *op. cit.*, Vol. I, p. 603.

8 I owe this information to Professor Carl Ernst, Pomona College.

9 Hess, *op. cit.*, p. 22 mentions *Deḥêm, Deḥmen* as terms of endearment for *'Abdur Raḥmān*.

10 This story about two government officials was told to me in Dhaka in November 1986.

11 *Encyclopedia of Islam*, 2nd ed., s.v. *laḳab.*

12 Nawawī, *op. cit.*, p. 368; A. Fischer, 'Vergöttlichung', p. 311 ff.

13 For the 'name-mysticism' see Annemarie Schimmel, *And Muhammad is His Messenger*, Chapel Hill 1985, Ch. 6.

14 Stowasser-Freyer, *op. cit.*, p. 26.

15 Nūrbakhsh, *Farhang*, p. 15.

16 The poem is quoted in Sājid Ṣiddīqī -Walī Āsī, *Armaghan-i na't*, a collection of poems in praise of the Prophet, Lucknow 1962, p. 49.

17 The problem is dealt with in detail in A. Fischer, 'Vergöttlichung'.

18 Such epithets are *rasūl-i akram*, 'the noblest Messenger', *ān haẓrat*, 'That Excellency', or in Turkey, *peygamber efendimiz*, 'our lord the Prophet', which corresponds to the North African custom of adding *Sī, Sīdī* 'lord' and similar polite forms of address to the Prophet's name.

19 K. M. Saif-ul-Islam, 'Cataloguing Bengali Muslim names', *UNESCO Information Science Journal* 2 (1980), p. 39.

20 A useful list of such compounds in Bihniyā, *Nām*, s.v. Muḥammad.

21 In India all the four qualities – *wasīm, qasīm* etc. – can be used for names with *ad-dīn*: Qasīm ad-dīn, Wasīm ad-dīn, etc.

22 Bihniyā, *Nām*, p. 36, even found a man called by the blessing formula *Allahummā ṣalli 'alā Muḥammad wa āl Muḥammad.*

23 The reason for the use of compounds with *hudà* for women's names may be that Arabic nouns ending in *alif maqṣūra* are generally feminine; but more probably it reflects ignorance of the name's implications or is done

merely for euphony.
24 Muḥammad Iqbāl, *Rumūz-i bēkhudī*, Lahore 1917, p. 190.
25 There is a problem as to whether names like *'Abdul maḥbūb* or *'Abdul ḥabīb* refer to the Prophet, God's beloved friend, or to God as the ultimate Beloved. In the case of *'Abdul-Khātam*, 'servant of the Seal', the reference to Muḥammad as the 'Seal of the Prophets' seems likely.
26 Aṣ-Ṣafadī, *Das Biographische Lexikon*, Vol. 13, p. 103.
27 Nūrbakhsh, *Farhang*.
28 Iqbāl, *Bāng-i Darā*, Lahore 1924, pp. 78, 242.
29 Iqbāl, *Payām-i Mashriq*, Lahore 1923, p. 150 in the poem *Al-mulk lillāh*, 'Kingdom belongs to God', and *Bāl-i Jibrīl*, Lahore 1936, p. 142, *Ṭāriq kī du'ā*, 'Tariq's prayer'.
30 Nūrbakhsh, *Farhang*, p. 230.
31 *ibid.*, p. 221 on 'the names of *Ḥażrat 'Alī*'. In India, the compound *Maulā 'Alī* is common.
32 Nawawī, *op. cit.*, p. 374; Nöldeke, 'Zur tendenziösen Gestaltung', p. 30.
33 In contemporary Iran I found a person called *Yad Allāh 'Alī-dōst Khaybarī* with a threefold allusion to the first imām.
34 Names like *Panāh 'Alī, Dildār 'Alī* belong here; they are, according to Garcin, *op. cit.*, p. 434, mainly used by *sayyids*, but have apparently proliferated into other groups.
35 Badāonī, *op. cit.*, Vol. III, p. 604.
36 Lists of compounds in Bihniyā, *Nām*, p. 109.
37 Combinations like *Shabbīr Ḥusayn, Shabbar* or *Shibr Ḥasan* occur in contemporary Pakistan.
38 Brockelmann, *GAL, S* II, p. 1021.
39 Marty, *op. cit.*, p. 402.
40 *ibid.*, p. 402.

CHAPTER IV

1 Caetani, *op. cit.*, deals with women's names on pp. 99-100. Special studies are Emil Gratzl, *Die altarabischen Frauennamen*, Leipzig 1906; Heinrich Ringel, *Die Frauennamen in der arabisch-islamischen Liebesdichtung*, Leipzig 1938; Laślo Rasonyi, 'Türklükte kadin adlari', *Türk Dili Araştírmalarí Yíllígí Belleten*, 1963.
2 Hess, *op. cit.*, p. 28; cf. Marty, *op. cit.*, p. 376: at the birth of the third or fourth girl one calls her *Dalanda*, which may be a magic formula.
3 Among Hindus in Bengal one find names like *ghairnâ* (despised) or *khainto* (cessation), Temple, *op. cit.*, p. 29.
4 Feminine names with superlative and following genitive, like *Akram as-sādāt, Ashraf al-, Aqdas al-*, are given in great quantity by Bihniyā, *Nām*. The genitive is then usually omitted in speaking, hence Princess *Ashraf* and similar names.
5 Nūrbakhsh, *Farhang*, p. 52.
6 Caetani, *op. cit.*, p. 100; vgl. Fritz Meier, *Die schöne Mahsati*, Wiesbaden 1963, p. 47.
7 Littmann, 'Eigennamen im heutigen Ägypten', p. 92.
8 Başgöz, *Name and Society*, p. 1, mentions a girl called *Aysel* (moon-like), because she was born on the day the first man landed on the moon. Similar explanations may lie behind many perfectly 'normal' names.
9 Caetani, *op. cit.*, p. 99.
10 Bihniyā, *Nām*, attests the *Ilāha-yi sādāt* for modern Iran. In Muẓaffar ad-dīn

Aḥmad, *Islāmī Nām*, even *Asmā' al-ḥusnà*, 'The Most beautiful Names' is given as a woman's name.

11 Meier, *op. cit.*, p. 47.

12 Littmann, 'Eigennamen im heutigen Ägypten', p. 85.

13 Muẓaffar ad-dīn Aḥmad mentions forms like *Aḥmad an-nisā, Fārūq an-nisā* and *Yūsuf an-nisā* as perfectly acceptable for Muslim women.

14 See Hess, *op. cit.*, p. 28.

15 Al-Qalqashandī, *Ṣubḥ al-a'shà*, gives a long list of titles to be used for high ranking ladies. This list, along with the variegated use of titles and forms of address in the various Islamic countries, would be worthy of investigation; the work of Ḥasan al-Bāshā, *Al-alqāb al-islāmiyya*, Cairo 1957, deals with the Arabic ones, but the use in Turkish and Indian areas, confusing to the student of medieval history, awaits a researcher; some useful remarks about women's names in different strata of Indian society (*Sayyid, Mughal, Pathan, Shaykh*) can be found in Temple, *op. cit.*, 15-17.

CHAPTER V

1 Caskel, *op. cit.*, Vol. 1, p. 49. For the subject in general see the works mentioned in Ch. I.

2 For antiphrastic forms see Theodor Nöldeke, *Neue Beiträge zur semitischen Sprachwissenschaft: Wörter mit Gegensinn,* Strassburg 1910, p. 88. A. Fischer, 'Arabisch *baṣīr* per antiphrasin "blind"', *ZDMG* 61 (1907) 425-34, 751-4; Fadwa Malti-Douglas, 'Pour une rhétorique onomastique: les noms des aveugles chez aṣ-Ṣafadī', *Cahiers d'onomastique Arabe* I (1979), 7-19.

3 Ibn Taghrībirdī, *An-Nujūm az-zāhira*, Vol. VII, p. 261.

4 Daulatshāh, *Tadhkirat ash-shu'arā*, ed. Muḥd. 'Abbāsī, Tehran n.d., p. 476.

5 Barbier de Meynard, *art. cit., JA* 10, p. 190.

6 aṣ-Ṣafadī, *op. cit.* Vol. 22, p. 298, No. 220.

7 Goitein, *op. cit.*, p. 521. Cf. Marty's story (*op. cit.*, p. 401) that some French officers in Algiers enjoyed putting together military units from soldiers whose *ism* or *laqab* was connected with foodstuffs.

8 *Encyclopedia of Islam*, 2nd ed., Vol. III, p. 950.

9 *ibd.* s.v. Ḥayṣa Bayṣa.

10 Pianel, 'Sobriquets marocains', *Hespéris* 37 (1950) p. 327.

11 Barbier de Meynard, *art. cit., JA* 10, p. 233.

12 Nawawī, *op. cit.*, p. 373.

13 Tha'ālibī/Bosworth, *op. cit.*, p. 67; the whole of Chapter 3 contains most amusing examples; cf. also the *laqab Ibn dahn al-ḥaṣā*, 'son of the "Fat of the pebbles"', the teacher of the historian *Ibn al-'Adīm.*

14 Brockelmann, *GAL S* II, p. 644.

15 R. Blachère, *Un poète arabe du IVe siècle de l'Hégire, Abou'ṭ-Ṭayyib al-Motanabbi,* Paris 1935, p. 150.

16 Maltzan, *op. cit.*, p. 620.

17 Pianel, *op. cit.*, p. 397.

18 Barbier de Meynard, *art. cit., JA* 10, p. 84.

19 Caetani, *op. cit.*, p. 152.

20 One important *laqab* in the Eastern Islamic world is *ṣāḥib qirān*, 'the lord of the auspicious conjunction',, which was first applied to Timur and then to later rulers, especially Shāh Jahān. The development of regnal titles, which has been treated by B. Lewis, M. van Berchem and many more cannot be discussed in this study.

21 Barbier de Meynard, *art. cit., JA* 10, p. 226; the article contains many

interesting *alqāb* of poets, among which the *'A'id al-kalb* appears on p. 80. A related example is that of the famous historian Kamāl ad-dīn *ibn al-'Adīm*, 'son of the deprived person', which he explained as referring to an ancestor who, despite his wealth, constantly complained in his poetry about bad times and deprivation, *''udm*, and became known as *al-'adīm*, Aṣ-Ṣafadī, *op. cit.*, vol. 22, p. 423.

22 See Sellheim, '"Familiennamen"'; a good example is Marty, *op. cit.*, p. 399; the development of *stā (= ustād*, 'master') from a professional title to part of the family name: *Stā Murād, Stāmerād.*

23 The frequent Indian name *Majumdar, Mazumdar* is developed out of the Persian *majmū'adār*, 'the one who keeps the records'.

24 When a servant in the University of Ankara, who was always called *Emin Efendi*, had passed an exam in reading and writing, his wife proudly referred to him as *Emin Bey*.

25 Marty, *op. cit.*, p. 397: cf. also the studies of Fahrettin and Ali Rĭza Önder about names in north-eastern Anatolia.

26 A long list of titles combined with *-bāshī* and *-aghāsī* is given in the interesting study on Qajar Iran by Muḥammad Hāshim Aṣaf Rustam al-ḥukamā, *Rustam at-tawārīkh*, ed Muḥammad Mushīrī, Tehran 1348 sh/1969.

27 Ibn Taghrībirdī, *An-nujūm az-zāhira*, Vol. VII, p. 312.

28 One could add here the titles which the Aga Khan confers upon leading members of the Ismaili community, a custom attested from the 19th century. They begin with the *muk'hī*, the chief official of the local community, and comprise *Dīwān, Rāi, Vazīr, Ālījāh*, and *Ḥuzūrmuk'hī*, each of which can be given to a woman as well; in this case, *ṣāḥiba* is added: *Rāi ṣaḥiba.*

29 Abu'l-Fażl, *A'in-i Akbarī*, p. 612.

30 Barbier de Meynard, *op. cit., JA* 10, p. 94.

31 *Encyclopedia of Islam*, new ed., Vol. V, 618-31, s.v. *lakab;* see also *ibid.*, Vol. III, p. 294, *'Izz ad-dīn*, a good survey in Ḥasan al-Bāshā, *op. cit.*, p. 104ff., further Caetani, *op. cit.*, p. 221; Garcin de Tassy, *op. cit.*, p. 424ff.

32 The Seljukid vizier Niẓām ul-mulk (d. 1092) complained in his *Siyāsatnāme*, chapter 41, that even the lowliest person gets angry when he is addressed with less than ten *alqāb;* see H. Darke, *The Book of Government, or Rules for Kings*, London 1960, pp. 152-62.

33 Tha'ālibī, *Yatīmat ad-dahr*, Cairo 1375-77H/1956-58, quoted in *Enclopedia of Islam*, Vol. V, p. 230; cf. also A. Mez, *Die Renaissance des Islam*, Heidelberg 1922, pp. 78-79.

34 J. Kramers, 'Les noms musulmans composés avec Dîn', *Acta Orientalia* V (1926), esp. 63-67.

35 Quoted by Ibn Khaldūn, *Muqaddima*, Vol. I, p. 281.

36 al-Bīrūnī, *al-Āthār al-baqīya*, p. 132/ transl. p. 1129, quoted in *Encyclopedia of Islam*, Vol. V, p. 625, s.v. *lakab*. Ibn Taghrībirdī also stated in his *an-Nujūm az-zāhira*, Vol. II, p. 145, that the Persians cannot mention anything without adding *ad-dīn* to it.

37 I. Goldziher, ''Alī ibn Majmūn and sein Sittenspiegel des östlichen Islam', *ZDMG* 28 (1874), esp. p. 306f.

38 This connection was first pointed out by Simon Digby, ''Abd al-Quddūs Gangohi: The Personality and Attitudes of a Medieval Indian Sufi', in *Medieval India*, Vol. 3, Aligarh (1975) 43.

39 Albert Dietrich, 'Zu den mit *ad-dīn* zusammengesetzten islamischen Personennamen', *ZDMG* 110 (1960), 45-54.

40 In his poem 'The memoirs of Bishr al-Ḥāfī the Ṣūfī'.

41 Fadwa Malti-Douglas, 'The interrelationship of onomastic elements *isms-dīn*-names, and *kunyas*, in the ninth century AH', *Cahiers d'onomastique Arabe*, 1981, 27-55.
42 Ayalon, 'The enuchs in the Mamluk sultanate', *Memorial Gaston Wiet*, Jerusalem 1977, p. 278.
43 Caetani, *op. cit.*, pp. 199-203; Barbier de Meynard, *art. cit.*, *JA* 10, offers many examples for combinations with *az-zamān*.
44 Qalqashandī, *Ṣubḥ al- a'shā*, Vol. 6, p. 61.
45 Barbier de Meynard, *art. cit.*, *JA* 10, p. 81.
46 One finds *Shaykh Allāh, Nauf Allāh, Żayf Allah, Ḥayāt Allāh* and, in Bihniya, *Nām*, even *Wafāt Allāh*. This, like numerous other compounds, really makes no sense.
47 Garcin de Tassy, *op. cit.*, p. 451.
48 Maltzan, *op. cit.*, p. 617f.
49 Caetani, *op. cit.*, p. 165ff. South Arabian clan names were often formed with *dhū*, like *Dhū Yāzan, Dhū Nuwās*.
50 I. Goldziher, 'Über Dualtitel', *WZKM* 13 (1899), pp. 321-29.

CHAPTER VI

1. Goldziher, 'Gesetzliche Bestimmungen', *ZDMG* 51, 264-66.
2. Nawawī, *op. cit.*, p. 372.
3. Special studies are E. García Gomez, 'Hipocorísticos árabes y patronímicos hispanicos', *Arabica* I (1953); E. Littmann, 'Arabische Hypokoristika', *Studii Orientalia Ioanni Pedersen. . . dicata*, København 1953; T. Khemiri, 'Die Formen fa'ūl und fa''ūl', *Der Islam* 26 (1942), and also the remarks in Socin, *op. cit.*, and Marty, *op. cit.*, esp. p. 310.
4. Ibn Taghrībirdī, *Ḥawādith ad-duhūr*, ed. W. Popper, 4 vols, Berkeley 1930-42, Vol. I, p. 201.
5. Afia Dil, 'A comparative study of the names and nicknames' in *Studies in Bengal*, ed. W. M. Gunderson, East Lansing (1976), 51-71.
6. He explains in his autobiography *'Ilm al-kitāb* (p. 84) why he was called by *khwāja* and *mīr*, as his parents belonged to two different *sayyid* families, that of Bahā ad-din Naqshband (*khwāja*) and that of 'Abdul Qādir Gīlānī (*mīr*).
7. Nūrbakhsh, *Farhang*, s.v. *Akram as-sādāt* and related forms.
8. Tha'ālibī/Bosworth, *op. cit.*, p. 20.
9. Nawawī, *op. cit.*, p. 368.
10. Marty, *op. cit.*, p. 375.
11. D. Ayalon, *op. cit.*, pp. 278-80.
12. Ibn Taghrībirdī, *An-nujūm az-zāhira*, ed. W. Popper, 6 vols, Berkeley 1909-36, Vol. V, p. 367.
13. Zetterstéen, *Beiträge zur Geschichte der Mamlukensultane*, Leiden 1919, p. 101; J. Sauvaget, 'Noms et surnoms des Mamlouks', *JA* 238 (1950). In my unpublished study of 1945 on Mamluk society, I made an extensive study of Mamluk nomenclature.
14. The reading *qaniṣauh* was suggested in my study mentioned above; it was later 'discovered' by A. Zajaczkowski who, of course, was unaware of my material.
15. The comprehensive work is that of al-Qalqashandī, *Ṣubḥ al-a'shà*, which was analysed first by W. Björkman, *Beiträge zur Geschichte der Staatskanzlei*, Hamburg 1928, and more recently used by Ḥ. al-Bāshā, *op. cit.* An excellent introduction to the titles on the Mamluks is M. van Ber-

chem, *Materiaux pour un Corpus Inscriptionem Arabicarum, Vol. I, Le Caire,* Paris 1903.

16 Nawawī, *op. cit.*, pp. 371-72 has a whole chapter on the change of names.

17 Goldziher, 'Gesetzliche Bestimmungen', p. 257; Stowasser-Freyer, *op. cit.*, p. 26.

18 Marty, *op. cit.*, p. 373.

19 G. Pianel, *op. cit.*,.

20 Brockelmann, *GAL S I,* p. 391.

21 Snouck Hurgronje, *Mecca,* Vol. I, pp. 236-37.

22 Ibn Taghrībirdī, *An-nujūm az-zāhira fī mulūk Miṣr wa'l-Qāhira,* ed. W. Popper, Vol. VII, p. 422.

23 'Abdul Bāqī Nihāwandī, *Ma'āthir-i Raḥīmī,* ed. M. Hidayat Khan, Calcutta 1924-27, Vol. II, p. 485.

24 Marty, *op. cit.*, pp. 430-31.

25 Ahmad Sirhindi, *Selected Letters,* ed. Fazlur Rahman, Karachi 1968, Letter Nr. 23 to Khānkhānān 'Abdur Raḥīm.

26 Marty, *op. cit.*, pp. 430-31.

27 A good survey is Muḥsin Jamāl ad-dīn, *Al-asmā' wa't-tawāqī' al-musta'āra fi'l-adab al-'arabī* (about pseudonyms), Mecca 1969.

28 S. Wild, *op. cit.*, p. 160; *cf* also Marty, *op. cit.*, p. 384-85 on local varieties of names in Tunisia.

29 Marty, *op. cit.*, pp. 393-95; Socin, *op. cit.*, p. 497; survey in Caetani, *op. cit.*, p. 97.

30 Nūrbakhsh, *Farhang,* p. 18.

31 In Muẓaffar ad-dīn Aḥmad, *Islāmī Nām,* several *fatwās* against the mixing of Islamic and Indian names are given, and especially islamicised Tamil and Telugu names are criticised.

32 Snouck Hurgronje, *Mecca,* Vol. 2, p. 235.

33 Marty, *op. cit.*, p. 385.

34 A survey is found in Samarrā'ī, *op. cit.*, pp. 28-29.

35 Turkish names have been studied both by Turkish and Western scholars; among American publications one may mention Robert F. Spencer, 'The social context of Modern Turkish Names' *South-western Jnl. of Anthropology,* 17, no. 3, 205-18; Richard W. Bulliet, 'First names and political change in Modern Turkey', *IJMES,* 9, 489-95; Ilhan Başgöz, 'The Meaning and Dimension of Change of Personal Names in Turkey', Turcica, 15, 201-18; and the same, *Name and Society.* A good number of Turkish studies are found in the *Türk Folklor Araştĭrmalarĭ Dergisi,* such as Ali Riza Önder, *'Hĭnis'ta Insan Isimleri',* 63 (1955); the same, *'Göle'da Insan Isimleri',* 73 (1955), M. Cavit Aker, *'Muğla'da adlarla ilgili gelenek ve ĭnanmalar',* 132 (1960); Hasan Basrĭ, *'Carşamba ve Terme'de adlarla ilgili gelenekler ve ĭnanmalar',* 135 (1960) and the studies of Zeki Dalboy, Kadriya Ilgaz, Kĭrzĭoğlu M. Fahrettin and Sait Tazebayoğlu, to which we referred earlier. A classical source is Atalay, *Türk Büyükleri,* (1920), which offers names and short biographics of persons noted in Turkish history.

36 One can also interpret it as 'wooden sword' – but is this a good family name?

Bibliography

Abbreviations Used

GAL *Brockelmann, Geschichte der arabischen Literatur,* 3 vols. and supplements
GAS Fuat Sezgin, *Geschichte des arabischen Schrifttums,* 9 vols.
IJMES *International Journal of Middle Eastern Studies*
JA *Journal Asiatique*
JAOS *Journal of the American Oriental Society*
JRAS *Journal of the Royal Asiastic Society*
MFOBS *Mélanges de la Faculté Orientale de l'Université St. Joseph de Beyrouth*
MSOS *Mitteilungen des Seminars für Orientalische Sprachen, Berlin*
MW *The Muslim World*
REI *Revue des Études Islamiques*
SB *Sitzungsberichte*
WZKM *Wiener Zeitschrift für die Kunde des Morgenlandes*
ZDMG *Zeitschrift der Deutschen Morgenländischen Gesellschaft*
ZfKM *Zeitschrift für die Kunde des Morgenlandes*

General Bibliography

The usual auxiliary works, such as Brockelmann's *GAL*, Fuat Sezgin's *GAS* and Storey's *Persian Literature* are not listed, nor are the numerous Arabic and Persian historical and poetical works which yielded some of the names.

Y. ʿAbdallāh, *Die Personennamen in al-Ḥamdānī's al-Iklīl, und ihre Parallelen in den alt-südarabischen Inschriften,* Diss. Tübingen, 1975.

Abū'l-Fażil, *Ain-i Akbarī,* vols. I-III, ed. H. Blochmann, Calcutta 1867-77, 1939; transl. H. Blochmann and H. S. Jarret, 1868-94
Akbarnāma, transl. H. Beveridge, 3 vols., Calcutta 1897-1921

Enricho de Agostini, 'Indagini onomastiche ed etniche in Libia', *Ann. Istituto Universitario Orientale di Napoli,* NS 3, 1949, 168-78

Muẓaffar ad-dīn Aḥmad, *Mukhtār Islāmī nām* (Urdu list of names recommended by Muslim authorities), New Delhi n.d. (*ca.* 1985)

M. Cavit Akar, 'Muğla'da adlarla ilgili gelenek ve ĭnanmalar', *TFAD* 132 (1960), 2179

Richard T. Antoun, 'On the Significance of Names in an Arab Village', *Ethnology* 7 (1968), 158-70

Muḥammad Hāshim Āṣaf Rustam al-ḥukamā, *Rustam at-tawārīkh,* ed. Muḥd. Mushīrī, Tehran 1348sh/1969 (originally written in 1209h/1794)

Besim Atalay, *Türk büyükleri veya Türk adlarĭ* (compilation of names borne by historical personalities), Istanbul 1339h/1920-1

David Ayalon, 'The eunuchs in the Mamluk Sultanate', *Memorial Gaston Wiet,* ed. Maryam Rosen-Ayalon, Jerusalem 1977, 267-94

Dr. M. Azadeh, *Les Jolis Prénoms Iraniens – Beautiful Iranian First Names – Die Schönen Persischen Namen – I Bei (sic) Nomi Persiani* (a collection of mainly Persian names which are 'easy to pronounce for all nations'), Tehran 1971

ʿAbd ul-Qādir ibn Mulūk Shāh Badāūnī, *Muntakhab at-tawārīkh,* ed. W. Nassau Lees, Maulwī Kabīruddīn and Maulwī Aḥmad Alī, Calcutta 1864-69; transl.

Vol. I. G. Ranking, II, W. H. Lowe, III T. W. Haig, Calcutta 1884-1925
Nihat Sami Banarlĭ, 'Türklerde Soyadĭ', *TFAD*, 7 (1950), 37
M. S. Baqa, *Popular Muslim Names and their Meanings* (a publication for Muslims in Great Britain, which explains the meaning of numerous names – not always correctly – but does not mention the historical significance). Barking, Essex, n.d. (*ca.* 1982)
A. C. Barbier de Meynard, 'Surnoms et sobriquets dans la littérature arabe', *JA* lo[e] série 9 (1907) 173-244, 365-428; 10 (1908) 55-118, 193-273 (still very valuable)
Hasan Basrĭ, 'Çarsamba ve Terme'de adlarla ilgili gelenekler ve ĭnanmalar', *TFAD* 135 (1960), 2238-9
Ilhan Başgöz, 'The Name and Society. A Case Study of Personal Names in Turkey'. *Kungl. Vitterhets Historie och Antikvitets Akademiens Konferensar* 12, n.d. (after 1983), 1-14
'The Meaning and Dimensions of Change of Personal Names in Turkey', *Turcica* XV (1983), 201-18
Ḥasan al-Bāshā, *al-alqāb al-islāmiyya fī't-tārīkh wa'l-wathā'iq wa'l-āthār* (a useful survey of surnames and titles, mainly from medieval sources, especially al-Qalqashandī's *Ṣubḥ al-a'shā*, Cairo 1957
Max van Berchem, *Matériaux pour un Corpus Inscriptionum Arabicarum*, Cairo, 1903, Vol. I
'Abdul Karīm Bihniyā, *Nām: Pazhūhashī da nāmhā-yi Irāniān-i mu'āṣir*, Ahwaz 1360 sh/1981 (a study of 25,752 men, with 1,675 different names, and 12,714 women with 1,283 different names).
Walther Björkman, *Beiträge zur Geschichte der Staatskanzlei im islamischen Ägypten*, Hamburg 1928 (esp. pp. 110-13)
C. E. Bosworth, transl., *The Laṭā'if al-ma'ārif of Tha'ālibī, The Book of Curious and Entertaining Information*, Edinburgh 1968
Richard W. Bulliet, 'First Names and Political Change in Modern Turkey', *Intern. J. of Middle Eastern Studies* 9 (1978), 489-95
Leone Caetani e Giuseppe Gabrieli, *Onomasticon Arabicum, ossia repertoria alfabetica dei nomi di persona*, vol. I, Rome 1915
Werner Caskel, *Ǧamharat an-nasab, das genealogische Werk des Hišām ibn Muḥammad al-Kalbī*, 2 vols, Leiden 1966
Pierre Centlivres, 'Noms, Surnoms, et Termes d'adresse dans le Nord Afghan'. *Studia Iranica* I (1972), 89-101
Francesco Codera, 'Apodos o sobrenombres de Moros españoles', *Mélanges Hartwig Dérenbourg*, Paris 1909, 323-34
T. E. Colebrooke, 'On the Proper Names of the Muhammadans', *JRAS* 9 (1879), 171-237 (relies mainly on Hammer-Purgstall's study of names in the Viennese Academy of Sciences of 1852, Kosegarten – whose name is always spelled wrongly – and Garcin de Tassy)
Zeki Dalboy, 'Konya'da adlarla ilgili gelenek ve ĭnanmalar', *TFAD* 80 (1956), 2280-2
Khwāja Mīr Dard, *'Ilm ul-kitāb*, Delhi 1310/1892-3
Albert Dietrich, 'Zu den mit *ad-dīn* zusammengesetzten islamischen Personennamen', *ZDMG* 110 (1961), 45-54
'Das *kunya*-Wörterbuch des Muslim ibn al-Ḥaǧǧāǧ', *Festschrift W. Caskel*, Leiden 1968, 43-52
Afia Dil, ' A comparative study of the personal names and nicknames of the Bengali-speaking Hindus and Muslims', *Studies in Bengal*, ed. W. M. Gunderson, East Lansing 1976, 51-71

R. Y. Edier and M. J. L. Young, 'A list of the appellations of the Prophet Muḥammad', *MW* 66 (1976), 259-62
Encyclopedia of Islam, 2nd. ed., Leiden 1954-60, s.v. *ism, kunya*, and *laḳab*
Kĭrzĭoğlu M. Fahrettin, 'Kuzeydoğu Anadolu'da kullanĭlan Türkçe erkek adlarĭ', *TFAD* 5 (1949), 76
Fĭndĭkoğlu Z. Fahri, 'Türk Folklorĭnda Isim Meselesi', *TFAD 39* (1952) 609-10
I. Fazal, A. Khurshid, S. Qaysar, 'Cataloguing of Oriental Names', *Quart. J. Pakistani Library Association*, Vol. 2, Nr. 1 (July 1961), 5-16
August Fischer, *Muḥammad und Aḥmad, die Namen des arabischen Propheten*, Sächsische Akademie der Wissenschaften, Leipzig 1932
'Vergöttlichung und Tabuisierung der Namen Muḥammads bei den Muslimen', *Beiträge zur Arabistik, Semitistik und Islamwissenschaft*, ed. R. Hartmann und H. Scheel, Leipzig 1943, 307-39
'Arabisch *baṣīr*, 'scharfsichtig' per antiphrasin 'blind' *ZDMG* 61 (1907), pp. 425-34, 751-4
Wolfdietrich Fischer, *Grammatik des klassischen Arabisch*, Porta Linguarum Orientalium, Wiesbaden, 2nd ed. 1987
Karl Foy, 'Zu "der Personenname *Aydemir* und das Wort *demir*"', MSOS (1900), 216-17
Marc Gaborieau, 'L'onomastique moderne chez les Musulmans du Sous-continent Indien', *Cahier d'Onomastique Arabe*, 1985.
E. García Gomez, 'Hipocorísticos Árabes y patronímicos hispánicos', *Arabica* (1954), 129-35
Joseph H. Garcin de Tassy, 'Mémoire sur les noms propres et sur les titres musulmans', *JA* série 5, Nr. 3, (1854), 422-510 (interesting especially for Indo-Muslim customs)
S. D. Goitein, 'Nicknames as Family Names', *JOAS* 90 (1970), 517-24
Ignaz Goldziher, ''Alī ibn Majmūn al-Maġribī und sein Sittenspiegel des östlichen Islam', *ZDMG* 28 (1874), 293-330
'Gesetzliche Bestimmungen über *kunja*-Namen im Islam', *ZDMG* 51 (1897), 256-66
'Der Gebrauch der *Kunja* als Ehrenbezeichnung', in *Muhammedanische Studien*, I 267 (= *Muslim Studies* I 242)
'Über Dualtitel', *WZKM* 13 (1899), 321-29
'Verheimlichung des Namens', *Der Islam* 17 (1928), 1-3
E. Gratzl, *Die altarabischen Frauennamen*, Diss. München 1907
Joseph von Hammer-Purgstall, 'Über die Namen der Araber', *Denkschrift* K. Akad. d. Wissenschaften, phil.-hist. Cl., III (1852), pp. 1-72
David M. Hart, 'Tribal and place names among the Arab Berbers of Northwestern Morocco', *Hespéris Tamuda* (1966), 457-512
M. Hartmann, 'Zahlen- und Monatsnamen als Personennamen', *Z. Verein f. Volkskunde* II (1892), 320-22
Hayat Mecmuasĭ, Turkish weekly magazine, which was published during the 1950's; in every issue a list of Turkish names with useful explanations
M. Ḥashīshī, 'Ramaḍān as a personal name', *Folklore* 36 (1925), 280
J. J. Hess, *Beduinennamen aus Zentralarabien*. S. B. Heidelberger Akademie der Wissenschaften, Phil. Hist. K1. 1912
G. H. R. Horsley, 'Name Change as an indication of Religious Conversion in Antiquity', *Numen XXXIV*, 1, (1987), pp. 1-17
M. Th. Houtsma, *Ein türkisch-arabisches Glossar, Nach der Leidener Handschrift hersg. und erläutert*, Leiden 1895
Muḥammad Bāqir al-Ḥusaynī,' *al-kunà wa'l-alqāb 'alá nuqūd al-mamālīk*

al-baḥriyya wa'l-burjiyya fī Miṣr wa'sh-Shām', al-Maurid IV 1, 2 (1975), 55-104 (Titles on Mamluk coins)

Ibn al-Athīr, *Kitāb al-muraṣṣaʿ fī'l-abā'i wa'l-ummuhāti wa'l-banīn wa'l-banāt wa'l-adhwā'i wa'l-dhawāt,*, ed. Ibrāhīm as-Samarrā'ī, Baghdad 1971

Al-lubāb fī tahdhīb al-ansāb, ed. Muṣṭafā ʿAbdul Wāḥid Cairo 1971

Ibn Iyās, *Badā'iʿ az-zuhūr fī waqā'iʿ ad-duhūr*, ed. Paul Kahle and M. Mustafa, vols. 3-5, Istanbul 1932-1935, Indices by A. Schimmel, Istanbul 1945 (new edition and indices in press)

Ibn Qutayba, *Adab al-kātib*, ed. Muḥammad Muḥyī'ddīn ʿAbdul Ḥamīd, Cairo 1963, 4th ed. (esp. *bāb uṣul asmā' an-nās)*

Ibn Taghrībirdī, An-nujūm az-zāhira fī ta'rīh Miṣr wa'l-Qāhira, ed. W. Popper, Berkeley 1909–36; vols. V-VII

Ḥawādith ad-duhūr, ed. W. Popper, 4 vols., Berkeley 1930-42

Kadriye Ilgaz, 'Istanbul'da doğum ve çocukla ilgili adetler ve inanmalar', *TFAD* 93 (1957), 1481-82

Jaʿfar Sharif, *Islam in India*, transl. by G. A. Herklots, ed. William Crooke, Oxford 1921

Muḥsin Jamāluddīn, *Al-asmā' wa't-tawāqīʿ al-mustaʿāra fī'l-adab al-ʿarabī*, Mecca 1969 (about pseudonyms)

Otto Jastrow, 'Die Familiennamen der Türkischen Republik. Bildungs weise und Bedeutung', *Erlanger Familiennamen-Colloquium*, Neustadt an der Aisch 1985, lol-llo (relies mainly on Turkish families settled in Germany)

Umar Riḍā Kahhāla, *Aʿlām an-nisā' fī ʿālamayi'l-ʿarab wa'l-Islām*, 5 vols, Damascus 2nd ed. 1377-79h/1958-59

S. Kekulé, *Über Titel, Ämter, Rangstufen und Anreden in der offizieller türkischen Sprache*, Halle 1892

Schauki Khalifa, 'Die Personennamen in Ägypten. Bildung and Bedeutung', *Armant, Deutsch-arabische Kulturzeitschrift*, 13 (1974), 21-25

T. Khemiri, 'Die Formen faʿūl *und faʿʿūl*. Ein Beitrag zur arabischen Namenkunde', *Der Islam* 26 (1942), 159-60

M. J. Kister, 'Call yourselves by graceful names. . .'*Lecture in Memory of Professor Martin M. Plessner*, Jerusalem 1970

J. F. D. Kosegarten, 'Über den Vornamen oder die Kunje der Araber', *ZfKM* 1 (1837), 297-312

J. H. Kramers, 'Les noms musulmans composés avec *Din*', *Acta Orientalia* V (1926), 53-67

Giorgio Levi della Vida, 'Matronymics among Arab poets', *JAOS* 62 (1942), 156-171

S. Lieberson, 'What's in a name? – Some socio-linguistic possibilities', *International J. for the Sociology of Language*, 45 (1985), pp. 77-87

Enno Littmann, 'Beduinen-und Drusen-Namen aus dem Hauran-Gebiet', *Nachr. Akademie der Wissenschaften Göttingen, Phil.hist. Kl.* 1921, 1-20

'Eigennamen der heutigen Ägypter', *Studi Orientalistici in onore di Giorgio Levi Della Vida*, Vol. II, Rome 1956, 81-93

'Arabische Hypokoristika', *Studia Orientalia Ioanni Pedersen dicata*, Copenhagen 1953, 193-199

'Leben and Arbeit', hersg. H. H. Biesterfeld, *Oriens* 29-30 (1986), 1-101

Fedwa Malti-Douglas, 'Pour une rhétorique onomastique: les noms des aveugles chez aṣ-Ṣafadī, *Cahiers d'onomastique Arabe* I (1979), 7-19

'The Interrelationship of onomastic elements: *isms* - *dīn*-names, and *kunyas* in the ninth century AH', *Cahiers d'onomastique Arabe* II, 1981, 27-55

Heinrich Freiherr von Maltzan, 'Über Beinamen bei den Arabern des Magrib',

ZDMG 24 (1870) 617-23
D. S. Margoliouth, 'Names (Arabic)', *Hastings Encyclopaedia of Religion and Ethics* 9, 136-40
P. Marty, 'Folklore Tunisien: L'onomastique des Noms propres de personne', *REI* 10 (1936), 363-434
Fritz Meier, *Die schöne Mahsati*, Wiesbaden 1963
Die fawā'iḥ al-ǧamāl wa fawātiḥ al-ǧalāl des Naǧm ad-dīn al-Kubrā, Wiesbaden 1957
Adam Mez, *Die Renaissance des Islams*, Heidelberg 1922
Mīr Ma'ṣūm Nāmī, *Tārīkh-i Ma'ṣūmī*, ed. U. M. Daudpota, Poona 1938
Mefkure Molova, 'Noms orientaux en Europe Orientale: noms *en-lyq*',*Prilozi za Oriyentalnu Filologiyu* 27 (1977), 1-59
Ṣalāḥ ad-Dīn al-Munajjid, 'Une importante *Risāla* de Suyūṭī; *risāla fī ma'rifati'l ḥilā wa'l-kunā wa'l-asmā' wa'l-alqāb*', *MFOB* 48 (1973) 352ff.
Muḥammad Muqbil Beg, *ad-durr ath-thamīn* (about names in Egypt and Turkey), Cairo 1294H/1877
Naimur Rehman, 'The *kunya*-names in Arabic', *Allahabad University Studies* 5 (1929), 341-442; 6 (1930) 751-883 (mainly about *kunyas* for animals and plants)
Yaḥyā ibn Sharaf an-Nawawī, *Kitāb al-adhkār*, Cairo 1312 H/1894-5
Niẓām al-Mulk, *Siyāsetnāma*, transl. Hubert Darke: *The Book of Government or Rules for Kings*, London 1960
Theodor Nöldeke, 'Bemerkungen über hebräische und arabische Eigennamen'. *ZDMG* 15 (1861), 806-12
——, *Neue Beiträge zur semitischen Sprachwissenschaft: Wörter mit Gegensinn*, Strasburg 1910
Ḥusayn Nūrbakhsh, *Farhang-i nām: Nāmhā-yi irānī-i islāmī*, Tehran, 1360sh/1981
Ali Riza Önder, 'Göle'de Insan Isimleri', *TFAD* 73 (1955), 1180-82
——, 'Hĭnĭs'ta Insan isimleri', *TFAD* 63 (1955), 1099
G. Pianel, 'Sobriquets marocaines', *Hespéris* 37 (1950), 443-59
Anna Parzmies, 'Noms de personnes en Algérie', *Folia Orientalia* 20 (1979) 107-18
A. F. Pott, 'Eigennamen in ihrem Unterschiede von Appellativen, und mit der Namengebung verbundener Glaube und Sitte', *ZDMG* 24 (1870), 110-24
al-Qalqashandī, *Ṣubḥ al-a'shà bi-ṣinā'at al-inshā'*, 14 vols., Cairo 1913-20, especially Vol. 5
'Abdur Ra'ūf Raḥmānī, *'Nam̃ aur unkī tathīren'*, *Akhbār-i muḥammadī*, Delhi 15 May 1923
Laslo Rasonyi, 'Turklükte Kadĭn adlarĭ', *Türk Dili Araştĭrmalarĭ Yĭllĭğĭ Belleten* 1963, 62-87
Abū Ḥātim Aḥmad ibn Ḥamdān ar-Rāzī, *Az-zīnat on Arab and Islamic nomenclature*, ed. Ḥusayn al-Ḥamdāni, Cairo 1957-8
Heinrich Ringel, *Die Frauennamen in der arabisch-islamischen Liebesdichtung*, Diss. Erlangen, Leipzig 1938
Ṣalāḥaddīn Ḥalīl ibn Aibek aṣ Ṣafadī, *Das Biographische Lexikon, Bibliotheca Islamica* 6, Beirut 1931-87 (22 vols).
K. M. Saif-ul-Islam, 'Cataloguing Bengali Muslim names: problems and possible solutions', *UNESCO Information Science Journal* 2 (1980), 35-41
as-Sam'ānī, *Kitāb al-ansāb*, vol. 1-13, Hyderabad 1382-1402 / 1962-1982
Ibāhīm as-Samarrā'ī, *Al-a'lām al-'arabiyya. Dirāsa lughawiyya ijuti-mā'iyya*, Baghdad 1964 (a useful all-round survey of Islamic names)

Jean Sauvaget, 'Noms et nurnoms des Mamlouks', *JA* 238 (1950), 31-58
Annemarie Schimmel, *And Muhammad is His Messenger*, Chapel Hill 1985
——, *Mamluken, Emire und der Sultan – Studien zur Organisation der Mamluken*, Habilitationsschrift, Marburg 1945-46, unpublished
——, 'Some remarks about Muslim Names in Indo-Pakistan', in *Gilgul*, ed. S. Shakeb, D. Shulman, G. G. Stroumsa, Leiden 1987, pp. 217-22
Rudolf Sellheim, *Materialien zur arabischen Literaturgeschichte, 1*, Wiesbaden 1976
——, '"Familiennamen" im Islamischen Mittelalter', *Oriental and Classical Studies in Honour of Frithjof Rundgren*, Stockholm 1986
MacGuckin de Slane et Ch. Gabeau, *Vocabulaire destiné à fixer la transscription en français des noms de personnes et de lieux usités chez les indigènes de l'Algérie, I. Noms des personnes*, Paris 1868
Snouck Hurgronje, *Mekka*, transl. by J. H. Manaha, Leiden 1931, vol. 2.
Albert Socin, 'Die arabischen Eigennamen in Algier', *ZDMG* 51 (1897) 471-500
Robert F. Spencer, 'The Social Context of Modern Turkish Names', *Southwestern J. of Anthropology*, 17 nr. 3 (1961), 205-18
Anton Spitaler, 'Beiträge zur Kenntnis der *kunya*-Namensgebung', in *Festschrift W. Caskel*, Leiden 1968, 336-50
Barbara Stowasser-Freyer, 'Formen des geselligen Umgangs und Eigentümlichkeiten des Sprachgebrauchs in der frühislamischen städtischen Gesellschaft Arabiens', *Der Islam* 42 (1965), 26-40
Jacqueline Sublet, ed., *Cahiers d'Onomastique Arabe*, Paris 1979, 1981, 1982-84
Sait Tazebayoğlu, 'Kilis'te ad verme adetleri', *Halk Bilgisi Haberleri* 9 (1940), 57
Sir Richard Temple, *A Dissertation on the Proper Names of Panjabis*, Bombay 1883
ath-Thaʿālibī, *Laṭā'if al-maʿārif*, see Bosworth, C.E.
Ülkü Toksöz, *Anne ve çocuk*, Ankara 1968 (pp. 261-273: Çocuğumuza ne isim koyalĭm: how should we name our child?)
A. H. Waleh, 'Names and Titles in Afghan Families', *Afghanistan News*, Nr. 80, vol. 7 (1964), 4-6
Gaston Wiet, *Les Biographies de Manhal Ṣāfī* (of Ibn Taghrībirdī), Cairo 1932
Stefan Wild, 'Arabische Eigennamen', *Grundriß der arabischen Philologie*, ed. W. Fischer, Wiesbaden 1982, 154-61
Yavrunuz için, 'for your baby', list of Turkish names recommended by the Turkish government
Eduard de Zambaur, *Manuel de généalogie et de chronologie pour l'histoire de l'Islam*, Hanover 1927

Index of personal names

The reader should once more remember that the transcription and transliteration is not always the same (change of al- and ul-, different pronounciations of certain consonants in different areas: d = z = sometimes j; j in Egyptian pronounciation g, in Turkish transliteration c, etc).

'Ābidīn, 35
abla, apal, 'elder sister', 68
Abraham, s. Ibrāhīm
Abraṣ, al-, 12
Abṭaḥī 32
abū 'father', 4
Abū 'Abdallāh ('Umar ibn al-Khaṭṭāb), 6
Abū 'Alī al-Ḥusayn, 6
Abū 'Aṣīda (Bou asside; d. 1295), 7, I 25
Abū 'aql, 12
Abū 'aṣr, 7
Abū Bakr (aṣ-ṣiddīq, d. 634), X, 5, 11, 12, 33, 39, 64, II 41
Abu 'd-dawāniq, 7
Abū Dharr (al-Ghifārī, d. 652), 7
Abū Fāṭima, I 13
Abū Firās (d. 967), 75
Abū Furāt, 75
Abū Ḥanīfa an-Nu'mān (d. 767), 11
Abū Ḥafṣ, 6 (+ 'Umar)
Abū Hurayra (d. 678), 7, 69
Abu'l-ḥuṣayn (= the fox), 8
Abū 'Īsā, 5, 7, I 12
Abū Isḥāq, 6, 7 (+ Ibrāhīm)
Abū Ismā'īl, 6 (+ Ibrāhīm)
Abū 'iẓām, 7
Abū Ja'far (Hārūn ar-Rashīd), 6
Abū Jahl (d. 624), 5, 7
Abū Khashab, 7
Abū Lahab (d. 624), 5
Abū Laylā ('Umar ibn al-Khaṭṭāb), 5, 6
Abū'l-'Atāhiya (d. 825–6), 7
Abū'l-'Aynā', 51
Abū'l-baqā, 6, 20 (+ Ya'īsh, + Khālid)
Abū'l-barakāt, 6
Abū'l-faraj (al-Iṣfahānī, d. 967), 5, 7
Abū'l-futūḥ, 6
Abū'l-Ḥasan, 6, 7 (+ 'Alī)
Abū'l-Ḥusayn, 6 (+ 'Alī)
Abū'l-'izz, 6 (+ 'Abdul 'Azīz)
Abū'l-Jafnā', 6
Abū'l-khayr, 5
Abū'l-Maḥāsin, 6, 16, 61 (+ Yūsuf)
Abū'l-misk, 13 (+ Kāfūr)
Abū'l-Qāsim, 7
Abū'l-yumn, 7
Abū Madyan (d. 1126), X
Abū Muḥammad (Hārūn ar-Rashīd), 6
Abū'n-najm, 6 (+ Badr)
Abū Naṣr, 7; Abū'n-naṣr, 7
Abū raqība, 7
Abū ra's, 7
Abū Rīḥāna (Rayḥāna), 5
Abū rījl, 7
Abū rujayla, 66
Abū Ruqayya, 5
Abū Shāma (Shihāb ad-dīn, d. 1266), 66
Abū'ṣ-ṣabr, 6 (+ Ayyūb)
Abū Sa'īd Khar (12th c.), 52
Abū'sh-sharr, 5
Abū Sinna, 66
Abū Ṭālib (d. 619), 14, 36
Abū Turāb (= 'Alī), 7, 34
Abū Yaḥyà Shu'ayb, 6
Abū Ya'rab, 75
Abū Yazīd (Bāyazīd), 7
Açkurt, 83
Adalet (f), 47
Adam (Abū'l-bashar, 'Father of mankind'), IX, 29, 64
'Adarūh, 76
Ādhar P, 22
'Adhbān, 76
'Adhrā (f), 43
'Adīd al-alf, 54
Adīgüzel, 14
'Ādil, 70
'Adīm, Ibn al- (d. 1262), V 13, 22

Adīna, 22; Adīna Muḥammad, 30
'Adnān, 17, 75
Adonīs, 'Alī Aḥmad, 75
'*Aḍud*, 'pillar', 61; — ad-daula, 60
Adsiz, (Abū Muẓaffar, d. 1156), 20
Afḍal ash-shu'arā, 59
Afet (f), 46
'Affāf (f), 70
'Afīf ad-dīn at-Tilimsānī (d. 1291), 54
Afram, al-, 72
Afrāsiyāb, 78
Afsāna, (f) 47
Afshār, 13, 67
Aftāb, 3; — ad-dīn, 62, 76; — az-zamān, 64
Aga Khan, 16, 23, V 28
Aghāz ad-dīn, 62
Ağzïbüyük, 10, 82; Ağzïbüyükler, 10
Agrō, 67
Aḥad, 31
Aḥlām (f), 43
Aḥmad, 31, 61, 69, 77; — un-nisā, IV 13
Aḥmad al-Badawī (d. 1278), 37
Aḥmad Sirhindī (d. 1624), 74
Aḥmad-bakhsh, 32
Aḥmadlā, 76
Aḥmad-yār, 32
Aḥsānā, 76
Aḥwal, al-, 50
'Aid, al-, 22
'A'id al-kalb, 55, V 21
'Ā'isha (Umm 'Abdallāh, Bint Abī Bakr d. 678), 6, 20, 33, 36, 43, 45, 69
Aishāṅ, 76
Aït Aḥmad, 9
'Ajamī, al-, 12
'Ajūz al-Yaman, 53
ak(aq) 'white', 3, 50, 81; – bulut, 81; — doğan, 3; — kaş, 82; — kuzu, 81; — üzüm, 81; — yürek, 80; — zanbak, 81
Akālī, 23
akbar, 50
Akbar, Jalāl ad-dīn (Mughal emperor, d. 1605), 15, 37, 48, 59, 73, 74
Akbar Allāhābādī, Ḥusayn Riżwī (d. 1921), 62
Akbarī (f), 48
akhi (ahi), 58
Akhtar (f), 3, 45; — as-sādāt, 40
akhū, gen. *akhī*, 'brother of', 8
ākhūnd, 57
Akram: as-sādāt (f), 40, IV 4
Akwa', al-, 50
Āl 'family', 9; — Hāshim, 9; — Sa'ūd, 9; — Ṣabāḥ, 9; Āl-i Aḥmad, 9, 36; Āl-i nabīy, 36; Āl-i Ḥaydar, 36
Alam son of Dard (18th C.), 75
A-lam nashraḥ, 25
'*ālam* 'world', in compounds, 64
'Ālam-ārā (f), 46
Alaverdiev, 77
'Alawī, Alvi, 11, 40
Alay, 19
Alev, 17
Alexander the Great (Iskandar), 66
Alfī, al-, 72
'Ālī, 74
'Alī (ibn Abī Ṭālib, first imām of the Shia, d. 661), 6, 7, 8, 11, 14, 23, 33-6, 39, 40, 43, 52, 64, 65, 69, 74, 76, II 7, 41
'Alī -dōst, III 33; — Gul, 34; — Ḥaydar, 34; — Madad, 36; — Mardān, 34; — Nūr, 34; — Qul, Qulī, 35; — Shīr, 34; — Yār, 34
'Alī Aṣghar (d. 680), 35
'Alī Hamadhānī, Sayyid (d. 1385), 37
'Alī an-Naqī (d. 868), 33, 40

'Alī ar-Riḍà (Rażà) (d. 818), 35, 40
Alids 6
'Alījiq (Alicik), 69
'*ālījāh*, V 28
'Alimukhamadov, 77
'Alīyūsh, 69
'Alkā, 76
Allāh, compounds with, 64, 65
Allāh-bakhsh, 18
Allāh bas (f), 42
Allāh — beren, 18; — dād, 18; — diyā ,18; — qulī, 28; — rakhiyā, 18; — varāyō, 18; — virdi (berdi), 18, 77
Allāhumma ṣalli 'alā Muḥammad, III 22
Allāh-yār, 66
'*allāma*, 58
Allan Faqīr, 39, 58
'Allūn, 75
'Allūsh, 69
Almās (f), 46; — ad-dīn, 62
alp, T 'hero', compounds with, 78, 81
Alptegin (d. 962), 81
'Alqama (d. *c.* 598), 3
Alṭāf Ḥusayn, 35
Altĭ parmak, 51
Altin (Altun) T 'gold': — baş, 82; — bughā, 2; — diş, 82; — ören, 82
Al'umar, 9
A'mā, al-, 50
Amadou (= Aḥmad), 77
Amān Allah (Amānullah), 65
A'mash, al-, 50
Amat, 'slave girl', 28, 44; — al-Ḥafīẓ, 44; — al-Jāmi', 44, 47; — al-Karīm, 28, 44
'Ambar, 63
'Ambarīn-qalam, 58 ('Abdur Raḥīm, d. after 1653)
Āmina, the Prophet's mother, (d. c. 577), 32, 43, II 41
Amīn (Emin), 12, 32, 82; Amīna (Emine) (f), 32
Amīnā, 63
Amīr, 34, 40; — 'Alī, 34; — A(r)slān, 34; — qūlī, 35; — un-nisā (f), 48
amīr ash-shu'arā, 58
'Āmir, 16
Amrīkā (f), 24
'Amrun, 1, 16
'Anādil (f), 43
anāli, 72
Anaverdi, II 19
Anayasa (f), 17
'Andalīb, Nāṣir Muḥammad (d. 1758), 74, II 13
angā, 'wet nurse', 58
Anjuman-ārā (f), 46
Ankaralĭ, 12
Anṣārī, 39
Anwār al-Karīm, 66
Anwar (Anvar), 48; Anwarī (f), 48
Anvarī (Anwarī) (d. *c.* 1190), 74
Anwari-Husayni, Shams, XI
apa, 68
aq, s. *ak*
-*aqāsī*, *aghasī*, PT 'master of', as suffix, 57
Aqdas as-sādāt (f), 40, IV 4
'Aqil, Muḥammad, 74
'Aqīq: — ad-dīn, 62
'Aqlān, 76
Aqqoyunlu (Akkoyunlu), 50
Aqqūsh (Akkuş), 61
Aqṭauh (= Akdağ), 72
-*ārā* P 'adorning' (f), as suffix, 46
'Arabī, 32
A'raj, al-, 2, 50
'Araq al-maut (9th C.), 54
Araz, 81
arbāb, 56
Ardalān, 67

Armaghān (f), 3
Armān, 20
Arseven, Celâl, 82
ʿarsh-ashiyānī, 59
Arshad: — az-zamān, 64
Arslān, Aslān, 2, 34, 78, 81; — doğmuş, 19; — korkut, 82
Ārzū (f), 20
Asad, 2, 14, 33, 61; — ad-dīn, 61
Asad Allāh (Asadullāh), 33, 64, 74
— ar-Raḥmān, 65
Asʿad, 2
Aṣamm, al-, 50 (Ḥātim al-, d. 852)
Asani, Ali S., XII
Aṣghar, 50
Aʿshà, al-, 50; — (banī Asad, 7th c.), 55
Ashʿath, al- (Abū Jaʿfar ibn al-, d. 970), 50
ʿĀshiq: — ʿAlī, 34; — Allāh, 65; — Muḥammad, 32
ʿĀshiqpāshāzāda (fl. *c.* 1500), 10
Ashraf (f), 42; — as-sādāt (f), 40, IV 4; — jahān (f), 46
ashrafī, al-, 71; — Qaytbay, 71; — Tūmān Bay, 71
ʿĀshūr, ʿĀshūrā, 22
Asiya (f), 43
Asker, 19
Aslān Khātūn (f) (11th c.), 46
Aslī (f), 17
Asmā' (f), 43
Asmā' al-ḥusnā (f), IV 10
Asmar, 2
Asrā, 25
Asrār al-īmān, 64
ʿAṣūḥ, 76
Āsumān (m, f), 3, 45
Aswad, al-, 51; Asyūd, 14
ʿAṭā' Allāh, 2, 8, 64
ʿAṭā Ḥusayn, 18; — Muḥammad, 18
atābeg, 72
Atadan, 80
Atatürk, Mustafa Kemal (d. 1938), 80
Ateş (Atish), 17
Athar son of ʿAndalīb (18th c.), 74
ʿAtīq Allāh (Abū Bakr), 64
ʿAṭīyat Allāh, 18
ʿAuḍ, 21
Aʿūdhū, 25
Auḥad az-zamān, 64
aulād 'sons', 9; — ʿAlī, 36; — Ḥaydar, 36
Aurangzēb (Mughal emperor, r. 1658–1707), 48, 74
Aus, 2
Auṣāf ʿAlī, 34
al-ausaṭ, 50
Avencerrage (= Ibn as-Sarrāj), 8
Avenzoar (= Ibn Zuhr), 8
Averroes (= Ibn Rushd), 8
Avicenna (= Ibn Sīnā), 8
Aʿwar, al-, IX, 50
Awān, 13, 67
Ay, T 'moon', 3, 45, 81; compounds with, 45, 81;
Aydemir 78; — doğmuş, doğdu, 4, 19; — ışık (f), 45; — kut, 19; — melek (f), 45; — peri (f), 45; — ten (f), 45
Āyat Allah (Ayatullah), 58, 65
Ayet (f), 41
ʿAyn Allāh (= ʿAlī), 34, 64
ʿAyn al-Ḥayāt (f), 47; — az-zamān, 64
Ayşegül (f), 44
Aysel (f), 45, IV 8
ʿAyshūsha, 69
ʿAyyād, ʿAyyāda, 22; ʿAyyādī, 22
Ayyūb (Job), 6, 29, 43
Āzād Bilgrāmī, Sayyid Mīr Ghulām ʿAlī (d. 1784), 25
Azhar, al-, 51
Azhār (f), 43

'Azīz aṣ-Ṣamad, 66
Azraq, al-, 51
'Azza (f), 55, 77
'Azzūj, 'Azzūz, 69

Bābak (d. 838): Bābak Husayn, 4
Babbaghā', Abū' l-Faraj (d. 1007), 52
Bābur, 2, 19, 58, 59 (Emperor, d. 1530)
Badāūnī, 'Abdul Qādir (d. after 1605), 15
Baddū, 70
Bādharr (= Abū Dharr), 7
Badhl (f): — ar-Raḥmān, 65
Badī' al-'ālam, 64; — az-zamān (Hamadhānī, d. 1008), 64
Badr, 3, 6, 45, 61; — ad-dīn, 16, 60, 63, 70, 74; — ad-dujà, 16; — al-'ālam, 64; — al-budūr (f), 45; — as-sādāt (f), 40
Badr, al-, 63
Ba'du bi'd-dīn, 25
Baghdādī Begum (f), 39; al-Baghdādiyya (f), 10
Bāghdagül (f), 44
Bahā, 63
Bahā' ad-dīn, 60, 63
Bahā' ad-dīn Naqshband (d. 1389), VI 6
Bahār (f), Bahār Bānū (f), 45
Bahārlū, 67
Bahjat (Behcet), 3
Baḥr, 3
Baḥr al-'ulūm, 59
Baḥriyya (f), 43
Baḥrūn, 75
-bakhsh (-bux) P 'gift', compounds with, 18, 49
Bakhshīsh 'Alī, 34
Bakkā', al-, 58
Bakraj, 3
Bakrī, 11
Balāsim, 20
Balban (Sultan of Delhi, d. 1266), 2
Baloch, 67
banāt, 'daughters', 8
banda P 'servant, slave', 28; — 'Alī ,35
Bandanawāz (Gēsūdarāz, d. 1422), 38
Bangash, 67
Bannā' (Ibn al —, d. 1321), 56
-bānū P 'lady', 48
banū, gen. *banī*, 'sons of', 8
Banū Asad, 55
Banū'azīzī, 9; Bānū Isrā'īl, 9; — Mughwiya, 72; — ar-Rushda, 72; — Muḥawwala, 72; — Umayya, 9
Banīfāṭima, 9, 36
Bāqī Billāh, Khwāja (d. 1603), 38
Bāqir (Muḥammad al-, d. 733), 35
Baqr'īdī 22
Baraka, 70
Barakāt, 19
Barbier de Meynard, XI
Barlas, 13, 67
Barq, 3
Barqūq, al-Malik aẓ-Ẓāhir (d. 1389), 71
Başbeş (f), 3
bāshā, Paşa, 19, 57
al-Bāshā, Ibrāhīm, XI
-bāshī (başĭ), T 'head of. . .' as suffix, 57
Bashīr, 31; — Aḥmad, 31
Baṣīr, 51
Bāsiṭ, 16
Baṣl (Baṣal), 52
Bassām ad-dīn, 62
Batt (Butt), 67
Batūl, 36, 44
Bāyazīd (Abū Yazīd), 7
Bayezit I Yĭldĭrĭm (d. 1403), 79
Bayram, 22

Bayt Allāh, 64
Bayṭār (Ibn al —, d. 1248), 56
Bāz, 31; al-bāz al-ashhab, 52
Bāzargān, 56
Bechai, 21
Bēdil, 'Abdul Qādir (d. 1721), 74
Bē-dīn, 62
Behdin, 60
Begum 'lady', 48, 49, III 3
Bēkas, 74
bel = abu'l, 7; = Ibnu'l-, I 21
Bēkhud, 74
Bekir, 33
Bel-Aid, 22
Bel Ḥasan, 7
Belli (= Ben 'Alī), 73
Bēnaẓīr (f), 46
Benli, 51
Bentürk, 79
Berat, 22
Beşbine (f), 21
-bey, T 'Mr.', 57
Beyatlĭ, Yahya Kemal (d. 1958), 82
Bī, Bībī, Bīwī, 'lady', 49
Bībī al-munajjima (f) (13th C.), 9
Bihniyā, A. K, XI
bih, P 'good', 19; — nām, 19; — rūz, 19; Bihtar, 2; Bihzād, 19
Bilāl (ibn Rabāḥ, d. 641), 33
Billā, I 2
Bilqīs (f), 43
Binbashi, 19
Binbirçeşit, 82
Binnāz (f), 46; Binnūr (f), 45
bint, 'daughter', 8
Bint 'Abdallāh, 8
Bint Baṭṭūta, 'Iṣmat Khānim, 75
-berdi, T 'he gave' (s.a. *verdi, virdi*)
Birsen, T (f), 46
Bīrūnī, al- (d. 1048), 61
Bismillāh, 25; — Begum, III 3
Bismillī, Ibn al-, 11
Biṭṭīkh, 3, 52
Bĭyĭklĭ, 51; Muṣṭafà, 51; — oğlu, 80
Boğazgōren, 83
Borjel (Abū rijl), 7
börü, T 'wolf', 2, 21, 51, 81
Bostancĭbaşĭ, 57
Boubker (= Abū Bakr)
Boumédienne, X
Bou ras, 7
Bourghiba (= Abu raqība), 7
Boynubazĭq 51; Boynueğri, 51
Bozkurt, 2, 81
Bseisa (= Busaysa), 2
Bū'aqlī, al-, 12
Bū Dīnār, 7; Bū Khobza, 52; Bū zbīb, 52
būbū, 'lady', 49; Būbū Rāstī, 49
-bughā T 'steer', 2
Bukhārī, Muḥammad ibn Ismā'īl al- (d. 870), 11
Bukhārī *sayyids*, 40
Bulāqī, 21
Bulbul, I 9
Bulbula (f), 46
Bülent (Buland), 17
Bunna (f), 47
Burghūth, 2
Burhān ad-dīn, 61
Burlay, 77
Burunsuz, 51
Busḥāq, 7
Būṣīrī, Muḥammad al- (d. 1298), 29
Būstān (f), 44
Būyid, Buwayhid dynasty, 60, 78
büyük T 'great', 50

Caetani, Leone IX, XI 16, 27
Casem, s. Qāsim, 000
Caskel, Werner, 7
Cavid, Cavide (f), (s. Jāvīd)
Cebesoy, 10
Ceyhan (m, f), 46

Celâl, Celâle (= Jalāl), 38
Çelebi (s.a. Shalabī), 19, 57
Cemile Sultan (f), 49
Çingiz (Chingiz), 79
Chādli (= Shādhilī), 37
Chagatay, Chughtay, 66, 81 (Çağatay)
Chaghrï Beg (d. 1059), 46
Chashma-i ʿAlī, 51
Chatoui (= shitāwī), 23
Chaudhry, 56
Chébinou, 20
chelab, chelb s. *kalb*, 76
Chelebi s. Çelebi
Chilrā, 21
Chīma, 67
Chirāgh, 62; — ad-dīn, 62
Chirāgh, Sirāj ad-dīn, 74
Chishtī, Muʿīn ad-dīn (d. 1236); Chishtī un-nisā Begum, 39
Çiğdem T (f), 44
Çorbaçi (Chorbachi), 56

dād, P 'gift', 18; Dād-ʿAlī, 18, 34; Dād-i Khudā, 77
dāgh (ṭāgh, ṭauh) T 'mountain', 3
Daḥmān, 76
Dahn al-ḥaṣā, Ibn (13th c.), V 13
Dalanda (f), IV 2
dāmād PT 'son-in-law', 58; — Ibrāhīm Pasha (d. 1730), 58
Danānīr (f), 43
Dānyāl son of Akbar (d. 1604), 59
Daqīq al-ʿīd, Ibn (d. 1302), 53
Dār 67
ad-dār (f), 49: — *al-ʿaliyya*, 49
Dārā, 55, 78; Dārā-Shikōh, prince (d. 1659), 55
Darāhim (f), 43
Dard, Khwāja Mīr (d. 1785), 40, 74, II 13
Ḍarīr, 50
Darwīsh, 39
Daryā, 3
Daryā Khān, 24
Dastgīr Bī (f), 39
Dasūqī, Ibrāhīm ad- (d. 1277), 37
Dā'ūd, 5, 16, 29
Dā'ūd-pōtā, 10
daula, daulat, X, 46; in compounds — ad-daula, 60; — ad-daula wa'd-dīn, 60
Daulatshād (f), 46
dawādār, 72
dawla , s. *daula*
Ḍayf Allāh, 65
Dean = ad-dīn, 73
Dede Korkut, 79
Dēgōl, 54
Dehlīwālī (f), 12
Deḥmen, Dehem, III 9
deli (teli) T 'crazy', 51; — Hüseyin Paşa (d. 1659), 51
demir (timur) T 'iron', 78, 81; Demirağ, 83; Demirbughā, 2; Demirci, 82; Demirdağ, 82
Demet T (f), 44
Deniz (f, m), 3
Denktaş, 82
devlet s. *daula*
Dewan Muhammad, 30
Dhabīḥ Allāh (Ismāʿil), 29
Dhahab ad-dīn, 62
Dhahānat ʿAlī, 26
Dhākir (Zakir), 16
D'haṇī-dinā, 18
Dharr, 2;
dhāt - (f), s. *dhū*, 66
Dhi'b, 2
Dhībān, 76
dhū- 'owner of', 66; Dhū'l-fiqār, 34
Dhū'l-fiqār ʿAlī Shāh Bukhārī, Sayyid, 40
Dhū'n-Nūn (Yūnus), 66
Dhū'n-nūrayn (ʿUthmān), 33

Dhū Nuwās, V 49
Dhu'l-qarnayn, 66; Dhu'r-riyāsatayn (al-Faḍl ibn Sahl, d. 818), 66; Dhū'r-Rumma (d. *c.* 735), 66; Dhū'sh-shamālayn, 66; Dhū'l-wizāratayn, 66; Dhū'l-yamīnayn, 66; Dhū Yāzan, V 49
Diamond, 23
Dībāja, 54
Dietrich, Albert, 61
Dijla (Dicle) (f), 24
Dīk al-jinn (d. 849), 52
dil P 'heart', T 'tongue', compounds with, 81
Dildār 'Alī, III 34
Dilek T (f), 20
Dilshād (f), 46
Dimishq Khan, 23; Dimishqī, 10
ad-dīn, compounds with, 1, 16, 22, 48, 60f., 73, V 36
Dīndōst, 62; Dīnyār, 62
Ḍirghām, 2, 61; — ad-dīn, 61
dīwān, V 28
dīwāna, P 'crazy', 51
Dīw-dād (d. 879–80), 18
Djilani, Djelloli (= Jīlānī), 38
Dodikhudaev, 77
Doğan (Toğan), 3, 81
Doğru, 83
Döne (f), 42
dōst P 'friend': Dōst-Muḥammad, 32
dovleh, dowle s. *daula*
Dozy, Reinhart, 75
-dukht P 'daughter', 10, 48
Dukhtarbas P (f), 42
Dümdüz, Kaya, 83
Dunyā (f), 24, 47
Duqmāq, Ibn (Ṣārim ad-dīn, d. after 1394), 78
Duran, 20
Durmuş, 20
Durr: Durr-i shahwār (f), 46; Durrdāna (f), 46
Durrānī, 67
Dursun, 4, 20
Durustawayh ('Abdallāh ibn, d. 956), 78
Dzumaev, 77

efendi, 57
Eid Muḥammad, 22
Ekmekçi, 56
Elāhe (s. Ilāha) (f), 47
Enamulkabir Brahma, I 9
Engin, 3
er T 'man', 81
Erdal, 81
Erdmann, Erdmuthe, 20
Ernst, Carl, III 8
Erol, 81
Ertem, 3, 47
Ertuğrul, 81 (d. *c.* 1285)
Esengeldiev, 77
Eti, 81
Etmekji (= Ekmekçi), 72
Evliyā Chelebī (d. *c.* 1697), 38
Evrenosoğullari, 80
eyt, īt, Berber 'sons', 9
Eyyübe (f) (*s.a.* Ayyūb), 43
Ezel (f) (Azal), 47

Faḍl (Fażl), 3, 19, 68; — Allāh, 19; — al-Ghanī, 19; — al-Mannān, 19; — ar-Razzāq, 19; — Muḥammad, 59; — ar-rasūl, 32; — Rabbī, 19
Fahd, 2, 51
Fahlawān, 57
Fakhr: ad-dīn, 11, 80; — (i) Imām, 36
Fakhrī, 11
Falāfil, 52
Falak (f), 45

Falakī (d. after 1157), 59
Fallāḥ, 23
Fanā fī'Llāh, 38
Faqīr, 39, 58; — ad-dīn, 62
Fār adh-dhahab, 52
Farazdaq (d. *c.* 732), 52
Farfūr, 52
Farghānī, al- (d. after 861), 11
Farhād, 43
Farḥūn, 75
Farīd, 73; — ad-dīn, 60; — al-Islām, 63; — un-nisā, 39
Farīd ad-dīn Ganj-i Shakar (d. 1265), 39, 53
Farīda (f), 46, 73
Farīdūn, 60, 78
Farkhunda Akhtar, 55
Farrukh Siyar (Mughal emperor, d. 1719), 55; Farrukhzād, 19
Farṭūṭ, 52
Fārūq, al- ('Umar), 12, 33, 39; — an-nisā, IV 13
Fārūqi (Faruki, Farooghi a.o.), 39
Farwān, 76
Faṣīḥ ar-Raḥmān, 65
Fatali s. Fatḥ 'Alī
Fatḥ 'Alī, X, 34; — Allāh, 63, 64
Fatḥ Mubārak, 73
Fāṭima (d. 633) 11, 15, 34, 35, 36, 40, 44, 69, 70, 76; I 2, II 29, 41; diminutives of – 69
Fāṭimī, 11, 40
Fāṭimids (969–1171), 40, 60
Fattāḥī, Sībak (d. 1448), 75
Faṭṭūm 69; Faṭṭōsh, Faṭṭūsh, 69
Fayḍ, Fayż, 19; — al-Ḥasan, 35; — ar-Raḥmān, 19
Fayṭama, 69
Fażā'il 'Alī, 34
Fazilet (Faḍīla) (f), 47
Fażl (faḍl): — Aḥmad, 19; — 'Alī, 19; — (i) imām, 36
Fażlī, 19
Fērōz (Fīrūz) (i) dīn, 62
Fetḥī; Fethiye (f), 63
Fidā' Ḥusayn, 35
Fifi (f), 70
Fĭndĭkoğlu (Fĭndĭklĭoğlu), 80
Finjān (f), 47
Firāq (d. 18th c.), 75
Firdaus (Firdevs) (f), 47; — al-islām, 63; — *firdaus-makān*, 59
Firdausī (d. 1020), 17, 74, 78
Firishta (m, f), 29, 47
Fīrūz, 71
Fitna (f), 46
Fōtī, Fōtō, 70
Frähn, Christian (d. 1851), 4
Fuḍayl (ibn 'Iyāḍ, d. 803), 68
Fulān ad-dīn, 62
Furay'a, 2
Fuṭayṭih, 69
Fuṭayṭūm, 69

Gabriel (Jibrā'īl), 5, 35
Gadjali, 77
Gafurov, Gapurov, 77
Galen (Jālīnūs) (d. 201), 59
Gamāl 'Abdun Nāṣir (d. 1970), 17
Ganj-i shakar (Farīd ad-dīn), 53
Garcin de Tassy, X, XI, 4, 66
Gassem, Gaçem = Qāsim, X
Gauhar (m, f), 46; Gauharshād (f), 46
Gāw, 52
Gāyumarth, 4
Genç, 83; Gençer, 81
Gēsūdarāz Bandanawāz, Sayyid (d. 1422), 38
Geyik T (f), 46
Gezdiren, 82
Ghāda (f), 46
Ghaḍanfar, Ghażanfar, 2, 34
Ghaffār, 28
Ghairnā (f), IV 3

Ghālib, Mirzā Asad Allāh (d. 1869), 74
Ghamdān, 76
Gharaj, Gharja, 76
Gharbāl lekdūb, 54
Gharībnawāz (Mu'īn ad-dīn Chishtī), 38
gharīq, al- (d. 1439), 59
ghasīl al-malā'ika (Ḥanẓala) (d. 625), 13, 59
Ghasim = Qāsim, X
Ghauth-i a'ẓam ('Abdul Qādir Jīlānī, d. 1166), 38; Ghauth-bakhsh, X, 18, 38; Ghauth-dinā, 38
Ghauthiyya, 39
Ghazāla (f), 46
Ghazālī, Abū Ḥāmid al- (d. 1111), 77
Ghāzān Khan (d. 1304), 71
Ghāzī, 58, 61; — ad-dīn, 61
Ghaznavids, 16
Ghaznī Khān, 23
Ghiyāth ad-dīn (Tughluq, d. 1325), 60
Ghousbux = Ghauthbakhsh
Ghūl, 53
Ghulām 'servant of -': — (i) Āl-i Muḥammad, 36; — 'Arabī, 32; — Bhīk, 21; — Dastgīr, 38; — Farīd ad-dīn, 39; — Gharībnawāz, 39; — Ghauth, 38; — Ghauth Begum, 38; — Hamadhānī, 37; — Ḥasanayn, 12; — Jīlānī, 38; — Kāẓim, 36; — (i) Kibriyā, 66; — Ma'ṣūm, 36; — Muḥyī ad-dīn un-nisā, 39; — Mu'īn ad-dīn, 39; — Murshid, 39; — Murtażà, 16; — Muṣṭafà, 16; — Qādir, 38; — nabīy, 28; — rasūl, 28, 32; — Rižā, 36; — Sarwar, 32; — Sayyidayn, 35, 12; — Shabbīr, 35; — Yāsīn, 32
Ghurrat az-zamān, 64
Gidi T (f), 42
Giese, Alma, XII
gil, T 'son', 10, 80
Gītī P (f), 47
Gleimid, 14
Goitein, S. 53
Gōk, kōk T, 81
Göktürk, 81
Gölge, Nuri, 83
Gonanrā, 21
Gorg, 21
Gözdüren, 82
Gözübüyükzade, 51
Gredhi, 14
Gubaidullin, Gubaidullina, 77
Güçbilmez, 82; Güçüyener, 82
Gul (Gül, Gol) P 'rose', 44: Gul'adhār, 44; Gulbadan (Mughal princess, d. 1603), 44; Gülbahar, 45; Gulbarg, 44; Gülbün, 45; Gülfatma, 45; Gülfiliz, 44; Güldalĭ, 45: Gülçin, 45; Gülperi, 45; Gulrang, 44; Gülru, 44; Gülrukh, 44; Gülseren, 45 (all f)
Gulistān (f), 44
Gulshan (f, m), 44
Gul-i ranā (f), 44
Gul, 'Abdul Ahad (d. 1714), 74
Gülbenk, 41
Gülümser, 46
Gümüşbuğā, 2
Gün, T 'day, sun', 3, 81; Günay (f), 45; Gündoğmuş, 19
Güneş, 3; Güneşsoy, 80
Güngör, 4; Günkut, 19
Gürpĭnar, 83
Güven, 4; Güvendik, 82
Güvercin T (f), 46
Güzide (f), 48

Ḥabīb Allāh. 66
Ḥaddād, al-, 56
Ḥaddī (f), 42
ḥafīd, 'grandson', 9
Ḥāfiẓ (Muḥammad Shams ad-dīn, d. 1389), 57, 74
Ḥafīẓa, 44
Ḥāfiẓak, 69
Ḥafṣ, 3
Ḥafṣa bint 'Umar (d. 665), 6, 44, 68
Ḥafṣūn, 75
Ḥājj, 22; Ḥājjī, 22, 57; Ḥajjigeldi, 22
Hak s. *ḥaqq*
Hākadhā, 53
Haliči, 56
Ḥalīma, II 41
Ḥallāj, al-Ḥusayn ibn Manṣūr (d. 922), 13, 56; *ḥallāj al-asrār*, I 38
Hamasa (f), 48
Ḥamd Allāh, 65
Ḥamdān, 31; Ḥamdī, 31; Ḥamdīn, 31; Ḥamdīd, 31; Ḥamdīs, 31; Ḥamdūn, 31, 75; Ḥamdūd, 31; Ḥamdūna, 75
Ḥāmid, 31, 69
Hamīd, 28, 31; — Allāh, 65; — ad-dīn, 65; — az-zamān, 64
Ḥamīda, 31
Ḥamīdān, 31
Ḥā-mīm, 31
Hamīnbas P (f), 42
Ḥammād, 31; Ḥammādī, 31; Ḥammādū, 31; Ḥammūd, Ḥammūda, 31, 69
Ḥamza (ibn 'Abd al-Muttalib, d. 625), 3, 33
Ḥanafiyya, 11
Ḥanbalī, al-, 11
hanïm s. a. Khanum, 48
Ḥanẓala (d. 625), 3, 13, 59
Ḥaq, Ḥaqq, 28, 30; compounds with *al-ḥaqq*, 65
Haqqī, 28, 79
Haqqverdi, 18
Haque s. Ḥaq
Harawī, 11
Ḥarb, IX, 14, 20, 28, 72
Ḥārith, al-; Ḥāritha, 1, 69
Hārūn ar-Rashīd (d. 809), 6
Ḥasan, al-Ḥasan (ibn 'Alī, d. 669), 1, 6, 11, 16, 33, 35, 69, 76, 77, II 41
Ḥasan Abdāl, 38
Ḥasan (al-) 'Askarī (d. 874), 35
Hasan al-Baṣrī (d. 728), 38
Ḥasanān, I 2
Ḥasanāt (f), 41
Ḥasanayn, 35; — dōst, 35; — nawāz, 35
Ḥasanī, al-, 11, 40
Ḥasanlū, 76
Hāshim, 10, 39, 72; Hāshimī, 10, 32, 39
Ḥaskā, 76
Ḥaṣkafī, 'Alā ad-dīn al- (d. 1678), 12
Ḥassō, Ḥassū, 69
Ḥassūna, 69
Hastī P (f), 47
Ḥauthān, 76
Ḥayāt Allāh, V 46
Ḥayāt al-qulūb, 75
Ḥayāt-bakhsh (f), 49
Ḥaydar, 2; Ḥaydara, 14, 34
Ḥaydar-bakhsh, 18; Ḥaydar-dost, 34
Ḥayṣa Bayṣa, Shihāb ad-dīn (d. 1179), 53
Haytham, 2
Hazār P (f), 46
Hazārasp (Luristani dynasty), 55
Heinrichs, Wolfhart, XII
Helvacïzade, 10
Hepşen T (f), 46

Herātī, 11
Ḥerz, Ḥerouz (= ḥirz), 41
Hess, J. J., 76
Hibat Allāh, 18, 64
Hidāyat, 16
Hidāyat al-ḥaqq, 65
Ḥifẓ Allāh, 65
Ḥijāz Khān, 23
Hilāl (m, f), 45
Hilālī, Badr ad-dīn (d. 1529), 74
Ḥīlān, 76
Ḥimār, 51, 52
Hindāl son of Babur (d. 1551), 19
Hiyām (f), 17
Ḥizb Allāh, 65
Hĭzĭr (s.a. Khiḍr), 29
Hōshang, Hūshang, 78
Hūd, 29
Ḥufayṣa, 68
ḥujjat al-islām, 58
Ḥulyā P (f), 46
Humā P (f), 46
Ḥumayd, Ḥumaydān, Ḥumaydūd, 31
Ḥumayrā, 43
Humāyūn, Mughal emperor (d. 1554), 27, 59
Huq s. Ḥaqq
Ḥūrīye (f), 47
Hürriyet (Ḥurriyya) (f), 17
Ḥusām ad-dīn, 16, 60; Ḥusāmak, 69
Ḥusayn (ibn ʿAlī, d. 680), 11, 15, 16, 21,, 35, II 41
Ḥusayn (Hüseyin) Ghāzī, 37
Ḥusayn Shāh Rāshdī, Sayyid, 40
Ḥusaynappa, 76; Ḥusaynayya, 76
Ḥusayn-bakhsh Qalandar, 39
Ḥusaynqulī, 35
Ḥusayn-i Manṣūr s. Ḥallāj, 9
Ḥusaynī, al-, 11, 40
Hüsrev s. Khusrau
Ḥuṭay'a, al- (d. *c.* 678), 53
Ḥuwayrith, 69
ḥużūrmuk'hī, V 28

Ibbo, Ibish, 29, 69
Iblīs, 5
ibn, 'son of', *ibnat*, *bint* 'daughter of' : to form the *nasab*, 8
Ibn Ạbbād, aṣ-Ṣāhib Abū'l-ʿAbbās (d. 995), 6
Ibn ʿAbd Allāh, 8
Ibn Abī Laylā (d. 765), 8
Ibn ʿAfīf ad-din at-Tilimsānī, 54
Ibn akhī ash-Shāfi'ī, 8
Ibn Akhī Turk, Ḥusām ad-dīn (d. 1284), 58
Ibn al-ʿAdīm (d. 1262), IV 13, 27
Ibn al-badhrā', 54
Ibn Baṭṭūṭa, Muḥammad ibn ʿAbd Allāh (d. 1377), 62, 75
Ibn Bībī (after 1285), 9
Ibn Bint al-Aʿazz, 9
Ibn ad-dāyā (d. betw. 941 and 951), 9
Ibn dhī'l-liḥya, 8
Ibn al-Fāriḍ, ʿUmar (d. 1235), 8
Ibn Ḥanbal, Aḥmad (d. 855), 11
Ibn Hirrat ar-ramād (10th c.), 54
Ibn al-Jauzī (d. 1200), 9
Ibn Jinnī (d. 1002), 18
Ibn al-Khaṭīb, Lisān ad-dīn (d. 1374), 60
Ibn Khurdadhbih, II 19
Ibn al-mar'a (d. 1214), 9
Ibn Maryam, 9
Ibn Maymūn (d. 1511), 61
Ibn Muṭahhar al-Ḥillī (d. 1326), 58
Ibn Qutayba (d. 889), 3
Ibn al-Qūṭiyya, Muḥammad (d. 977), 9
Ibn Rashīq (d. 1064), 60
Ibn ar-Rūmiyya (d. 1239), 9
Ibn Rushd (d. 1198), 8
Ibn as-Saʿātī (d. 1230), 8

Ibn as-Sarrāj, 8
Ibn as-Sikkīt, Ya'qūb (d. 859), 8
Ibn as-sitt, 9
Ibn Sīnā, 'Alī (d. 1037), 8
Ibn Tumart (d. 1131), 77
Ibn ukht Ghānim (d. 1130), 9
Ibn az-Zarqā, Marwān (d. 684), 9
Ibn az-Zayyāt, (Shams ad-dīn, d. after 1401), 8
Ibn Zuhr (family), 8
Ibrāhīm (Abraham) 6, 12, 16, 29, 61, 64, 69
Ibrāhīm al-Mauṣili (d. 804), 5
'Idī, 'Idō, 'Idū, 22
Idil T (f), 24
Idrīs, 29, 64
Iffi, 70
Iftikhār ad-dīn, 70; al-ḥukamā', 58; — as-sādāt, 40
Iḥsān, 19, 76, 79; — i ḥaqq, 19, 65; — rabbī, 19
Iḥtishām ad-dīn, 62
I'jāz al-ḥaqq, 65
Ikrām al-ḥaqq, X ; — 'Alī, 18
'Ikrima, 2
Ilāh-dād, 18
Ilāha as-sādāt (f), 40, iv 10
Ilāhī-bakhsh, 18
Ilknur T (f), 45
Iltutmiş, Sultan of Dehli (d. 1236), 4
Ilyās, 29
Imām, 57; compounds with, 36
Imāmqulī. 36
Imām al-ḥaramayn, al-Juwaynī (d. 1085), 57
Imdād 'Alī, 34
'Imrāñ, 43; 'Imrāna, 43
Inal, Inan, 71, 73, 82
Inal, Ibnülemin, 82
In'ām, compounds with, 19; – ul-ḥaqq, 19; ul-Kabīr, I 9
'Ināyat, 16, 19; — ar-Raḥīm, 19; — ar-Raḥmān, 19; — i Kibriyā, 19, 66
Inci T (f), 46
Incil (f), 47
Inshā Allāh, 25
Iqbāl, [Muḥammad (d. 1938)], 3, 17, 18, 32, 33, 46, 58, 62; — ad-dīn, 62; — un-nisā (f), 48
Iqrār an-nabīy, 32
Iraj, 78
Iram (f), 47
Irān Khātūn (f), 24
'Irāq Khātūn (f), 24
Irtiḍà, Irtiżā, 3; — Ḥusayn, 35
'Īsà, 29, 59, 65
'Isākhēl, 10
Iṣfahānī (Abu'l-Faraj al-, d. 967), 12
Isfahsālār, 56
Isfandiyār, 78
Isḥāq, 16, 29
ishrāqī, 11
Iskandar, 78
-al-Islām, compounds with, 63
Islām, 44
Islām Khān, 44; — ad-dīn, 62
Ism 'Alī, 34
Ismā'īl, 16, 29
Ismā'īlīs, XI, 16, 17, 23, 33, 36, 48, V 28
Isminăz (f), 46
'Iṣmat (Ismet) (m, f), 3; 'Iṣmat Khānim, 75
Istabraq (f), 26
Istanbullu, 12
ithnā''asharī, 11
'Itrat: — 'Ali, 36; — Ḥusayn, 36
Ittahirān, 9
'Iyād, 21
'Iyūshā, 69
Izmirli, 12
'Izz: — ad-daula wa'd-dīn, 60; — al-batūl, 36

Jabal, 3
Jabbārbirdi, 18
Jabbūr, 28
Jābū Allāh, 18
Ja'far ibn Abī Ṭālib al-Ṭayyār (d. 629), 43, 59
Ja'far aṣ-Ṣādiq (d. 765), 35
Ja'far Ju'ayfirān, 69
Ja'farān, 76
-*jahān*, P 'world', compounds with, 46
Jahānāra (Mughal princess, d. 1681), 46
Jahāngīr (Mughal emperor, r. 1605–27), 37, 59
Jāḥiẓ, (the Goggle-eyed) 'Amr ibn Baḥr al- (d. 868), 12, 75
Jahlān, 76
Jalālā, 63
Jalāl ad-din (s. Rūmī), 38
Jalāl ad-dīn Istarjānī Qurbān (12th c.), 52
Jale (f), 44
Jālīnūs az-zamān, 59
Jamal, al-, 51
Jamāl ad-dīn, 61, 63
Jamālāt (f), 43
Jamālī (Kanboh, d. 1534), 74; al-Jamālī, 63
Jamālzāda, 10
Jāmī, Mollā 'Abdur Raḥmān (d. 1492), 74
Jāmi'a (f), 44
Jamīla (Cemile) (f), 42, 68, II 41
Jamshīd, 70
Jāmūs, al-, 51
-*jān*, compounds with, 49
Jānjānān, Mirza (d. 1781), 76
Jannat (Cennet) (m, f), 47; — un-nisā (f), 48
jannat-ashiyānī, 59; — *makān*, 59
Japanwālā, 12
Jaqmaq, (al-Malik aẓ-ẓāhir, d. 1453), 71
Jār Allāh, 64; Mūsā – (d. 1949), 64
Jarrāḥ, al-, 56
Ja'shān, 76
Jashnagīr (Baybars al-, d. 1309), 72
Jāsim, 76
Jasīm 32; Jasīm ad-dīn (d. 1974), 32
Jasmine (f), 47
Jauhar [ar-Rūmī, d. 992], 71
Jāvīd (Cavid), 20, 43
Jawāhir (f), 43, 47; — raqam, 58
-*jee*, suffix of endearment, 68
Jesus ('Īsā), 5
-*jī* (ci, çi), T suffix for professions, 56
Jiā, Jiān, 20
Jibrā'īl, Jibrīl, 29
Jibrā'īl ibn Bukhtīshū' (d. 830), 5
Jihād (Cihat), 41
jihat, al- (f), 49; *ash-sharīfa*, 49
jik, jug (cik, çik) T, suffix for diminutives, 69
Jīlānī ('Abdul Qādir); — Begum, 39
Jimmy, 70
Jīndo, Jīnī, Jīwī (f), 20
Jonah (Yūnus), 66
Joyn ad-dīn, 76
Jūj kalmāt, 53
Jum'a (Cuma), 22, 77
Jumayla, 68
Jūnā, 20
Junayd (d. 910), 38; Junayd un-nisā (f), 48
Juwayriya, wife of the Prophet, 8, 47

Ka'b ibn Zuhayr (d. after 632), 43
kabīr, 50
Kaçim, Kasim (= Qāsim), X
Kāfī (f), 42

Kāfirak, 69
Kafsh ʿAlī, 35
Kāfūr (d. 968), 13, 71
Kaḥlān, 76
Kā'ināt (f), 47
Kākākhēl, 10, 67
kālān, 50
Kalb, 20; Kalb ʿAlī, 35; — al-a'imma, 36; — Allāh (s. *chelb*), 65
Kalīm Allāh (Moses), 12, 29
Kallāshay', 54
Kamāl, 63; — ad-dīn, 63
Kamālā, 63
Kamāngar, 56
Kāmdēn, 60
Kāmrān (m, f), 19
Kāmyo (f), 54
Kanʿān (Kenan), 29
Kanbōh, 67
Kanīz (f), 36, 44
Kaplan (Qablān), 81
Karacaoğlan (17th c.), 10
Karam ʿAlī, 34
Karamāt, 16
Karīm, compounds with, 66
Karīm Khan Zand (d. 1779), 67
Karīma (f), 28, 44
Kartal, 81
Kathīr. 69
Kauthar (m, f), 47
Kawākibī, ʿAbdur Raḥmān al- (d. 1902), 11
Kaya, 83
Kayf al-Islām, 63
Kayğusuz Abdal (d. *c.* 1444), 38
Kayhān (f), 24, 47
Kayqōbād, 78
Kāẓim, 23, 76
Kāẓimī, 40
Keçi T (f), 46
Kediā (f), 77
Kerem (Karam), 17
-kibriyā, compounds with, 66
Kifāḥ, 17
Kifāya (f), 42
Kiluwwah (f), II 39
Kishile, 21
Kishmish (f), 47
Kishwar (f), 24
Kĭzlar ağasĭ, 57
Kohandil Khān, 16
kök, gök T 'sky', 81
Kökbörü, 51
kōkā, 'foster brother', 58
Köprülü, 80; — zade, 10, 80
Korkmaz (Qorqmaz), 19
Köroğlu (16th c.), 10
Kosegarten, 4, 6
Kramers, J., 60
kubrà, al-, 50
Kubrà, Najm ad-dīn al- (d. 1220–1), 26
kūchik (küçük), 50; — Hüseyin Pasha, 51
Kūfī, al-, 10
Kufrī, 74
Kül Kedisi (d. 1574), 54
Kulthūm-shamā'il, 55
Kumīn, 3
Kumru (Qumrī) (f), 46
Kurāʿ an-naml (d. 922), 52
Kurd, 67
Kurt T 'wolf', compounds with, 2, 81
Kurtaran, 82
Kushājim (d. 961), 76
Kuthayyir ['Azza (d. 723)], 55, 69
Kutlu s. qūtlū
Kutlubugha, 2, 78

Khadīja (Hatice), (d. 619), the Prophet's wife, 23, 36, 43, 77, II 41; al-Kubrā, 50; Srinavas, I 9
Khaḍir, Khiḍr, 29
Khaintō (f), IV 3

khalaf, 'decendant, successor', 15
Khaldūn, 75
Khālid (Halit) X, 2, 6, 69
Khālid ibn al-Walīd (d. 648), 64
Khalīl Allāh (Ibrāhīm), 12, 29, 64
Khalīlī, Khalīl Allāh (d. 1980), 74
Khāliqbirdī, 18
Khalīq: — as-Subḥān, 66; — az-zamān, 64
Khamīs, Khamīsa, Khamīsū, Khamsī, Khemisse, 22
Khān, 67
Khān Bahādur, 59
Khān Jamālī, 67
Khānkhānān ('Abdur Raḥīm, d. 1627), 15, 77, VI 25
Khānum, Khānim (Hanïm), 'lady', 48, 49, III 3
Khansā, al- (d. *c.* 664) (f), 51
Khar, 52
Kharīfī, 23
Khaṭak, 67
Khātima (f), 42
Khatma, 41
Khawāja, khwāja, 40, VI 6
Khawāja Mir Dard (d. 1785), 40
Khawand, 54
Khayālī, 74
Khaybarī, III 33
khayr, al-, 50; Khayr Allāh, 23; Khayr al-hudā, 16; Khayrulbashar, 32; Khayr un-nisā, 43; Khayr uz-zamān, 64
Khayrān, 76
Khayrāt 'Alī, 34; Khayrātī, 21
Khayriyya (f), 43
Khayṭ al-bāṭil, 54
Khayyām ['Umar, d. 1123], 56
Khayyāt, al-, 55
-khēl 'clan'; compounds with, 10, 67
Khiḍr s. Khaḍir
Khiḍrawayh, Khiḍrūye (d. 854), 78
Khiljī (Khalji, Ghilzay), 67
Khonfashār, 75
Khosrof s. Khusrau
Khudābanda (Öljäitü, d. 1317), 28
Khudāberdi 18; Khudā-dād, 18
Khudā-dōst, 66; — yār, 66
Khumārawayh [ibn Aḥmad ibn Ṭūlūn (d. 905)], 78
Khurdādhbih, Ibn (d. 913), II 19
Khurshīd, 3; — al-Islām, 63; Khurshīd-jahān (f), 46; -i dīn, 76
khush, P 'pleasant, nice', compounds with, 19
Khush-dil, 19; — ḥāl, 19
Khushgū (18th C.), 74
Khushḥāl Khān Khaṭak (d. 1689), 67
Khush khush, 53
Khushqadam (al-Malik aẓ-Ẓāhir, d. 1467), 71
Khushknānja (10th C.), 52
Khusrau (Parvīz, d. 628), 43, 78
Khusrau, Amīr (d. 1325), 52
Khuwaylid, 69
Khwārizmī, Abū Bakr al- (d. 993), 60

Lājīn, 61, 78
Lak'hiārī *sayyids*, 40
La'l Shahbāz Qalandar (d. *c.* 1267), 18, 52
lālā, lālla (f), 49
Lāle (f), 44
Lamine (al-Amīn), 32
Landoulsi (al-Andalusī), 11
Lansiné, 77
Laqīṭ/a, 73 (ibn Bakr al-Muḥāribī, d. 806)
Larbeh (al-Arba'), 22
Lasker (al-'Askar), 57
Lassoued (al-Aswad), 51
Laṭā'if, 16
Laṭīf, 16
Laṭīm ash-shayṭān, 53

Layl ash-shitā', 53
Layl u nahār (f), 47
Laylà, Leylī (f), 43
Laylatulqadr (f), 22
Layth, 2
Lazaar (al-Azhar), 51
Lazreg (al-Azraq), 51
Leghārī (Laghārī), 67
Levent, 17
-li, T suffix for *nisba*, 12
Liḥyat at-tays, 54
Lily, 70
Lisān ad-dīn, 60
Littmann, Enno, 23
Lōdī (dynasty 1451–1526), 67
Lubnà (f), 43
Lucien (= Munīr), 73
Lugal, 81
Lu'lu'a (f), 46, 70
Lund, 67
Luṭf, 19: — al-Bārī, 19; — 'Alī, 34; — Allāh, 19

Mā' as-samā' (f, m), 47, 54
Mabrūk, Mabrūka (f), 70
Machhai, 20
Madīna Khān, 23
Madīnī (correct: Madani), 32
Mafīz ad-dīn, 62
Magda (= Mājida) (f), 12
maghfūr, 59
Magomedov, 77
Māh, Mah P 'moon', 3, 45; Māham, 45; Māhbānū, 48; Māhdukht, 45; Māhin, 45; Mahliqā (Mehlika), 45; Mahnāz, 46; Mahpāra, 45; Māhpeykar, 45; Māhrukh, 45; Mahsittī, 48; (all f)
Maḥammad, 30
Maḥbūb (m, f.): Maḥbūba (f.), 42
Maḥbūb az-zamān, 64
Mahdī, 35; Mahdīqulī, 36
Mahdi, al-, caliph (d. 785), 6
Maḥfūẓ, 2
Maḥmūd, 31, 61, 63, 70; Maḥmūd an-nabīy, 33; Maḥmūda (f), 31
Maḥmud Hüdayi, 37
maḥrūsa, al-, 49
Mahsatī, Mahasti (f), 45 (also Mihisti, poetess, 12th c.)
Mahtāb (Mehtab) (f), 17, 45; — ad-dīn, 62
Mā'il, 74
majdhūb, 58
Majnūn, 43
Majūmdar, Mazūmdar, V 23
Makhdūm, 37: — zāda, 37
Makhfī (Zēb un-nisā, d. 1689), 74
Makhlūf, 15
Makkī, 32
Malāḥa (Melâhat) (f), 42
Malā'ika (f, m), 13, 47
Mal'ak (f), 47
Malbay min Ṭarābay, 71
malik, 56; — *ash-shu*'arā, 58
Mālik, 28
Mamadī, Mamadou, 77
Mambetaliev, 77
Māmō, 30
Ma'mūn, al-, caliph, (d. 833), 5
Manasse, 25, 73
Manērī, Sharaf ad-dīn (d. 1381), 37
Mānda, 20
Manēzha (f), 78
Manṣūr, 77; = Ḥallāj, 9; — ad-dīn, 62
Mantūf, al-, 53
maqtūl, 59
Marḍīya, 36
Marḥabā, 70
marḥūm, 59
Marjān, 70, 71
Marty, P., XI
Marwān ibn al-Ḥakam (d. 684), 9
Marwazī, 11

Maryam, 23, 43
Maṣābīḥ (f), 43
Masarrat (f), 20
Māshā' Allāh (d. *c.* 815), 25, 26, 73
Mashīsh, 52
Mashriqī (d. 1405), 74
Masīḥ, 29; — az-zamān, 59
maslūkh, 59
Mastūra (f), 49
Mas'ūd, 2, 70; — un-nisā' (f), 48
Ma'ṣūm, 36; Ma'ṣūma (f), 36
maṣūna, al- (f), 49
Maṭīr, 23
Maudūd ibn Mas'ūd ibn Maḥmūd of Ghazna (d. 1049), 16
maulā, 57; — *amīr al-mu'minīn*, 57; Maulā 'Alī, III 31
Maulānā (Mevlâna), 57; Maulānāqul, 28
Maulūd (Mevlût), 22; Maulūdiyya (f), 22
maulvī, 57
Mausiqār, 75
Māzin, 2
Mecca, 23; Mecca Beg, 23
Medīna (f), 24
Mehmed, Mehmet, 30
Melek (Mal'ak) (f), 29, 47
Memish, 69
Mēmō, 30
Menāra (f), 41
Menderes, 17
Mengübirti (Jalāl ad-din, d. 1231), 18
Meral T (f), 46
Miān, miyān, 68
Miānkhēl, 10
Miḥammad, 30
Mihr, 45; Mihrbānū (f), 48; Mihrdil Khān, 16
Miḥrāb, 41
Mihrī (f), 22
Mihrimāh (f) (daughter of Sulṭān Sulaymān, d. 1578), 45
Mīkā'īl (Michael), 29
-al-milla, compounds with, 63
Miloud, 22
Mīm, 30; — Kemāl, 70; — Nūn, 70
Mīmūna (= Maymūna, lucky) (f), 49
Minā (f), 3
Mingli, 51; — Aḥmad, 51
Minnat: — 'Alī, 34; — Allāh (f), 18
Mīr s. Amīr, 40, VI 6
Mīr 'Alī (Harawī, d. *c.* 1550), 40
Mīrān Shāh, Pīr Sayyid, 70
Mīrānbakhsh, 23
Mi'rāj (Mehraj, Merāj), 22; — ad-dīn, 22
Mirzā, 56
Miṣbāḥ al-Karīm, 66
Miskawayh, Ibn (d. 1030), 78
Miṣr Beg, 23
Mithqāl, 71
miyān s. *miān*
Mīzān ar-Raḥmān, 65
Moghul, 67, 72 (s.a. Mughal)
mollā, 57
Moodi, 70
Moses s. Mūsà
Mu'āwiya (d. 680), IX, 1
Mubāraka (f), 36; Mubārakzadī (f), 10
Muddaththir, 31
muftī, 57; Muftīzāda, 10
Mughal (dynasty, 1526–1857), 15, 16, 19, 27, 35, 44, 48, 58, 59, 64
Mughīra ibn Shu'ba, al- (d. 666), 1
Mughīth, al-, I 38
Mügül, XI
Mūḥ, 30
Muḥaddatha (f), 36
Muḥammad 7, 15, 21, 29ff., 34, 61, 69, 77; I 2, *s.a. Prophet*
Muḥammad Akhtar, 30
Muḥammad 'Alī, 77
Muḥammad Ghauth, 39
Muḥammad Ḥamīd Allāh, 30; — Rasūl Allāh, 32

Muḥammad at-Taqī (d. 835), 35
Muḥammad ibn al-Ḥanafiyya (d. 700), 9
Muhammad Kala Gāw (12th c.), 52
Muḥammad Krishna, I 9
Muḥammada (f), 31; Muḥammadī (f), 31
Muḥammad - dōst, 32; — qulī, 32; — yār, 32
Muḥammadūh, 76
Muḥarram, 21
Muḥayyar, al-, I 38
Muḥibb 'Alī, 34; — an-nabīy, 32
Muḥsin, 2, 16, 35, 63
Muḥyī'd-dīn (= 'Abdul Qādir Jīlānī), 38; — un-nisā Begum (f), 38
Mu'īn, 2
Mu'īn ad-dīn Chishti (d. 1236), 37, 38
Mu'īn ad-dīn un-nisā Begum (f), 39
Mu'īna (f), 39
Mu'īnī, 37; — Begum (f), 39
Mujīr ad-dīn, 71; Mujīrī, 71
Mujtabà, 35
mujtahid, 58
muk'hī, V 28
Mukhliṣāy, 63
Mūlāy Idrīs (d. 792 or 793), 57
al-mulk, compounds with, 60
Mulūk (f), 43
Mumayyiz, al-, I 38
Mumcu, 82
Mumtāz (m, f), 70; — ar-Raḥmān, 65
Mūnā (f), 12
Munawwar (m, f), 2
Munīr, 32, 42, 73; — az-zamān, 64
Munīra (f), 32, 42
Munji'a (f), 72
munshī, 56
Munyā(t) (f), 20; — al-munà (f), 47
Muqanna', al- (d. 780), 53
Muqīt, al-, I 38
muqri', 57
Muqtafī, al-, caliph, (d. 1159), 55
Murād Farīd, 73
Murād son of Akbar (d. 1598), 59
Murr, 20
Murra, 14, 28
Murshid, 37, 58
Mursī, al- (Abū'l-'Abbās, d. 1287), 37
Murtaḍà (Murtażà), X, 35, 70, 76 Murtajā, X; Murtalā, 77
Mürüvvet (Muruwwat) (f), 46
Mūsā (Moses), 12, 29, 35, 43
Mūsà al-Kāẓim (d. 799), 23, 35, 36, 40
muṣannifak, 69
Müsavat (Musāwat), 17
Mūsawī, 40
Muṣḥaf (f), 41
Muṣṭafà (= Muḥammad)
Mustafa Kemal [Atatürk (d. 1938)], 70, 80
Mustafīż ar-Raḥmān, 65
Mustalim, al-, I 38
mustaufī, 56
Mu'tamid, al- (caliph, d. 893), 54
Mutanabbī, Abū Ṭayyib al- (d. 965), 55
Mutawakkil, al- (caliph, d. 861), 13
Mu'tazila, 11; Mu'tazilī, 11
Mutlu, 17
Muẓaffar (m, f), 2
Muzhān, 70
Muzhgān (f), 48
Muzzammil, 31

Nabāhat (Nebahat) (f), 42
Nabāt (f), 44
Nabībakhsh, 18, 32; Nabībakhsh Khān Balōch, 67
Nād 'Alī Beg, 36
Nādān, Muḥammad 'Āqil, 74
Nadhr: — al-Islām, 63, I 9

Nadhīr, 31; — Aḥmad, 31
Nādīda (f), 46
Nadīm (Nedim): — al-Islām, 63
Nādir: — al-'aṣr, 58; — az-zamān, 58, 64
Nādirpūr, 10
Naḍr, an- (m, f), 3
Nafīsa (f) (Sayyida —, d. 824), 37, 44
Nafṭawayh (d. 937), 78
Nāhīd (f), 45
Najaf (Nazaf), 23
Najāḥ, 70
Najīy Allāh (Noah), 64
Najjār, an-, 12
Najm, 3, 61; — ad-dīn, 61; — al-Ghanī, 66; — ath-thāqib, an-, 25, 45; — un-nisā', II 41; Najma (f), 45
Nakhwāsta (f), 42
Namir, 2
Nāmwar, 19
Naqī, 'Alī an- (d. 868), 40
Naqwī, 40
Nāranj (f), 47
Nargis (f), 44; — Khānum (f), 48
Narmīn (f), 2
Nasīm, 32; — al-Ḥaqq, 65
Nāṣir, an-, 61, 63; — ad-daula wa'd-dīn, 60; — ad-dīn, 61, 63
Naṣīr: — ad-dīn, 61
Naṣr, 3
Naṣr Allāh, 61; Abū naṣr, 7; Abu'n-Naṣr, 7
Naṣrum min Allāh, 25
Naṣūḥ, 25, III 2
Nauf Allāh, V 46
Naurūz, 22
nawāb, nawwāb, 56; Nawwābzāda, 10
Nawawī, Abū Zakarīyā Yaḥyà an- (d. 1277), 6, 15, 53
Nawāz 'Alī, 34
Nāyāb ad-dīn, 62
nāz P 'coquettery', compounds with, 46
Nāzī, Nāzli (f), 46
Nazīha (Nezihe) (f), 42
Nāẓim, 2
Necabet (Najāba) (f), 42
Necati (Najātī); Necatioğlu, Necatizade, Necatigil, 10
Nehru, 17
Nfeyid (f), 24
Nidāl, 17
Nīkū Siyar, 55
Nīlufar (f), 44
Nimr, 2
Niqāb al-'anaz, 54
-un-nisā, compounds with, 48
Niẓām (m, f): — al-ḥaqq, 65; — ad-dīn Auliyā (d. 1325), 38, 62
Niẓām ul-Mulk (d. 1092), 60, V 32
Niẓāmī (d. 1209), 43, 78
Notker Balbulus (d. 912), 50
Nūḥ (Noah), 29, 64
Nu'mān, Abū Ḥanīfa, 11
Nu'mānī, 11
Nūn, 67
Nuqaybān, 76
Nūr, 'light', 33, 43, 45, 61, 63; — ad-dīn, 42, 63; — Allāh, 34, 65; — 'aynī (f), 47; al-Bāqī, 66; — al-Ḥasan, 35; — al-hudà (f), 16, 32; — Muḥammad, 30; — an-nabīy, 33
Nūrān, 76
Nūrhān (f), 45
Nūr Jahān (f) (Mughal queen, d. 1645), 46
Nurten (f), 45
Nūr un-nisā' (f), 45
Nūrbakhsh, 19
Nūrī, 33, 43, 63, 83; Nūriyya (f), 43, 63
Nuṣayb, Abū'l-Jafnā' (late 8th C.), 6

Nuṣrat (m, f), 3
Nuwayhī, 12

- *oğlu*, T suffix 'son of', 10, 80
- *oğlan*, T suffix 'son', 10
Oghuz Khan, 79, 81
ok- T 'arrow', 81
Ökkeş (= 'Ukkāsha), 37
Okumuş, 19
Ölmez, 20
Omar Sharif (s. 'Umar), 17
Ömer (s. 'Umar), 33
Önder, 80; Öner –, XII
'Oqbī, 37 (s. 'Uqba)
Ördek (f), 46
Orhan (d. *c.* 1359), 79
Oruç, 22
Osman (s. 'Uthmān), 33
Ovezberdiev, 77 (*s.a.* Uways)
Oysul (*s.a.* Uways), 33
öz - T 'self', 81
Özbek min Ṭuṭukh, 71
Özdil, 81; Özer, 81; Özgül (f), 45; Özkan, 81; Özsüt, 81; Öztemiz, 81; Öztürk, 81

Paksüt, 81
Panāh 'Alī, III 34
Panja 'Alī, 34
Parī, P 'fairy' (f), 46; Parī-bakhsh, 49; Parī-jān, 46; Parīkhān (Perihan), 46; Parihan Hanĭm, 49; Parīsīmā, 46; Parīzād, 46
Parvāna (f), 47; Parwāna, Sirāj ad-dīn, 74
Parvīn (f), 45
Parvīz, Parvēz, 78 (Khusrau, d. 628)
Pāshā, 57
Pattūm, 69; Pattumapa, 76 (f)
Pāyinda Khān (19th C.), 16
Paymāna (f), 47
Peygamber-qul, 32
Peynir ad-dīn, 62
Peyniryemezgil, 13
Pīltan, 54
Pīr, 37, 58
Pīr-i dastgīr ('Abdul Qādir Jīlānī), 38
Pīr-dād, 38; Pirden, 38; Pirnur, 38
Pīr Sayyid Mīrān Shāh, 70
Pīrzāda, 10, 37
pisar, P 'son', 10
Piyār 'Alī, 34
Platinum, 23
Poonawala, 12
Pōpalzay, 10
Portakal (f), 47
-*pōtā, potrā*, Sindhi 'son', 10
Prophet, Muhammad the, 3, 5, 6, 7, 8, 11-15, 18-22, 27, 28, 29 ff., 34, 36, 37, 39, 40, 43, 55, 59, 65, 66, 68-70, 72, I 12, II 1, III 16, 18, 25
pūr, P 'son', 10
Pūr-i Bahā, 10
Pūrāndukht, 78
Purdil Khān, 16
Pūstīndūz, 56

Qabāqūlāq (Kabakulak), 51
Qablān (Kaplan), 2, 16
Qabīḥa, 13
Qāḍāmīrī (Ḥasan al-, d. 1498), 12
Qaddūr, 69
qāḍī, 57
Qādir, II 41
Qādirī, al-, 11; Qādirī Begum, 39
Qādirqulī, 28
Qādirūh, 76
Qaḥṭān, 75
Qajar (dynasty 1721–1925), 27, 58, 67
Qalandar, 39; Qalandarbakhsh, 18
Qalānisī, Abū Ya'là al- (d. 1160), 56

Qalqashandī, Aḥmad al- (d. 1418), 12, 64, 71
qamar, A 'moon': – ad-dīn, 16, 23
Qamḥān, 76
Qand 'Alī, 34
Qanṣauh (al-Ghūrī, d. 1516), 72, VI 14; — Khamsmi'ah (d. 1501), 72
qarā (kara), T 'black', 3, 50, 81
Qarāgöz (Karagöz), 72; Qarāqāsh (Karakaş), 51
Qarāqōyūnlū (Karakoyunlu) (*c.* 1378–1470), 23, 50
Qarāsonqur, 3
Qarāyelek (Karayelek) (d. 1428), 52
qāri', 57
Qaṣab as-sukkar, 53
Qāsim (Qassem), X, 76
Qasīm, 32; — ad-din, III 21
Qaṭā'if, 53
Qātil al-jū', 54
Qawārīrī, 11, 56
Qaymāz (Kaymaz), 3
Qays, 43
Qayṣar al-hudà, 64
Qaytbay, al-Ashraf (d. 1496), 71; al-Qaytbāhī, 71
Qayyim al-Jauziyya, Ibn (d. 1350), 58
Qibchaq (Kĭpçak), 67
Qilich 'Alī, 34
qizil (kĭzĭl), T 'red', 51; qiziljā (kĭzĭlca), 72
Qizoghlu (Sibṭ ibn al-Jauzī), 9
Qoch 'Alī, 35
qōjā (koca), T 'great, old', 50
Qonṣol al-kilāb, 54
Qoṣrauh, 71
Qudrat Allāh, 65; Qudrat-i khudā, 28
qul, qūlī, T 'slave', 28
Qul huwa Allāh, 25, 40
Qunfudh, 14; Ibn Qunfudh (d. 1406–7), II 3
Quraysh, 11, 39; Qurashī, 11, 39; Qurayshī, 11, 39; Quraeshī, 39; Qureshī, 39
Qurbān 'Alī, 35; Qurbānverdī, 22
Qurrat ul-'ayn (f), 46
quṭ (kut), T 'good luck', 19; quṭlugh (kutlu), 2, 17, 19
Quṭlūbughā, Ibn (d. 1474), 78
Qūt al-qulūb (f), 47
Quṭāmiy, 2
Quṭayṭ, 52
quṭb, 'pole, axis', 38; Quṭb ad-dīn, 68; Quṭb al-'ālam, 64; Quṭb un-nisā' (f), 39
Quṭb ad-dīn Bakhtiyār Kākī (d. 1235), 39
Quwaydir (Ḥasan, d. 1847), 69

Raba', 22
Rab'ī, 23
Rābi'a (f), 23, 42, 44; — of Baṣra (d. 801), 44; — of Quzdār (10th c.), 44
Rachel, II 18
Raḍīya (Rażiya) (Sultana of Dehli, d. 1240), 36
Radmān, 76
Rafī' Allāh, 64; Rafī' az-zamān, 64
Rāfi'a (f), 23
Rafīq al-islām, 63
Rafraf, 26
Rāḥat Allāh, 65
Rahīm ad-dīn, 65; Raḥīm Allāh, 65; Raḥīm-bakhsh, 23
Raḥīm-dād, 18; Raḥīm-dinā, 18
Raḥīmāṅ, 76
Raḥimtolla, 65
Raḥīm, Khwāja A. of Lahore (d. 1974), 28
Raḥīmī, 11

- ar-Raḥmān: compounds with, 30, 65
Raḥmān-dād, 18
Raḥmānqulī, 28, 77; Rahmanqulov, 77
Raḥmān, Justice S.A. (d. 1979), 28
Rahmaninoff, S. (d. 1943), 77
Raḥmat Allāh, 65
Raḥmūna, 75
rā'ī, V 28
Rajā' al-Karīm, 66
Rajab 21; Rajab ad-dīn (17th c.), 22; Rajab ʿAlī, 35
Ramaḍān, Ramażān, Ramjān, X, 21, 83; Ramjān ʿAlī, 22
Ramazanoğlu (dynasty in Adana, 1379–1593), 10
Ramzan Idi, 22
Ra's al-ghāba, 53
Rashīd ad-dīn, 63
Rashīdā (mid-17th c.), 63
Rasūl (Resul), 32; Rasūl-bakhsh, 32; Rasūl-i akram, III 19
Raunaq-jahān (f), 46
Raushan Akhtar (Naṣīr ad-dīn Muḥammad, d. 1748), 55;
Raushanjabīn (f), 46
Raymond (= Raḥmān), 73
Rāz-i ilāhī, 38
Rażavī s. Riḍawī, Rizvi, 40
Rāzī, (Fakhr ad-dīn ar-, d. 1209), 11
Rehmani, 11
Riḍawī, Riżvi, 40
Riḍwān (Riżwān), 29; Riḍwāna (f), 29
Rifāʿī (Aḥmad ar-, d. 1178), 37
Rifʿat, 3
Rīḥāna (Rayḥāna), 44
Rijl aṭ-ṭā'ūs, 53
Riyāḍ (f), 43; Riyāż ul-Islām (m), 43, 63
Rizq Allāh, 65
Ruby, 70
Rūḥ Allāh, 65
Rukhshāna, 70, 78
Ruknā, 63
Rumayḍān, 21
Rūmī, Jalāl ad-dīn (Celalettin) (d. 1273), 25, 38, 57
Ruqayya, Muḥammad's daughter (d. 624), 33, 44
Rūs, 72
Rustam, 34, 78; Rustam-ʿAlī, 34, 78
Ruswā, Mirzā Ḥasan Muḥammad (d. 1931), 49
Ru'yā (f), 46
Rūza, 22
Rūzbih, 19

Saʿādat (f), 19; — al-islām, 63
Saʿātī, as-, 56
Ṣabʿān, 76
Sabbatī, 22
Sabīḥ: — al-ʿālam, 64
Sābiq ad-dīn, 71
Ṣābir; Ṣābira (f), 42
Ṣabrun jamīl (f), 25
Ṣabūr-dād, 18
Saʿd, 61; — ad-dīn, 61; — Allāh, 65
Saʿd ibn Zengī (d. 1231), 74
Ṣadaqa, 41
Saddōzay, 10
Saʿdī, Muṣliḥ ad-dīn (d. 1292), 17, 32, 74
Ṣadr, 61; — ad-dīn, 61, 63; — ash-sharīʿa, 63
Ṣadr ad-dīn Sag (12th c.), 52
Ṣadrā, Mollā (d. 1640), 63
Ṣafar, 21; — Bey, Khoja, 21
Ṣafīy Allāh, 64
Ṣafīyat ad-dīn (f), 63
Ṣafwat ad-dīn (f), 63
Sag, 52
Sağ, 83
ṣaghīr, 50, 69

Sağlam, 82
ṣāḥibqirān, V 20
Saḥnūn, 'Abd as-Salām (d. 854), 52
Sa'īd, 2, 77, II 41; — az-zamān, 64
Saif-ul-Islam, 30
Ṣā'im, 22, 83; Ṣā'ima (f), 22
Sā'indinō, 18
Sājid: — ar-raḥmān, 65
Ṣakhr, IX, 13
Ṣalāh ad-dīn (Sultan Saladin, d. 1191), 70
Ṣalāḥ 'Abd aṣ-Ṣabūr (d. 1982), 62
Salām Allāh, 65
Salāma, 3; Salāmat, 16
Ṣalāt, 41
Salāṭīn (f), 43
Ṣāliḥjī, 68
Salīm (Selim), 37; — az-zamān, 64
Salīma (f), 42
Salīm Chishti (d. 1571), 37
Sallūm, 69
Salm, 3
Salmà (f), 43
Salmān (al-Fārisi, d. after 656), 33
Sally, 70
Samā' (f), 33; — ad-dīn, 62
Sām'ānī, Abū Sa'īd Muḥammad (d. 1166), 11
Sāmarrā'ī, Ibrāhīm, XI
Samīna (f) (= Thamīna), XI
Samrā' (f), 2, 42
Samūrkaş, 82
Sanam (f), 46
Sanjar, 78
Ṣannū', 28
Sapi'i, Sapingi, 77
Ṣaqar, 2
Sāqī — al-islām, 63
Sarāb (Serab) (f), 17, 46
Sarāwīl al-ba'īr, 54
Sarḥān, 76
Sarshār, Ratan Nath (d. 1903), 25
Sarymsakov, 77
Satĭ (f), Satĭlmĭş, 37
Satkandi, 21
Satr Allāh, 65
Sattarov, 77
Sa'ūd, 2
Saudā'ī, Bābā (12th c.), 52
Sayf; — ad-dīn, 63; — Allāh, 64; — al-mulk, 59, 60; — ar-Raḥmān, 65
Ṣayfī, 23
Ṣayrafī, aṣ-, 56
sayyid, 40, 53, 66, 70, III 34, VI 6
sayyid as-sādāt, 40; — un-nisā, 48
sayyidat un-nisā (Fāṭima), 36
Sayyidayn, 35
Schulze, 56
Sebtī, 22
Sebüktigīn (d. 997), 60
Seddenā (f), 42
Sédou, 77
Şehsüvaroğlu, 82
Sékou, 77
Selcuk, Seljuk, 9, 81; Seljukids, 46, 55
Selim I Yavuz (d. 1520), 79
Sema'nur (f), 41
Şemsi, 80
Şen, 2
Şenay, 45
Servet (Tharwat), 79
sēthī, 56
Sevil, 46; Sevin, 46; Sevinç, 46 (all f)
Seyfi (= Sayf ad-dīn), 63
Sī (= sayyidī), 9, III 18
Siāl, 67
Sībawayh (d. 770), 78
Sībak (= Fattāḥī), 75
Ṣibghat Allāh, 65
sibṭ 'grandson through the mother', 9, 35
Sibṭ-i Ḥasan, 9, 36; — Haydar, 36; — rasūl, 9

Sibṭ Ibn al-Jauzī (d. 1257), 9
Ṣiddīq, Abū Bakr as- (d. 634) (Sĭtkĭ), 12, 39
Ṣiddīqī, 39
Sidra (f), 47
Ṣīfī (= Ṣayfī), 23
Sihām (f), 17
Silm, 72
Şimşek, 3
Sinān, Miʻmār (d. 1578), 79
Sinān ad-dīn, 16
Sindhī, 11
Sirāj, 32; — ad-dīn, 32, 62, 74, 76; — al-ḥaqq, 32; — al-islām, 32; — al-maulā, 66
Sirājā, 63
Sirḥān, 2
Sĭtkĭ s. Ṣiddīq, 33
Sīstān Khanim (f), 24
Sitt 'lady', 37, 48; — il-ahle, 48; — il-beyt, 48; — al-budūr, 45; Sittuhum (f), 48
- *sitti* 'lady', in compounds, 48
Siyāwush, 78
Siyavuşgil, 10; Siyavuşoğlu, 10
Sliman (= Sulaymān), X
Snouck Hurgronje, Ch., 73, 77
Sōdāwāterwālā, 56
Sönmez, 82
Soraya (f, m) (= Thurayyā), 45
-*soy* T 'family'; in compounds, 10, 80
Stā (= *ustā*), Stāmerād, V 22
Suʻād (f), 43
Subḥānverdi, 18
Ṣūf al-kalb, 54
Ṣūfī, 39; Ṣūfiyya (f), 39; Ṣūfiyak, 69
Ṣughayyir, 69
Ṣughrà, aṣ-, 50
Suhayl (Süheyl), 3
Suhrawardī (Abū Ḥafṣ ʻUmar, d. 1234), 37
Suhrawardī *al-maqtūl* (d. 1191), 59
Sukkar wa'l-līmūn, as-, 53
Sulaymān (Solomon), X, 16, 29, 69, 70; — shikōh, 55
Sulmà bint Abī Sulmà, 5
Sulṭān, Sulṭāna (m, f), 49
Sulṭān (for *sayyids*), 40
Sulṭān un-nisā' (f), 48
Sulṭān- ʻAlī (Mashhadi, d. 1519), 40
Sümer, 81
Sumroo. 67
Ṣunʻ Allāh, 65
Suna T (f), 46
Sundus, 26
Ṣunqur, Sonqor, 2, 78
Süreyya (= Thurayyā), 45
Sürerçeker, 82
Suwaydān, Suwayyid, 14
Swēlā, 53

Shaʻbān, 21 (al-Malik al-ashraf, d. 1366); — al-milla (d. 1359), 22
Shabban, 70
Shabbar Ḥasan, III 37
Shabbīr, 35; — Ḥusayn, III 37; Shabbīra (f), 35
Shābb aẓ-ẓarīf, ash-, 54
-*shād*, P 'happy' compounds with, 46
Shaddād, 47
Shādhilī (Abū'l-Ḥasan ash-, d. 1258), 11, 37
Shafīʻ: — ad-dīn, 62
Shāfiʻī, ash- (d. 820), 8, 77
Shāhbāz, 3, 52
Shāh Jahān (ruled 1628-58, d. 1666), *V 20*
Shāhjahānābādī, ash-, 11
Shāh (-i) Mardān, 34
shahīd, 59
Shāhīn (m, f), 3, 46

Shahr Allāh, 22
Shahrbānū (f), 78
Shahzadī (f), 48
Shāhwirdī, 34
Shāʿir, 69
Shajarat ad-Durr (d. 1250) (f), 46
Shakarnāz (f), 46
Shakeb, Ziauddin A., XI
Shākir, Shākira (f), 42
Shakūfa (f), 44
Shalabī, 19, 57
-*shamā'il*, 'good qualities', compounds with, 55
Shāmlū, 67
Shams, 3, 45, 61, 80; — ad-dīn, 61; — al-ʿārifīn, 38; — aḍ-ḍuḥà, 16; — ash-shuʿarā, 59; — al-ʿulamā, 59;
Shams wa'ḍ-ḍuḥà, 25
Shamsa, Shamsha (f), 45
Shamsān, 76
Sha'n al- ḥaqq, 65
Sharaf: ad-dīn, 37; — al-ḥukamā', 58; — al-udabā', 58
Sharāfat ʿAlī, 26
-*ash-sharīʿa*, compounds with, 63
Shaʿrānī, Shaʿrāwī, 53
Sharīf ul-Ḥasan, XI
Sharīk ibn al-Aʿwar, IX
ash-sharr, 50
Shash angusht, 51
Shasht kalla, 55
Shāṭibī (Abū'l- Qāsim ash-, d. 1194), 11
Shauqī, 74
shaykh, 58, 77; — Allah, V 46
shaykh al-islām, 58
Shemissa (= Shamsa), 3
Shērdil Khān, 16
Shia, Shiites, 7, 11, 14, 15, 17, 19, 21, 23, 25, 27, 28, 32 ff., 39, 40, 44, 55, 57, 58, 78, I 2, II 7
Shiblī, 2
Shiblī Nuʿmānī (d. 1914), 11
Shibr, 35; — Ḥasan, III 37
Shihāb, 72; — ad-dīn, 60, 61, 70
-*shikōh*, P 'glory', compounds with, 55
Shīr, Shēr, 2, 16, 34
Shīrawayh, 78
Shīrāz ad-dīn, 76
Shirāzī sayyids, 40
Shīrīn (f), 43, 78
Shīrzād, 2
Shitāwī, 23
Shōrish Kashmīrī (d. 1975), 28
Shuʿayb, (Abū Yaḥyà), 6, 29
Shujāʿ, 63; Shujāʿā, 63; Shujāʿat, 16
Shukr Allāh, 40, 65
Shuwayʿir, 69

Ta'abbaṭa Sharran (d. *c.* 530), 12, 55
Taazait, 77
Tabassum (m, f), 42
Ṭabāṭabā, 40, 53
Tabrīzī, 12
Tadhrū (f), 46
Tafaẓẓul Ḥusayn, 35
tāgh (dağh, ṭauh) T 'mountain', in compounds, 81
Taghrībirdi, Abū'l-Maḥāsin ibn- (d. *c.* 1469), 18, 51, 57, 69, 71, 72, 73, 78, V 36
Ṭāhā, 31
Ṭāhira (f), 36
Tahmīna (f), 78
Tahmurath, 78
Tahtakïlïç, 82
tāj, 'crown', compounds with: — al-ʿārifīn, 38; — al-ʿāshiqīn, 38; — ad-dīn, 48, 61; — ash-sharīʿa, 63
Tajammul Ḥusayn, 35
Tājīde (f), 48

Tājdukht (f), 48
Ṭalḥa, 68, I 2
Ṭālib, 23, 36
Tālpūr, 67
Tamanṣūrt, 77
Tamīm ad-Dāri, Abū Ruqayya (d. *c.* 661), 5
Tamra (f), 47
Tamūt (f), 20
Tamyīz ad-dīn, 62
Tanrī, Tenri, T 'god' compounds with, 18
Tanzīl ar-Raḥmān, 65
Taqī (Muhammad at- d. 835), 43; Taqī ad-dīn, 42, 61, 63; Taqīzāda, 10; Taqiyya (f), 43; Taqīyā, 63
Tarāna (f), 47
Ṭāriq (ibn Ziyād, d. after 712), 33
Tarlan, 3
Taṣadduq Ḥusayn, 35
Taslīm (Teslim; Teslime f), 43
Tasnīm (m, f), 47; Tasnīma (f), 47
taş T stone, 81
Ṭaṭar, 67
Tatwānī, at- (Abū 'Abd Allāh, d. 1696), 11
Taubat an-naṣūḥ (f), III 2
Taufīq (Tevfik; Tevfika f), X, 3, 43
Tauḥīd (Tevhid; Tevhide f), 43
Tawaddud (f), 3, 42
Ṭawīl, aṭ-, 50
Ṭayyār, Ja'far at- (d. 629), 59
Ta'ẓīm ad-dīn, 63; Ta'ẓīmā, 63
Tehrān Bībī (f), 24
Temuçin (= Chingiz Khan), 79
Tengiz (= deniz), 71, 81
Tevrat (f), 47
Tha'ālibī, Abū Manṣūr ath- (d. 1077), 54; 56
Thālij, Thalīj, Thalj, Thalja (f), Thallāj, 23
Tha'lab, 2
Thamīna, XI
Thaqīf, 11; Thaqafī, 11
Thāqiba (f), 45
Thaur, 2, 52
Thurayyā (m, f), 3, 45
Tigīn, Tekīn, 78, 81
Tilkī, 51
Timsāḥ, 51
Tīmūr-i lang (Tamerlane, d. 1405), 51, V 20
Tirmidhī, Abū 'Īsà at- (d. 892), 5
Tito, 17
Tiwāna, 67
Tökin, 81
Tourzeur (f), 24
Ṭūbà (f), 47
Tūghān (Toğan, Doğan), 3
Tughril (Togrul), 3, 78
Tuhādā (f), 48
Ṭulayḥa, 68
Tumāḍir (f), 51
Tūmart, Ibn (d. 1131), 77
Tuna (f), 24, 81
Tunis (f), 24
Turāb 'Alī, 34
Tūrān Khātūn (f), 24
Turandot (f), 10, 48; Tūrāndukht (f), 10, 48
Turğut, 3
Türksen, 79
Ṭurṭūshi, Ibn Abī Randaqa aṭ- (d. 1126), 11
Turunj (f), 47
Ṭūṭā, 3
ṭūṭī-yi Hind (Amīr Khusrau), 52

'ubayd, 68
'Ubayd Allah, 'Ubaydullāh, 28, 69, 77
'Ubaydullah Aḥrār (d. 1490), 38
Üçok, 81
'Udd wa'skut (f), 42
Udhn al-ḥimār, 53

Ufuq (Ufuk), 3, 17
Ughur (Uğur), 3, 19
Uhuvvet (Ukhuwwa), 17
ukht 'sister', 8
'Ukkāsha (ibn Miḥṣan, d. *c.* 632), 37
ūlad (= *aulād*) 'sons', 9
Ülker T (f), 45
Ülkütaşïr, 82
'Umar (ibn al-Khaṭṭāḅ reg. 634–644), 1, 5, 6, 12, 17, 28, 33, 39, 77, II 41; — ad-dīn, 62
'Umar akhū al Juwayriya, 8
Umarov, 77
'Umayr, 16
Umayya, IX; — ibn Abī Umayya, 8; Umayyads (661–749), 8
Umayyat aṣ-ṣalāt, 55
Umīd (m), 3
umm 'mother', 44 — 'Abdallāh, 6; — 'Alī, 44; — al-banīn, 44; — Faḍl, 44; — Fahd, 44; — Ḥākim, 44; — Islām, 44; — Khālid bint Khālid, 15; — al-Khayr, 70; — Kulthūm (d. 630) XI, 17, 33, 44, 55; — Ma'shar (*c.* 630), 32; — Salāma, 44
Ümmü Gülsüm, XI
Umm arba' wa arba'īn, 8
Umrāo Jān Adā (f), 49
ün – T 'honour', compounds with, 81: Üner, 81; Ünsev, 81; Ünver, 81
'Uqāb, 2
'Uqba ibn Nāfi', Sīdī (d. 683), 37
'Urfī (d. 1591), 30, 74
Ürkmez, 19
'Urs, 22; 'Ursān, 22
U'rūj, 51
'Urwa ibn al-Ward (d. *c.* 596);
'Urwat al-wuthqà, al-, 25
Usāma (ibn Zayd, d. 673), 2, 69
'Uṣayrān, 76
Ushqūlāq (= üçkulak), 51
'Uthmān (ibn 'Affān, d. 656), 33, II 41
Uṭrūsh, 51 (Al-Ḥasan al-, d. 917)
Utturuja, 52
Uways (al-Qaranī) (d. *c.* 658), 33; — berdi, 77
Uzayriq, 69
Üzlifat, 25
Uzun, 50
Uzunağacaltïndayataruyaroğlu, 81
Uzūn Ḥasan (d. 1478), 50

Vatansever, 82
Veysel (= Uways), 33
Viqār un-nisā, 73
-virdī (*wirdī, berdi*) T 'he gave', in compounds, 18

Wadād (Vedat) (m, f), 3
Wafāt Allāh, V 46
Wāḥid, 28
Wajh al-kabsh, 54
-wālā, wālī, Suffix for *nisbas*, 12, 56
Walad, 'son', 9
Walī, 39; Walī Allāh (Shāh, d. 1762), 39
Walī Deccani (d. after 1707), 74
Wāmiq, 43
Ward, al-, 52
-wāṛō, -wāṛī, 12
Warrāq, al-, 55
Wasīm, 32; — ad-din, III 21; Wasmā (f), 42
Waṭwāṭ, Rashīd ad-dīn (d. 1177), 74
Ways s. Uways
Wilāyat Khān, 16
Wild, Stefan, XII, 75, I 2
wuld 'son', 9

Yabqà, 20
Yād ʻAlī, 34; Yādgār ʻAlī, 34
Yad Allāh (= ʻAlī), 4, 34, 64, III 33
Yaghmūr, 3, 71
Yaḥyā, 5, 16, 20, 29
Yaʻīsh, 3, 20
Yakhlaf, 15
Yakshanbahī, 22
Yaʻmur, 20
Yamūt, 20
Yaʻqūb (Jacob), 16, 29, 73, II 41
Yāqūt, 71; — al-Mustaʻṣimī (d. 1298), 71
yār, P 'friend', in compounds: Yār Muḥammad, 30
Yaʻrab, 75
Yasar, 70
Yaşār, 20
Yaşat, 82
Yasawī (Aḥmad, d. 1167), 11
Yāsīn, 31
Yasmīn (f), 44
Yaʻsūb, 52
Yāvar ʻAlī, 34
Yavuz, 79
Yazansoy, 80
Yazdān: -bakhsh, 18; — yār, 66
Yazdagard III (d. 651), 78
Yazĭcĭoğlu, 10
Yazīd (caliph, 680–683), 1, 3
Yegāne (f), 46
Yemlīkhā, 33
Yener, 4
Yenişehirlioğlu, 80
Yesārī, 51
Yeter (f), 42
Yĭldĭrĭm (Bayezid I), 3, 79
Yĭldĭz T (f), 3, 45, 81
Yĭlmaz, 19
Yūnus, 66
Yurdagül T (f), 44; Yurdakul, Mehmet Emin (d. 1944), 82; Yurdanur (f), 45; Yurdatap, 82; Yurdaydĭn, 82
Yūsuf (Joseph), 16, 29, 43, 61, 63, II 41; — un-nisā, IV 13; -jamāl, 55; -shamā'il, 55
Yūsufzay, 10, 67
Yusrà, 25

Zabīb, az-, 52
Zabīdī, As-Sayyid al-Murtaḍà az- (d. 1798), 11
- *ẕada* P 'son', compounds with, 10, 48
- *zādī* (f), 10, 48
Ẓafar (m, f), 19
Ẓafar Allāh (Ẓafrullāh), 64
Zaghlūl, Saʻd (d. 1927), 52
Zāhid, az-, 12
Zahrā' (f), 36, 44
Zajaczkowski, A., VI 14
Zakīy, 2; Zakiyya (Zekiye) (f), 36
Zakariyā, 16, 29
Zamakhsharī, Abū'l-Qāsim Maḥmūd (d. 1144), 5, 64
az-zamān, compounds with, 54, V 35
Zamzama (f), 47
Zand, 67
Zaouia (= Zāwiya), 41
Zarrīn-qalam, 58 (Muḥammad Ḥasan, d. after 1597)
Zarrsitti (f), 48
-zay 'descendant' (Pashto), 10, 67
Zaydān, 76
Zayf (= Ḍayf) Allāh, V 46
Zaynab, 37, 44; aṣ-ṣughrà, 50
Zayn al-ʻābidīn (ibn Ḥusayn, d. 714), 15, 35, 78; Zayn ad-dīn 61, 63, 71, 76; Zaynal, Zaynul, 35; az-Zaynī, 63
Zayyāt, az-, 1, 8
Zēb un-nisā (d. 1689) (f), 48, 74
Zeno (Ṣafdār Mīr), 75

Zhinda Pīl, Aḥmad-i Jām (d. 1141), 51
Zibālah, 21
Ziegenbalg, Ziegenspeck, 54
Ẓill; — ar-Raḥmān, 65, 70; — ash-shayṭān, 54
Zīnat un-nisā (d. 1721) (f), 48
Ziqq al-ʿasal, 53
Ziyād ibn Abīhi (d. 675), 8
Ziyā (Ḍiyā') Allāh, 65; — al-Ḥaqq, 65
Ziyārat, 22
Zoë Anṣārī, 70
Zubayda Begum (f), 49
Zubdat un-nisā (f), 48
Zuhra (f), 45
Ẓuhūr al-Islām, 63
Zulaykhā, 43
Zulf-i ʿAlī, 51
Zurāfa, 51

Index of places, ethnic groups, and languages

Abivard, 52
Abū Qubays, Mt., 14
Abyssinia/n, 43, 70
Afghans, Afghanistan, X, 10, 21, 45, 66, II 36
Africa: East, XII, 48;
North —, X, 7, 9, 18, 22, 30, 31, 49, 51, 54, 73, 75, III 18
Ajmer (Rajasthan), 37
Algeria/n, 73, 80, II 3
America/n, 26, 27
Anatolia, 19, 26, 43, 46, 47, 69, 83, V 25
Ankara, XI, 37, 82, V 23
Arabia, 23, 46, 54, 76;
South — 7, 76, V 49.
Arab/s X, 1, 5, 7, 14, 17, 20, 23, 29, 32, 38, 43, 45, 47, 52
Arabic IX–XII, 1–3, 8–10, 12, 13, 18–20, 23, 25, 28, 29, 31, 36, 39, 42, 43, 45, 48–51, 54–58, 62, 63, 66, 68–75, 77–80, 82, III 23
Armenia/n, 43
Aurangābād (Deccan), 25
Azerbaijan, 51

Baghdad, 10, 13, 39, 54, I 38
Baluchistan, 22
Basra, I 38
Bedouins, 2, 7, 14, 23, 24, 42, 47, 49, 76
Bengal, X, 21, 22, 24, 32, 36, 42, 76, IV 3; Bengali, 16, 30, 62, 70, I 9
Berber, 9, 77
Bihar, 37
Bonn, XII
Bukhārā, 11
Bursa, 54
Byzanz, 71

Cairo, 52, 71
Canarese, 76
Caucasus, 71
Central Asia, 11, 28, 34, 38, 67, 71, 73, 77, 78
Circassian, 61, 71
Cologne, XI

Damascus, 7, 10
Deccan/i, XI, 16, 31, 32, 49
Dehli, 11, 38, 39, 40, 52, 74, 78, II 13
Dhaka, 47, 66, III 3

Egypt 17, 18, 21, 25, 26, 37, 42–4, 46–8, 51–4, 61–3, 71, 73, 75, 80, II 39
English, British, X, 17, 70
Erzerum, 47
Ezbekiyya (in Cairo), 71

Farghana, 11
Fars, I 38
France, French, X, 53, 70, 73, 82, III 18, V 7

Gebes, Oasis, 37
German, Germany, 17, 54, 56, 73
Georgian, 71
Gibraltar (= gabal Ṭāriq), 33
Gilgit, 31
Granada, 8
Gujarat, X, 15, 22, 76

Hamadan, 76
Ḥanīfa (Arab tribe), 9, 11
Harvard, XII
Ḥaurān, 23
Herāt, 11, 31, 40
Hindi, 10, 34, 47, 70
Ḥiṣn Kayfā, 11
Ḥodayda, 76
Hyderabad Deccan, XI, 16, 26, 39, 47

India/n, IX, XII, 4, 10, 11, 19–21, 23, 29, 31, 36, 38, 39, 43–47, 49, 54, 56, 58, 59, 62–6, 70, 73, 74, 76, 78, I 38, II 13, III 2, 21, IV 15, V 23
Indian subcontinent, 3, 25, 27, 32, 40, 48, 57, 58, 59, 62, 66, 68, 70, I 9, III 3
Indo-Muslim, 22, 33, 53, 56;
Indo-Pakistan, 9, 12, 17, 19, 35, 47, 63, 65, 67;
Indo-Persian, 30
Indonesia, 62, 77
Indus Valley, 11, 40, (s.a. Sind)
Iran/ian, 4, 7, 9, 12, 18, 22, 24, 28, 34, 35, 40, 42–9, 51, 56, 57, 62, 63, 66, 67, 73, 76, 78, 80, II 18, 19, III 33, V 26
Iraq/i 13, 20, 23, 55, 65, 75, 76
Iṣlāḥiya, 37
Islamabad, XII
Istanbul, 21, 37, 47
Izmir, 17

Japan, 12
Java, 73, 77
Jew/s, 25, 73
Jordan, 39

Kabul, 16
Kairouan, 37, 52
Karachi, 12
Kaṣhmir, 37, 67
Kazak, 77
Kerbela, 35, 40
Khurasan, 53, I 38
Khūzistan, 21, 76, I 38
Kirgiz, 33
Konya, 20, 83
Kūfa, 10
Kurds, Kurdish 20, 67

Lahore, 28, 66
Lak'hi range (Sind), 40
Lebanon, Lebanese, 75
London, XI
Lucknow, 49

Maghrib, 7
Malaṭya, 14
Malaysia/n, 32
Marw, 11
Mecca, 22, 32, 47, 57, 59, 64, 73, 77
Medina, 39, 57
Mehrauli near Dehli, 39
Mongol, 71
Morocco, Moroccan, 53, 57, 60

Najaf, 23
Najd, 76
Nefud, 24
Nīshāpūr, 54
North West Frontier, 10, 56

Ottoman, 19, 45, 51, 57, 58, 63, 72, 78, 79

Pakistan/i, X, 4, 10, 17, 18, 22, 33, 43, 46, 49, 58, 62, 63, 66, 75, III 37
Pākpattan, 39
Pashto, 70
Pathans, 10, 25, 67
Persia/n, IX-XII, 1–4, 9–11, 13, 15, 18, 19, 22, 26, 28, 29, 32, 34,

35, 42–8, 50–4, 56, 58, 60–4, 66, 69, 70, 71, 74, 75, 78, 82, II 13, V 23, 36
Punjab, Panjabi, 13, 18, 20–3, 67, I 2

Qumm (Ghum), 36

Rayy, 11, 76
Russia/n, 71, 77

Ṣanʿā, 51
Saudi Arabia, 28, 75, I 27
Sāva, 76
Sehwān (Sind), 18
Seville, 8
Shebā 43
Shīrāz, 74
Siberia, 81
Sind, Sindhi, 10, 12, 15, 18, 40, 42, 52, 67, 70, 76
Spain, Spanish, 11, 60 75
Swahili, 22
Syria/n, 7, 37, 51

Tajik, 77
Tamil, VI 31
Ṭanṭā (Egypt), 37
Tashqurgān (Afghanistan), 15, 21, 22, 42
Tatar, 64, 77
Telugu, 76, VI 31
Tetuan, 11
Tihāma, 76
Tortosa, 11
Tunis, Tunisia/n, XI, 3, 11, 20, 21–4, 37, 38, 41, 42, 51, 54, 57, 70, 72, 73, 75, 78, 80, VI 28
Tūrān, 78, 81
Turcomans, Turkmen, 13, 23, 50, 52, 67, 77
Turk, X, 20, 22, 44–6, 51, 71
  Turkey, XI, 10, 12, 15, 17, 21, 24, 30, 33, 38, 42–8, 58, 63, 70, 78, 79, 80, ff., III 18
  Turkish, IX–XII, 1, 2, 9, 10, 12–14, 17–19, 22, 25, 28, 29, 35, 37, 43–7, 49–51, 56, 57, 61, 64, 67, 69, 71, 72, 77, 78, 79, 80 ff., V 15

Uḥud, 13, 59
Urdu, 18, 33, 39, 40, 74
USA, 31
Uygur, 81
Uzbek, 77

Xativa, 11

Yasī (Turkistan), 11
Yemen, XI, 7, 27, 33, 42, 50, 53, 54, 75, I 13
Yenişehir, 80
Yugoslavia, 48

Zabīd (Yemen), 11

Index of the Qur'ānic verses

Sūra 2/138, 65
2/157, 25
Sūra 12/59, 25
Sūra 17/1, 25, 27
17/81–2, 61
Sūra 18/105, 26
Sūra 20/1, 31
Sūra 27/40, 19
Sūra 36/1, 31
Sūra 37/21, 25
Sūra 49/11, 25
Sūra 53/1, 27
53/10, 31
Sūra 55/76, 26
Sūra 61/13, 25
Sūra 63/13, 27
Sūra 66/8, 25
Sūra 73/1, 31
Sūra 74/1, 31
Sūra 76/21, 26
Sūra 79/34, 26
Sūra 81/13, 25
Sūra 86/3, 25
Sūra 87/8, 25
Sūra 89/27, 36
Sūra 91/1, 25
Sūra 92/7, 25
Sūra 111, 5
Sūra 112/1, 25

Glossary of technical terms

abdāl: a group of usually forty saints in the mystical hierarchy
adhān, (T *ezan*): the call to prayer
Aḥmad bilā mīm: according to an extra-Qur'anic revelation, God said 'I am Aḥmad without the *m*, that is Aḥad,' One. Thus the letter *m* is the 'letter of humanity and mortality', by which Muḥammad-Aḥmad is separated from God
a'là: most high
'alam: proper name
'a.m.r: Arabic root 'to flourish, be prosperous'
amīr al-mu'minīn: 'Prince of the Believers', title of the caliph
amīr an-naḥl: 'Prince of the Bees', appelation of 'Alī ibn Abī Ṭālib who is connected, in legend, with bees who obeyed him.
anṣār: 'Helpers', the inhabitants of Medina who supported the Prophet when he left his hometown Mecca
'aqīqa: the first haircut of a new born child, connected with the sacrifice of a blemishless sheep or goat, usually on the sixth or seventh day after birth
al-'ashara al-mubashshara: the ten companions of the Prophets to whom Paradise was promised
ashrāf (pl. of *sharīf):* the nobility, descendants of the Prophet; in India: the Muslim upper class whose ancestors had immigrated to the Subcontinent
'āshūrā: the tenth of Muḥarram, the first lunar month. Ḥusayn ibn 'Alī, the Prophet's grandson, was killed on 10 Muḥarram 680 in the battle of Kerbela; it is therefore devoted to the memory of his and his family's sufferings.
al-asmā' al-ḥusnà: the 99 Most Beautiful Names by which God is described in the Qur'ān
al-asmā' ash-sharīfa: the names of the Prophet, often also thought to be ninety-nine
baqā': 'remaining', duration
baraka: 'blessing', power of a sacred object to bless
bē-dīn: 'without religion'
Bektashi: Sufi fraternity which developed in Turkey in the 14th century, with a strong inclination to letter mysticism and special rites
bid'a: innovation, something contradictory to the *sunna* of the Prophet, hence often 'heresy'
bismillāh: 'In the name of God [the Merciful the Compassionate]', formula with which every action should begin
Burda: 'Cloak', name of two poems, the first written by Ka'b ibn Zuhayr in the hope of being forgiven by the Prophet. The latter threw his cloak, *burda,* over him and forgave him. The second one was written by the Egyptian author al-Būṣīrī in connection with a dream in which the Prophet, by casting his *burda* upon him, cured his illness.
ezan adĭ: (T), name given to the child while reciting the *adhān*
faqīr: 'poor', usually designation of a Sufi
fatwà: legal opinion pronounced by the *muftī*
ghauth: 'help', title of the highest member of the hierarchy of saints, especially

of ʿAbdul Qādir Jīlānī
gh.l.b: Arabic root 'to be victorious, to overcome'
göbek adĭ: (T) name given to the child while cutting the umbilical cord
ḥadīth: saying of the Prophet, or tradition describing his actions
ḥadīth qudsī: extra-Qur'anic Divine saying
ḥajj: pilgrimage to Mecca in the last lunar month of the year, incumbent upon every Muslim provided he or she has the means
ḥ.m.d: Arabic root 'to praise'
h.y.y: Arabic root 'to live'
īshān: 'they' (P) term for the mystical leader in Central Asia
ishrāq: 'illumination' – mystico-philosophical school developed by Suhrawardī (d. 1191)
ism: personal name
izafet: (iḍāfa) connection, in Persian, of two nouns by a genitive construction, or of a noun and an adjective, expressed by a short *i* which is not written (except for certain cases): *pisar-i* ʿAlī ''Ali's son', *Ḥasan-i kūchik* 'the little Ḥasan'
jadhba:, 'attraction', overwhelming spiritual experience
jalāl: Divine Majesty, Power, Wrath; *jalālī* Divine names that express this power, like 'The Mighty', 'The Bestower of death'
jamāl: Divine Beauty and Loving kindness; *jamālī* Divine names expressing this aspect: 'The Merciful', 'The Forgiving' etc.
jī: Panjabi-Urdu root 'to live'
khiṭāb 'address': form of addressing a person
kināya: 'allusion'
kunya; patronymic, forms consisting of *abū* or *umm* with the following name or qualifying noun: *Abu Aḥmad, Umm al-faḍā'il* 'mother of virtues'
laqab: (T lakab) nickname
laylat al-barā'a (P shab-i berāt): the night of the full moon in the eighth lunar month, Shaʿbān; one believes that human fate is controlled and rewritten in heaven during this night, which is often celebrated with illuminations
laylat al-qadr: 'Night of Destiny', one of the last three odd nights in Ramaḍān, in which the first revelation of the Qur'ān took place; according to Sūra 97, it is 'better than a thousand months'.
luṭfī: connected with Divine kindness, *luṭf*
madrasa: theological college
Mevlevi: Sufi fraternity, the 'Whirling Dervishes', inspired by Maulānā (T Mevlâna) Jalāl ad-dīn Rūmī
mīlād an-nabīy: birthday of the Prophet Muhammad on 12 Rabīʿ al-awwal, the third lunar month. It is also the day of his death.
muʿammà: riddle, enigma, usually one in which a name has to be found by a complicated process of allusions and changes of letters
nabaẓ: insult
nafs muṭma'inna 'the soul at peace' (Sūra 89/27), the highest stage of the soul from where she returns to God.
Nādi ʿAliyyan: 'Call ʿAlī, the manifester of miracles . . .' Shia prayer which is widely used from the early 16th century onward
nasab: relation of a person with his ancestors: ʿAlī ibn Ḥusayn
nisba: form to express relationship to one's country, creed, loyalty, formed in Arabic by adding *-iyyun* to the place name or the name with which an affiliation is expressed; in Persian by adding a long *ī*, in Turkish *-li*, in Urdu *wālā*

peygamber efendimiz: 'our lord the Prophet', Turkish way to speak of the Prophet

quṭb: 'pole, axis', designation of the highest mystical leader of his time

rasūl-i akram: 'the most noble Prophet', Persian and Turkish way of expressing respect for the Prophet

sayyid: descendant of the Prophet through his daughter Fāṭima and her husband ʿAlī ibn Abī Ṭālib

sharʿi: connected with religious law, *sharīʿa*

sharīf: descendant of the Prophet

ṣūf: 'wool'; hence the Sufi, ascetic and mystic, 'who wears a woollen frock'

sunna: 'custom', the custom of the Prophet, whose imitation is binding for every Muslim

taḥnīk: to put saliva into an infant's mouth

taḥqīr: insulting, libeling

takhalluṣ: pen-name of a writer

takniya: to address someone by his/her *kunya*

takrima: honouring someone

taʿrīf: description

tashrīfī: honouring

taskhīf: declaring someone for stupid; insult

ʿurf: custom; also the name by which someone is usually called in the family or among friends

ʿurfī: customary law

ʿurs: lit. 'wedding', anniversary of a saint's death (because his soul is united with God)

ustād: 'master' in arts and crafts

walī: 'friend of God', hence 'saint'

ʿ.y.sh: Arabic root 'to live'